VICKERS-ARMSTRONGS WELLINGTON

VICKERS-ARMSTRONGS WELLINGTON

Ken Delve

First published in 1998 by
The Crowood Press Ltd
Ramsbury, Marlborough
Wiltshire SN8 2HR

British Library Cataloguing-in-Publication Data
A catalogue record for this book is available from
the British Library.

ISBN 1 86126 109 8

Photograph previous page: A very low level pass by
a Wellington I. Peter Green Collection.

Typefaces used: Goudy (*text*),
Cheltenham (*headings*).

Typeset and designed by
D & N Publishing
Membury Business Park, Lambourn Woodlands
Hungerford, Berkshire.

Printed and bound by Butler & Tanner, Frome

Dedication

To all those connected with a great British aircraft – the Vickers Wellington

Contents

Introduction and Acknowledgements

In *Flying Wartime Aircraft*, Hugh Bergal recalled:

> The Wellington was universally loved ... it was a docile and friendly thing ... its geodetic construction was more flexible than the normal all-metal monocoque construction and it had a habit of twitching slightly from time to time as it rattled along; it was almost as if it was wagging its tail at you. It was very easy to fly (though a bit marginal if one engine failed), and the view from the cockpit was good enough to make it one of the better aeroplanes for bad weather flying ... and it was exceptionally easy to land.

This comment has certainly been reflected in numerous interviews and correspondence with the author.

Much use has been made of official documents during the research for this history of the Wellington, and my thanks go to the ever-helpful staff of the Air Historic Branch of the MoD in London. Ex-Wellington air- and groundcrew have also contributed in large measure to the telling of this tale and I thank them all for their time, patience and memories. On the photographic side I am indebted to the *FlyPast* magazine archive, plus the personal collections of my friends and fellow researchers, Peter Green and Andy Thomas. Finally, many thanks to those authors who granted permission to use extracts from their published works, and especially to Bill Chorley for access to his excellent series of volumes on Bomber Command losses. Other material has come from a wide range of sources and I apologize for not being able to list every individual and organization by name.

This book cannot claim to be definitive as there are far more stories to tell, and too little space within a commercial publication to use more than just a few to add to the bare bones of the historic account. Aviation research is an on-going activity and the author would be delighted to hear from anyone with material to add to the story of that great British aircraft, the Wellington.

Ken Delve

CHAPTER ONE

Background, Development and Entry to Service

Design and Development

A July 1939 issue of *Flight* magazine carried a feature entitled 'Geodetics on a Grand Scale' in which the opening paragraph ran:

It is extremely unlikely that any foreign air force possesses bombers with as long a range as that attainable by the Vickers Wellington I, which forms the equipment of a number of squadrons of the Royal Air Force and of which it is now permissible to discuss structural details. The Wellington's capacity for carrying heavy loads over great distances may be directly attributed to the Vickers geodetic system of construction, which proved its worth in the single-engined Wellesley used as standard equipment in a number of overseas squadrons of the RAF ... it [the Wellington] is quite exceptionally roomy and it is amazingly agile in the air.

Though one should make allowance for pre-war jingoism, there was still a great deal of truth in these comments.

The Vickers Wellington was the only RAF bomber to serve throughout World War Two. For three years it shouldered much of the burden of RAF Bomber Command's bombing offensive against Germany; it served in both the Middle and Far East theatres of war; and it played a vital role in the maritime war against German U-boats – and yet by the time war broke out in September 1939 it, and the doctrine under which it was to be employed, were in large measure outdated.

The Wellington had its origins in Air Ministry Specification B.9/32 which required a twin-engined medium day-bomber:

This specification is issued [in response to Operational Requirement OR.5] to govern the production of a twin-engined landplane, which is to be designed for day bombing operations, with due regard to the possibility that the aircraft may frequently start on these operations before dawn and return after dark. The tare weight must be

less than 6,300lb. The main planes may be designed to fold (otherwise the span is not to exceed 70ft). All parts of the aircraft which contribute to its strength in flight are to be made of metal. The alighting gear is to be of a type which obviates the use of rubber in tension. Wheel brakes of an approved type are to be fitted.

The fuel tanks permanently included in the fuel system shall be large enough in aggregate to hold 73gal of fuel more than will be necessary for a range of 720 miles at 15,000ft. Auxiliary fuel tanks are to be supplied, to increase the total tank capacity to that required for a range of 1,250 miles at an altitude of 15,000ft.

Stability and Control: The aircraft when flying in its fully loaded condition shall:

i)   have positive stability about all axes;
ii) respond quickly to the controls and be fully controllable at any speed, especially near the stall and during a steep dive, when it shall have no tendency to hunt;
iii) be reasonably easy to manoeuvre;
iv) not be tiring to fly;
v)   form a steady platform for bombing and firing at any speed within its range;
vi) not experience excessive fluctuations in the speed for it to be trimmed if the throttle control is moved from the correct positions for that speed to either of its limiting positions.

Contract Performance: The performance of the aircraft, as ascertained by official type trials, shall reach the standards indicated hereunder:
i)   The height reached by the aircraft when it has travelled a distance of 600yd from its starting point is not to be less than 60ft.
ii) The speed at the rated altitude with the engines running at the maximum permissible rpm is to be not less than 190mph.
iii) Range – as stated above.
iv) The service ceiling is to be not less than 22,000ft.
v)   The landing speed shall not exceed 65mph.

Engines: Any suitably rated type of British engine which will have passed the 100 hours

Service Type Test within one year of the submission of tenders to this specification. The airscrews may be constructed either of wood or metal, but the aircraft will be tested as though metal airscrews were fitted.
Crew: One pilot, one navigator, one W/T operator and one gunner.
Armament: Single gun station, aft of mainplanes. Maximum bomb load 1,650lb.

It must be remembered that this was written in the early 1930s, a time when the RAF's front-line bomber force consisted of biplanes such as the Vickers Virginia with its top speed of 98mph, ceiling of under 10,000ft, bomb-load of 3,200lb and defensive armament of just three Lewis guns. It was also a time when the 'air standard' for strength and capability used France as the 'primary enemy': the rise of Germany as the primary threat was still some years away.

Four companies duly put forward proposals: Gloster with their B.9/32, Handley Page with their HP.52, Bristol with their Bristol 131 and Vickers with the Type 271.

Vickers put forward their proposal in October 1932 with the chief structures engineer, Barnes Wallis (who had been appointed to this post in January 1930), and the chief designer, R. K. Pearson (who had held this post since the early years of World War One), making various representations regarding elements of the specification. Both were of the opinion that the new aircraft should be powered by the most powerful engines that were available, regardless of the weight of the engines. This may seem an obvious point, but at the time the Air Ministry specifications rigorously imposed the tare weight of the aircraft: as the engine(s) were inevitably the heaviest element of the design, this often meant that 'less than ideal' engines had to be used in order for the design to stay within the weight limit.

This was to some extent the reason why Wallis had taken a close look at aircraft structures themselves; using his earlier

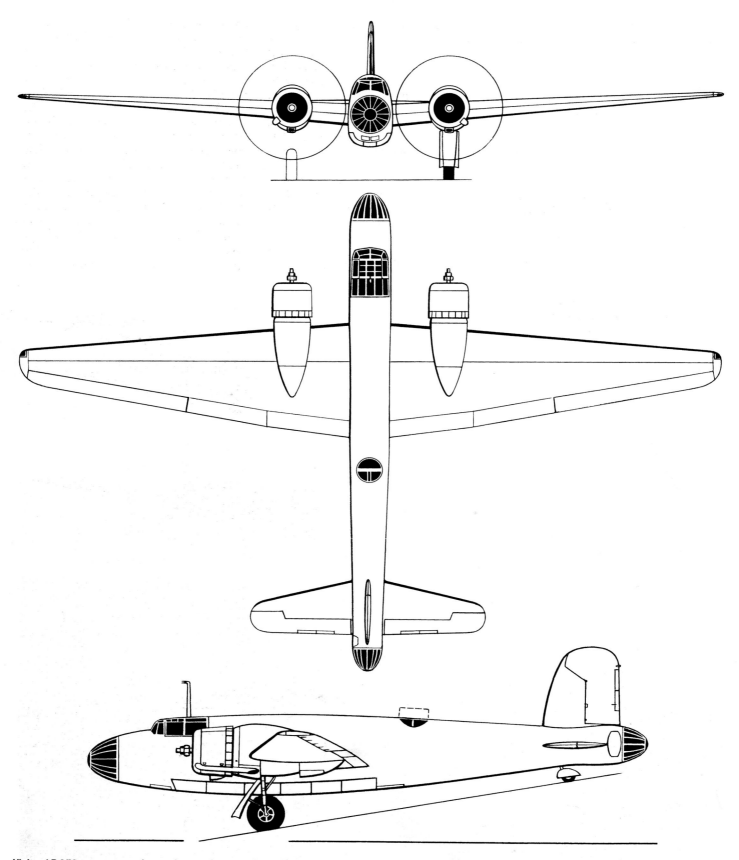

Vickers' B.9/32 entry to meet the requirement for a new heavy bomber for the RAF. FlyPast Collection

experience with airship construction, he was of the opinion that a new type of metal structure could be designed that would not only save weight but also be inherently strong. As the structures designer, he initiated a number of research programmes into strength:weight ratios, which led to the development of his 'geodetic' system of construction using stress-balancing members.

It is, at this point, worth taking a quick look at an aircraft design that preceded the Wellington and which, as intimated by the *Flight* article quoted above, was in some respects a 'prototype' for the design methods later employed on the Wellington. The Vickers Wellesley was designed to meet Specification G.4/31 for a general purpose bombing and torpedo aeroplane.

Using the experience that he had gained in the use of lightweight structures on the M.1/30 (the Vickers type 207, which 'Mutt' Summers first flew at Brooklands on 11 January 1933, although the aircraft disintegrated during a later test flight), Wallis designed a fuselage that comprised four light-alloy longerons around which was wrapped a metal lattice structure. The original design was for a biplane, although a monoplane version was soon developed and the two designs put through comparative tests. The biplane version, K2771, first flew on 16 August 1934, again in the hands of 'Mutt' Summers.

It was the monoplane version (a private venture by Vickers as the Air Ministry specification called for a biplane) that

proved superior and led in due course to the next development stage – the Wellesley. In September 1935 the biplane contract was cancelled and an order placed for ninety-six of the monoplane design, under Specification 22/35 and with the name Wellesley, for use as a medium bomber. The monoplane version, as K7556, was provided with operational additions, such as bomb panniers under the wings, and duly went to Martlesham Heath for testing in March 1936. What is of particular note is that we are now, time-wise, well down the development line with the Wellington: in effect, the two aircraft were under development at the same time, the Wellesley being slightly ahead but with little chance to apply any significant design lessons.

Wellesleys of 76 Squadron; this type was a precursor of the Wellington and, in some measure, a 'prototype'. Ken Delve Collection

(Below) **Vickers entered a very modern-looking, sleek aircraft for Specification B.9/32.** FlyPast Collection

B.9/32 prototype K4049 wearing new type number '7' for its appearance at the seventeenth RAF Display, at Hendon in June 1936. FlyPast Collection

There were so many new elements being incorporated within the design of the aircraft structure that Vickers at Weybridge established a large and sophisticated testing laboratory, including a number of structural test rigs, to prove the design concept of the geodetic structure. This was truly ground-breaking stuff, as C. F. Andrews said: 'Wallis's geodetics set a new high in strength factors which other structural systems did not match for a considerable time, particularly in high-aspect-ratio wings.'

The first production Wellesley (K7113) first flew at Brooklands on 30 January 1937 (eight months after the Wellington prototype had taken to the air) and the type entered service with 76 Squadron in April. The Wellesley had a relatively short life within Bomber Command, being replaced in Europe before war broke out but continuing to serve in other theatres during the early years of the war. (Ten RAF squadrons were equipped with the type, units in the Middle East seeing action in the early part

of the war; the Wellesley was finally declared obsolete in August 1943.) The final aspect of the Wellesley that is worth mentioning in this story is that of the Long Range Development Unit. This unit formed for an attempt on the world distance record and was equipped with five modified aircraft (L2637, L2638, L2639, L2680 and L2681); after a number of proving flights the record attempt took place in November 1938. Having positioned to Ismailia, three aircraft (L2638, flown by Sqn Ldr Kellett; L2639, Flt Lt Hogan; and L2680, Flt Lt Combe) took off on 5 November, bound for Australia. The aircraft flown by Kellett and Combe duly landed at Darwin some forty-eight hours later, having flown a distance of 7,157.7 miles, a record that was to stand until 1946.

Meanwhile, development work on the new heavy bomber – for the Wellington was classed as a 'heavy' until the advent of the four-engined 'heavies', at which point it was re-classified as 'medium' – was pro-

gressing steadily. Whilst work continued on the new bomber, the world into which it was to be born was rapidly changing. The somewhat 'anti-military' atmosphere of the early 1930s, in which war was to avoided at all costs and politicians spoke only of treaties and conventions, was shaken by the growth of nationalist parties in certain European countries. By 1935, when the Hitler regime in Germany formally announced the existence of the (previously secret) *Luftwaffe*, it was obvious to most military men, and a fair number of politicians, that war was once more a possibility in Europe. Although the British were slow to react, various measures were taken, with a number of expansion schemes being considered as a way of boosting RAF strength. To start with, these looked to the creation of a strong bomber force as being the decisive weapon of any future war – this was still the era when the strategic bombing theorists held sway – and so greater efforts had to be made to re-equip the RAF with adequate numbers of effective bombers. Handley Page Hampdens, Armstrong Whitworth Whitleys and Bristol Blenheims were all included within the late 1930s expansion plans, but it was the Vickers Wellington that appeared to hold the most promise of being the bomber best suited to Bomber Command's requirements. The thrust of air power doctrine was that a powerful bomber force would be able to destroy an enemy's military and industrial potential and thus the bomber was seen as 'the' war-winning weapon.

An initial order for 180 Wellingtons was placed in August 1936, only two months after the prototype had first flown. Powered by two 915hp Bristol Pegasus X engines, Wellington prototype K4049 had first flown, in the hands of Mutt Summers and with Barnes Wallis aboard, on 15 June 1936 . The basic aircraft weighed 21,000lb (9,500kg) and was considered capable of 250mph (400kph) at 8,000ft (2,400m), a fairly typical bombing altitude for the period (operationally, the Wellington would make most of its bomb runs between 10,000 and 14,000ft). K4049 was destroyed in a test flight on 19 April 1937 when it broke up in a high-speed dive; this led to a re-design of the tail section for the production Wellington I.

Technical Description

The 'geodetic' construction of the fuselage involved six main frames of varying sizes, the entire structure then being covered in fabric; the same basic technique was also applied to the wings and fin/tailplane assembly. Geodetic construction had its detractors, not on technical or structural grounds but rather on the grounds that it was considered too complex for mass production, especially if other companies were required to licence-build the aircraft. In the event, these fears proved unfounded as Wallis and his team created tooling and instructional material allowing the aircraft to be efficiently and speedily assembled by other factories with a minimum of skilled engineers supervising a semi-skilled workforce. The Vickers factories at Blackpool and Weybridge certainly played a full and active part in Wellington production, ably supporting the development and production work being conducted at Vickers' Brooklands works.

The aircraft's wings were equipped with Frise ailerons and split trailing-edge flaps.

A July 1939 shot of the Weybridge production line which shows to good effect the geodetic construction of Barnes Wallis's Wellington; note the early single-gun nose turrets waiting to be fitted.
Peter Green Collection

The wings contained three spars: a central main spar (in the thickest part of the wing, at the approximate centre of pressure), along with front and rear spars. Main wheels and tailwheel were all retractable via a hydraulic system, the main wheels also having a reversionary (back-up) hydraulic system. The construction of each wing allowed it to carry all six of the aircraft's fuel tanks, joined in threes; in addition there was a collector tank in the engine nacelle. The latter held 55gal (250ltr) of fuel and the total fuel capacity of each wing was 750gal (3,400ltr). If the Wellington needed more fuel than could be carried in the wings tanks, then overload tanks were fitted in the bomb bay.

The manufacturers claimed that the arrangement of the fuel tanks allowed for a rapid change of tankage in the event of a major problem; to remove the wing, change the tanks and replace the wing was said to take less than three hours. Having 'wet wings' gave the Wellington a number of advantages: they added to the structural integrity of the airframe (modern aircraft that have 'wet wings' tend to use the fuel they contain last for the same reason); and it allowed for an uncluttered fuselage design, permitting greater flexibility in the arrangement of the bomb bay and overall war loading. Unarmoured 'wet wings' were, however, to cause major concerns in the early months of the war.

According to a July 1939 report in *The Aeroplane*, 'Careful attention has been paid to the comfort of the crew. The incoming fresh air can be heated at will by the well-known Gallay system. Steam is raised in a boiler around the exhaust pipe of the port motor. It is fed to a heater in the fresh air duct. The walls of the cabin are soundproofed.' *Flight* carried a report the same month stating that:

> Equipment, in addition to an elaborate wireless and D/F installation, comfortable navigating facilities and an automatic pilot, includes an inflatable dinghy housed in the port engine nacelle, a lavatory, a rest bunk, stowage for ten Thermos flasks, sea markers, two retractable landing lights in the port wing, provision for landing flares in the wing roots, a launching chute amidships for parachute flares, and formation-keeping lights. Soundproofing is now being incorporated as standard.

All of this represented a vast improvement over previous designs.

The design parameters of the aircraft meant that careful thought had to be given

---

Specification 29/36 for Wellington Mark I

In part, Specification 29/36 stated:

29/36 FOR THE MANUFACTURE OF WELLINGTON AIRCRAFT, DATED 29/1/37.
The aeroplane shall be constructed in strict accordance with the drawings and schedules covering the design and construction of the experimental aeroplane no. K4049 in the form in which the aeroplane is accepted by DTD as the prototype of the production aircraft. A set of master parts will be held by the Air Ministry for use as standards of interchangeability. A separate contract will be issued to cover mock-ups and test specimens, also any flight test work which is done on the prototype aeroplane for the purpose of obtaining data relevant to the production type.

Special requirements:
1. Pegasus XVIII or XX engines are to be installed.
2. The bomb compartment is to accommodate internally the following: 18 × 250lb SAP or GP, or 9 × 500lb SAP or GP, or 9 × 250lb AS or LC, or 6 × 250lb B, or 2 × 2000lb AP, or 9 × 250lb bomb containers and 8 × 11½lb Practice.
3. A prone bombing position is to be provided.
4. The Frazer-Nash Mechanism is to be adopted for the gun turrets.
5. The amidships gun station is to be on the underside of the fuselage.
6. Rear gun station, power-operated with two Browning guns.
7. Front gun station, power-operated with one Vickers 'K' gun.
8. Central stowage is to be provided for 100 per cent reserve of ammunition.
9. The pilot's seat is to be padded and parachute stowage provided.
10. The pilot's instrument board is to be modified to take the new standard instrument panel and P4 compass in lieu of the P7 type.
11. The installation of a dual control conversion set.
12. A cockpit heating system will be developed.
13. Lavatory accommodation of a simple type is to be provided.
14. The W/T station is to be immediately aft of the pilot's station, with T.1083-R.1082 and DF.
15. A separate intercommunication set is to be fitted.
16. The arrangement of the normal tankage is to be twelve tanks in the outer wings and within the engine nacelles with capacity of 696gal and with special provision for accessibility of the wing tanks provided by special quick release attachment bolts.
17. The external surfaces of the aeroplane are to be camouflaged, particular care shall be taken to obtain a finish such as will reduce drag to a minimum.
18. Arrangements for fuel consumption measurements on the first aeroplane are to be made.
19. All metal parts shall be protected against corrosion.
20. The undercarriage shall comply with current requirements as regards the locking and emergency release. An audible warning device is to be fitted.

---

to its defensive armament. Front and rear gun positions open to the elements would no longer be viable: the new bomber would need enclosed turrets, and in order for these to be effective they would have to be powered, a far cry from the 'single gun station' of the original specification. This raised a completely new set of design problems that had be overcome. Initially, Vickers sought to use its own hydraulic experience to design a turret, but it soon became clear that more specialized knowledge needed to be called upon, in addition to which the Air Ministry stated that, as gun turrets were considered to be items of 'ancillary equipment', they were to be provided by independent manufacturers. This new weapon requirement, amongst other factors, led to the abandonment of the tare weight restrictions of the original specification.

The initial production order was followed in 1937 by orders to two other companies for the licence-production of Wellingtons: an order for one hundred Pegasus- and one hundred Merlin X-engined aircraft being issued to the Gloster Aircraft Company and one for sixty-four aircraft to Armstrong Whitworth. Neither of these went ahead, all orders being transferred to other Vickers factories following the establishment of the shadow aircraft factory scheme, whereby production levels and security were increased by diversifying centes of production.

A new specification, 29/36, had been issued to cover the production variant of the Wellington, the Mark I (*see* box), and much of this involved re-design work, which was carried out at the same time that design work was underway on the Vickers Warwick, a larger and heavier bomber to Specification B.1/35 (of which more later).

Amongst the changes brought into the Wellington was a deeper fuselage which was better able to accommodate the bomb bay and other equipment now required for the type; furthermore, the nose was lengthened for a new nose turret and bomb-aimer's position. Other changes included the use of constant-speed propellers and a retractable tailwheel as well as improvements in overall aerodynamics. At this stage it was also proposed to replace the Vickers ventral gun turret with a Frazer-Nash design despite some concern as to the weight of the turret and its effect on the aircraft's centre of gravity. Defensive armament was to be a problem during

Although it was planned for other manufacturers to undertake production of the Wellington, in the event all aircraft were produced by three Vickers Works: Weybridge, Chester and Blackpool. This photograph shows a royal visit to the Chester factory with a very pristine Wellington as a backdrop. Les Taylor

(Below) Putting together a classic – the workers at the Vickers plants were skilled craftsmen. Brooklands Museum

the early period of the Wellington's operational life:

I first flew a Wellington, L4381, on a Home Defence exercise with 215 Squadron on 11 August 1939 as an armourer/air gunner. On Friday 1 September the squadron, not being operational, flew to Little Rissington and then to Bramcote a few days later, and, finally, to Bassingbourn, to become a training squadron. The main reason for being non-operational was duff gun turrets, the aircraft being virtually defenceless. She was fitted with Vickers turrets, we had a single Browning in the nose and two in the rear, firing 1,200 rounds per minute (the old Lewis used to fire 300 rounds per minute) so we

reckoned it was a vast improvement – until we tried to use them! The problem was the ammo feed: this came via 'plastic' chutes from containers aft of the turret. They were fine firing up to 30-degree deflection, but being inflexible, the ammo belt could not follow the plastic chutes and jammed. We later partially overcame this by applying steam hoses to the chutes to bend them, but when attempting a beam shot it was always necessary to give the ammo belt a good tug to build up sufficient ammo for a burst. (John Whorton)

The Bristol Pegasus XVIII had been specified for the Wellington I but the first production aircraft, L4212, flew on 23 December 1937 powered by Pegasus XXs as the other engines were not yet type rated. There were few problems during the intensive flight trials as many of the aerodynamic parameters had been proven with the B.9/32. However, the Wellington I showed

a nose-heavy trend during diving; this was unacceptable in an operational bomber and so various modifications were made to the elevator balance and trim to rectify the problem. By this time the Pegasus XVIIIs were available, and they were duly fitted to the aircraft.

1939 scene at Brooklands with brand-new aircraft awaiting delivery – these are part of a batch of aircraft for New Zealand, as shown by the aircraft bearing the NZ302 serial. Peter Green Collection

Specification – Wellington I	
ENGINES	Two Bristol Pegasus XVIII
DIMENSIONS	Span 85ft 10in (26m); length 60ft 6in (18.33m)
PERFORMANCE	Max. speed 265mph (424km/h); ceiling 26,300ft (7,969m)
ARMAMENT	6 × 0.303in guns, 4,500lb (2,000kg) bombs
FIRST FLIGHT	15 June 1936
NUMBER BUILT	183

Entry to Service

The first RAF aircraft, L4215, was taken on charge by 99 Squadron on 10 October 1938 and by January this Mildenhall-based squadron became the first to be fully equipped with this modern bomber. The squadron gave up its antiquated Handley Page Heyford biplanes (which it had only had since late 1933) for the Wellington, and the change of capability and performance was startling (*see* box).

The second unit to re-equip, 38 Squadron at Marham, received its first aircraft in November 1938 whilst the third, another Mildenhall unit, 149 Squadron, re-equipped the following January. Although the pace of re-equipment accelerated in early 1939 there were still only ten Wellington bomber units when war was declared in September 1939.

The new bomber, whilst being universally seen as better than previous types did have its shortcomings:

The Wellington I had the Pegasus engine, which although very reliable was severely underpowered. Also, the propeller could not be feathered so a faulty engine 'windmilled' and created excessive drag that had to be overcome by the remaining engine. I was told that the only way to overcome this deficiency was to get rid of the faulty engine and that this could be done by very rapid movement of the pitch control lever from 'fine' to 'coarse' shortly before total failure – causing the propeller shaft to shatter and the propeller itself to fly off without hitting the aircraft. Luckily, I never had occasion to try this drastic action. (C. Mount)

In April 1939 a detachment of 38 Squadron went to Northolt to carry out trials at the Air Fighting Development Establishment (AFDE) along with a detachment of

	Maximum Speed	Ceiling	Bomb Load	Range
Heyford IA	142mph (227kph)	21,000ft (6,400m)	1,600lb (730kg)	920m (1,500km)
Wellington	245mph (392kph)	21,600ft (6,500m)	4,500lb (2,000kg)	3,200m (5,000km)

(Left) In the immediate pre-war period RAF aircraft flew joint exercises with their French allies; here, 149 Squadron Wellingtons fly over Paris in June 1939. Peter Green Collection

This aircraft overshot its landing at Montrose and ran on to the golf course in autumn 1939. Note the 'Beware of Airscrew' notice just below the cockpit – many pilots remember with mixed emotions just how close the prop was to their heads!
Ken Delve Collection

Rare shot of a Wellington of the New Zealand Flight at Marham in 1939; this aircraft is NZ305, one of a number of Wellingtons destined for New Zealand but held back in the UK at the outbreak of war.
Andy Thomas Collection

1939 crew shot of 115 Squadron; this Marham-based unit re-equipped with the type in April 1939 and operated various marks until March 1943.
Ken Delve Collection

Hurricanes from 111 Squadron. The results of the trials were published as an Air Fighting Committee paper (AFC 70) entitled 'Tactical experiments with high speed aircraft, trials with Wellington aircraft.' In part this stated,

... the bomber results are similar to those of the Whitley rear air gunners. It was hoped that they would be better, but the Wellington turrets are inclined to be jerky in movement and the air gunners had difficulty in controlling them accurately. In addition, the air gunners were untrained and it will be seen that their shooting improved somewhat towards the end of the trials. Due to the operation of the rear turrets being jerky, and except in dead astern positions, the air gunners frequently had to kneel on the

Wellington I L4212 with no guns fitted but showing the 'dumpy' lines of the aircraft when viewed from this angle. This particular aircraft was converted to DWI standard and served with a number of units.
FlyPast Collection

Feltwell in August 1939 and a 214 Squadron aircraft. Andy Thomas Collection

seat to sight correctly, thus being somewhat unbalanced, the bomber results on the whole are not up to expectation.

The Wellingtons flew in formations of three, one span apart for mutual cover, and this, too, caused problems:

[the] Wellington corkscrews well but on slightly larger lines than the Hampden. At first they tried all aircraft corkscrewing in unison but this was not found practical and they resorted to independent corkscrewing.

The bombers used a co-ordinated defence plan with,

… the fighting controller operating from the astro hatch in the middle of the top of the fuselage where he had a good all-round view, except below his tail. He was able to issue warnings of all fighter approaches. When flying high, or in cold weather, the astro hatch is unsuitable for use by the fighting controller, also the heat from the fuselage is sucked out through this opening. It is understood, however, that the astro hatch is being modified into a dome. This, it is considered, would provide a most satisfactory position from which to exercise aiming control. Until the astro hatch is domed, the Fighting Controller should occupy the rear gunner's position. From his position, the Fighting Controller was in communication with the remainder of the formation by R/T and, in addition, with his own crew by intercom. The CO of the Wellington Squadron was convinced of the necessity of having an officer as the Fighting Controller.

Conclusions. The Wellington for its size is a manoeuvrable and comparatively fast aircraft which formated and carried out evasive manoeuvres most satisfactorily. It provides a large target for fighter aircraft and its present defence of two Browning guns in the tail turret does not appear to be adequate. The addition of an underneath dustbin turret having two Browning guns, which it is understood is being made to this type of aircraft, will be a great improvement but it is thought that the aircraft will still be rather exposed to a diving attack.

The final appendices of this report were dated 19 September 1939 and all too soon it would be proved just how inadequate the Wellington's defences were during daylight attack by a determined fighter opposition.

The Bomber Offensive

Since its formation in 1936, Bomber Command had undergone a significant number of changes: new squadrons had been formed (often by dividing existing units whose flights then acted as the nuclei of the new squadrons), new airfields opened and antiquated aircraft replaced. Indeed, there was little time for consideration of the development of sound tactics, and so the old 'invincible bomber' concept continued to hold sway.

In September 1939 the Wellington strength was concentrated in No. 3 Group under Air Vice-Marshal J. E. A. Baldwin, with its HQ at Mildenhall; it comprised six mobilizable squadrons (99 and 149 at Mildenhall, 38 and 115 at Marham, 9 at Honington and 37 at Feltwell) plus two non-mobilizing reserve squadrons, 214 and 215. In addition there were two Group Pool squadrons, 75 and 148.

At the declaration of war, Bomber Command was in somewhat of a dilemma as the strategic targets upon which bombing doctrine was based – the enemy's industrial and economic heartland – were 'off limits'. With land targets banned, the command had only one option open: attacking German shipping at sea. (It was even forbidden to attack shipping in port in case the bombs fell on land.) Thus, on the evening of 3 September 1939, the Wellington opened its operational career with an armed reconnaissance, hunting the Schilling Roads area for shipping to attack. Nine aircraft were involved, six from 37 Squadron at Feltwell and three from 149 Squadron at Mildenhall.

The following day the first real encounter took place when twenty-nine Blenheims and Wellingtons were tasked to attack German warships reported in the Wilhemshaven area. The Operation Order stated that, 'The greatest care is to be taken not to injure the civilian population. The intention is to destroy the German fleet. There is no alternative target.' The poor weather made the mission difficult, but the first wave of Blenheims that found the target surprised the defenders; later waves were not so lucky and lost five aircraft. Meanwhile, the Wellingtons of 9 and 149 Squadrons attacked the *Scharnhorst* and *Gneisenau* (two ships against which Bomber Command was to expend a great

Not the best of photos, but highly significant as it shows a 149 Squadron aircraft at Newmarket on 3 September 1939 – the day that war broke out.
Andy Thomas Collection

deal of effort over the next two years) at Brunsbuttel. The formations faced intense *Flak* and opposition from Bf 109 fighters but completed their attack, unfortunately with no significant result. However, they did lose two aircraft, L4268 and L4275, both from 9 Squadron, one of these falling to fighters and thus being the first RAF bomber to be lost to enemy fighter activity (the claim being made by Fw Alfred Held flying a Bf 109 of II./JG77). The 9 Squadron ORB records the mission by its six aircraft thus:

Report by Sqn Ldr Lamb – commanding No. 1 Section. I was ordered to carry out a bombing raid on warships inside Brunsbuttel harbour. Towards the end a fighter attack was carried out by nine German fighters at approx. 1835 hours. I jettisoned my three bombs 'live and in stick' at 400ft in the south side of the harbour. At the moment of bombing I felt sure that there was no shipping in the vicinity but having pressed the bomb release I saw a merchant ship, approx 7,000 tons. I climbed rapidly, still being attacked by fighters and succeeded in reaching cloud cover. It was necessary for the safety of my crew that these bombs were jettisoned as the decreased load enabled the machine to successfully evade the attack … Report by Flt Lt I. P. Grant – commanding No. 4 Section. The bombs were dropped at 1812 hours at a battleship which was about 7–8 miles due south of the entrance to Kiel; height 6,000ft. Immediately after release were forced to pull up into the cloud owing to the very high concentration of anti-aircraft fire and turned for home without waiting to see the results. Six or eight cruisers as well the battleship and shore batteries were firing at us. We were hit three times. All three

machines dropped their bombs at the same time.

No. 1 Section comprised L4320 (Sqn Ldr Lamb), L4268 (Flt Sgt Borley) and L4275 (Flt Sgt Turner); the latter two aircraft were casualties. No. 4 section comprised L4278 (Flt Lt Grant), L4287 (Sgt Purdy) and L4262 (Sgt Bowen).

Newer variants of the Wellington entered service in September when 9 Squadron received a number of Frazer-Nash turret-equipped Mark IAs. The IA was in fact a design development of the Wellington II with the same higher all-up weight of 28,000lb (13,000kg) – and the associated strengthened undercarriage – Pegasus X engines (although the original requirement called for the ability to interchange between the Pegasus and the Merlin) and the fitting of Frazer-Nash turrets in nose, midship and tail positions. The nose (FN5) and tail (FN10) turrets were hydraulically powered and each carried two 0.303in Brownings, whilst the ventral position was given an FN9 retractable turret. However, the Wellington IA was not truly successful and was not produced in large numbers.

After the September operations the bombers saw little action until the end of the year: in the period between 8 October and early December only fifty-five Wellington sorties were flown, all anti-shipping missions on which no targets were found and no aircraft lost.

Specification – Wellington IA	
ENGINES	Two Bristol Pegasus X
DIMENSIONS	Span 86ft 2in (26.26m); length 64ft 7in (19.68m)
PERFORMANCE	Max. speed 265mph (424km/h); ceiling 26,300ft (7,969m)
ARMAMENT	6x0.303in guns, 4,500lb (2,000kg) bombs
NUMBER BUILT	187

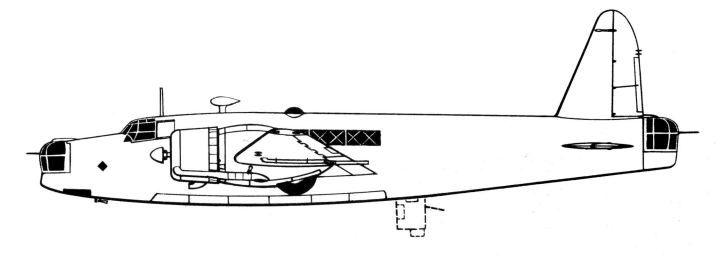

Wellington IA with its ventral turret extended. FlyPast Collection

Wellington squadrons were also involved in a number of exercises, especially in an endeavour to create effective wing operations. A major exercise for four squadrons of No. 3 Group (9, 37, 38 and 115 Squadrons) took place on 28 November, as recorded in the 9 Squadron ORB:

Six Wellingtons took off to carry out an exercise and proceeded to the first rendezvous (Upper Heyford). Co-ordination was good and the wing formed up after five minutes and proceeded to the second rendezvous (Rhyl). Heavy rainstorms were encountered on Welsh hills and the formation dropped from 6,000ft to 1,600ft at times. On passing over coast at Rhyl, wing was still in good formation and climbed steadily to 10,000ft. On approaching target clouds became more intense and a decision had to be made, either to deliver a high-level attack with a chance of gaps in the cloud or come down to below 2,000ft. As the main object of the exercise was high level, the wing commander decided to continue and carried out the attack at 10,000ft. The exercise was most useful and many points of instructional value were learned:

1. A force of twenty-four aircraft could put in a co-ordinated attack: first squadron to attack (9 Sqn) over target 1200 hours, last squadron to attack (115 Sqn) over target 1215 hours. This time could be reduced under more favourable weather conditions.
2. Rendezvous of squadrons can be carried out successfully provided that care is taken in co-ordinating prior to the exercise and if squadrons are not rushed.
3. It appears that we shall have to accept the fact that a wing is unable to form up again quickly after an attack and that flights of six will have to keep together for support after the attack.
4. Squadrons should be much closer together in wing formation for support on outward journey. It is considered that one type of formation should be adopted in wing formation i.e. 37 Squadron flew in pairs and other squadrons in vic.

Within a matter of weeks the Germans would show just how inappropriate was Bomber Command's concept of daylight bomber operations, and 9 Squadron would be one of those on the receiving end.

Although the command continued its war against German shipping, the contribution of the Wellington units was a series of invariably fruitless armed reconnaissance sorties. December, however, brought a return to major operations – and a num-

ber of disasters. On 3 December, twenty-four Wellingtons (from 38, 115 and 149 Squadrons) were tasked to attack warships in the Heligoland area; the bombers claimed at least one hit but were then attacked by Bf 109s and Bf 110s. A number of combats took place but the Wellingtons, employing their box defensive fire, suffered no real damage whilst claiming one Bf 109 shot down, for which LAC John Copley of 38 Squadron duly received a Distinguished Flying Medal (DFM). One of the most likely reasons for the German failure was their unfamiliarity with attacking targets the size of the Wellington, so most attacks were probably not pressed into effective range, and uncertainty as to the defensive capability of their opponents; to the RAF it appeared that the validity of daylight bomber formations had been proved. Less than two weeks later there would be a different picture.

Wellington ORBAT, November 1939	
No. 3 Gp	
Feltwell	37, 214 Sqns
Honington	9 Sqn
Marham	38, 115 Sqns
Mildenhall	99, 149 Sqns
No. 6 Gp	
Bassingbourn	215 Sqn

A posed publicity shot of crews after the initial Heligoland raids; the Wellingtons were confined to searching for, and attacking, 'naval targets at sea' in the first months of the war. Ken Delve Collection

Among the forty-four aircraft operating on 14 December were twelve Wellingtons from 99 Squadron out of Newmarket, tasked to attack shipping 12 mile south of Heligoland. The weather was very poor and the bombers had to go down to sea-level to attack from below cloud. Some twenty enemy fighters appeared and in the ensuing combats five Wellingtons were shot down, although some sources suggest that a number of the losses may have been due to the *Flak* from ships. The bomber gunners claim to have shot down five fighters, although German records con-

cede only one loss; according to RAF reports, 'The crews of the Wellingtons were very well satisfied with the mutual fire-power developed by the power-operated turrets. They had inflicted losses heavier than those they had themselves sustained.' With no definite proof either way as to the viability of such daylight attacks, the RAF planned another raid. On 18 December a force of twenty-four Wellingtons (9, 37 and 149 Squadrons) set out for the Wilhelmshaven area. Detected by German radar, the twenty-two bombers that reached the target area were met by

The theory that the bombers would be able to operate by day using mutual defensive fire in close formation was soon proved to be wrong; one of the 115 Squadron pilots involved in the December raids had this picture painted based on his recollection of the Bf 110 attack on his section.
Eric Scott

(Below) Crews kitting out for another sortie; sheepskin jackets and fleece-lined boots were one way of trying to keep out the cold – the Wellington had little in the way of heating.
Ken Delve Collection

heavy fighter opposition from II./JG77 and 1./ZG76. Although instructed to hold formation and bomb from above 10,000ft to avoid the worst of the *Flak*, the bombers were forced to spread out to reduce the danger from intense *Flak* over the port, leaving them vulnerable to fighter attack. The *Luftwaffe* took full advantage and shot down many of the bombers, others being so seriously damaged that they crashed back in England.

Of the 9 Squadron contingent, Sgt Petts had to force-land N2873 at Sutton Bridge: 'The starboard wing to the rear of the mid cell of wing tanks badly shot up and had been on fire, but the fire was localized. Armour plating kept fire from tank. The armour plating was pierced but the tank was not holed. Starboard side of fuselage freely peppered' (after repair the aircraft went to 20 OTU). Fg Off Macrae had to force-land N2871 at North Coates: 'The armour plating to the rear of starboard wing tank had been pierced and ragged edge had turned forward and holed tank. Rudder control rod pierced and roller bracket shot away causing partial jamming of rudder control. Starboard tailplane and fuselage peppered' (the aircraft was repaired and saw extensive service, eventually crashing at Mauripur in September 1944). One aircraft (N2983, Sgt Hewitt) was so badly damaged that it had to ditch off Cromer, Norfolk, one crewman having been killed in the fighter attack. Four aircraft of 9 Squadron failed to return: N2872 (Sqn Ldr Guthrie), N2941 (Fg Off Allison), N2939 (Fg Off Challes) and N2940 (Plt Off Lines). Meanwhile, 37 Squadron had two aircraft, N2888 (Fg Off Wimberley) and N2889 (Fg Off Lewis), shot down by Lt Helmut Lent (who went on to become one of the top-scoring night fighter pilots). A further three were also shot down by fighters: N2904 (Sqn Ldr Hue-Williams), N2935 (Fg Off Thompson) and N2936 (Sgt Ruse). (See Appendix V for a list of all Bomber Command operational Wellington losses.)

The Switch to Night Bombing

The 18 December raid had been a disaster, but even this did not convince all within Bomber Command's higher echelons of the futility of such missions: some argued that poor formation-keeping was the major cause of the losses. If they could have seen contemporary German reports they would have read that German fighter

A very pensive-looking Wellington crew member.
Ken Delve Collection

pilots considered that the close formation made their job easier! Nevertheless, this raid did bring to an end such missions by the Wellington units (although this was not entrenched official policy until April 1940). The Air Ministry ordered,

... cessation of attacks on naval bases and reconnaissance in force until the petrol tanks should be armoured, pending the fitting of self-sealing tanks. Many aircraft had been observed to have petrol pouring out, and most of the losses during the month were attributed to petrol tanks catching fire. This is confirmed by German reports, which note the extreme vulnerability of Wellingtons to fire in the wings ... the most important lesson learnt was that the heavy bombers could not economically be used by day. The firepower of their turrets did not compensate for their slow speed and they had numerous blind spots. (AHB *Narrative*; 'RAF in the Bomber Offensive against Germany')

From now on the Wellingtons joined the Whitleys of No. 4 Group on night leaflet-dropping (code-named *Nickel*) missions over Germany; indeed, the first such Wellington involvement had taken place on 8 September when four aircraft from 99 Squadron dropped 'Nickel 273' over Hannover and Brunswick.

Even the scant operational experience of late 1939 had shown up major defects with the aircraft and its concept of operations and these were gradually addressed. In January,

... a further modification was begun with the introduction of self-sealing (Semaped) tanks. The process was slow owing to the shortage of tanks, but aircraft were replaced by degrees, the aircraft with non-sealing tanks being passed on to the Group Pool squadrons for training purposes. The mods were not completed until May, in which month balloon-cutting equipment was also added. (AHB *Narrative*: 'RAF in the Bomber Offensive Against Germany')

Bomber Command was still very much an offensive organization in search of a worthwhile task. The decision to move to night operations meant a major change for the crews as up to this point very little night flying had been carried out either in training or on the squadrons. The night operations flown for leaflet-dropping were to prove invaluable in respect of crews acquiring experience in the art of night flying, although the effectiveness of the leaflet campaign itself was highly suspect. Typical of such operations was that by two 37 Squadron aircraft (N2937/R, Flt Lt Samuels, and P9216/O, Sgt Fletcher) of the night of 5–6 March, the former going to Bremen and the latter to Hamburg. The 37 Squadron ORB records:

0100. Both aircraft took off in snow storms, set course and climbed through 10/10 cloud, clear air was reached at 4,000ft, clouds over the German coast were 8/10 to 10/10. Line bearings were obtained from HF/DF at Feltwell during the first 100 miles of outbound flight. Aircraft then changed to MF/DF and a number of fixes were obtained. Fixes were obtained immediately before *Nickels* were released. No trouble was experienced and both aircraft released all *Nickels* in twenty-five minutes each.

In the same month, Bomber Command issued an instruction giving specific 'night reconnaissance' areas to each Group, that

Warnung

Großbritannien an das Deutsche Volk.

Deutsche,

Mit kühl erwogenem Vorsatz hat die Reichsregierung Großbritannien Krieg aufgezwungen. Wohl wußte sie, daß die Folgen ihrer Handlung die Menschheit in ein größeres Unheil stürzen, als 1914 es tat. Im April gab der Reichskanzler euch und der Welt die Versicherung seiner friedlichen Absichten; sie erwies sich als ebenso wertlos wie seine im September des Vorjahres im Sportpalast verkündeten Worte: „Wir haben keine weiteren territorialen Forderungen in Europa zu stellen."

Niemals hat eine Regierung ihre Untertanen unter geringerem Vorwand in den Tod geschickt. Dieser Krieg ist gänzlich unnötig. Von keiner Seite waren deutsches Land und deutsches Recht bedroht. Niemand verhinderte die Wiederbesetzung des Rheinlandes, den Vollzug des Anschlusses und die unblutig durchgeführte Einkörperung der Sudeten in das Reich. Weder wir, noch irgendein anderes Land, versuchte je dem Ausbau des deutschen Reiches Schranken zu setzen—solange dieses nicht die Unabhängigkeit nicht-deutscher Völker verletzte.

Allen Bestrebungen Deutschlands—solange sie Andern gerecht blieben—hätte man in friedlicher Beratung Rechnung getragen.

273

!!! Warnung !!!

— Seite 2 —

Präsident Roosevelt hat euch sowohl Frieden mit Ehren als auch die Aussicht auf materielle Wohlfahrt angeboten. An Stelle dessen hat eure Regierung euch zu dem Massenmord, dem Elend und den Entbehrungen eines Krieges verurteilt, den zu gewinnen sie nicht einmal erhoffen können.

Nicht uns, sondern euch haben sie betrogen. Durch Jahre hindurch hat euch eine eiserne Zensur Wahrheiten unterschlagen, die selbst unzivilisierten Völkern bekannt sind. Diese Zensur hält den Geist des deutschen Volkes in einem Konzentrationslager gefangen. Wie sonst konnten sie es wagen, die Zusammenarbeit friedliebender Völker zur Sicherung des Friedens fälschlich als feindliche Einkreisung darzustellen? Wir hegen keine Feindseligkeit gegen euch, das deutsche Volk.

Diese Nazi Zensur hat euch verheimlicht, daß ihr nicht über die Mittel verfügt, einen langen Krieg durchzuhalten. Trotz erdrückender Steuerlast seid ihr am Rande des Bankrotts. Wir und unsere Bundesgenossen verfügen über unermeßliche Reserven an Manneskraft, Rüstung und Vorräten. Wir sind zu stark, durch Hiebe gebrochen zu werden und können euch unerbittlich bis zur Enderschöpfung bekämpfen.

Ihr, das deutsche Volk, habt das Recht, auf Frieden zu bestehen jetzt und zu jeder Zeit. Auch wir wünschen den Frieden und sind bereit, ihn mit jeder aufrichtig friedlich gesinnten deutschen Regierung abzuschließen.

Leaflet No. 1   Copy No.1
E.H. 273

WARNING

German men and women,

The Government of the Reich have with cold deliberation forced war upon Great Britain. They have done so knowing that it must involve mankind in a calamity worse than that of 1914. The assurances of peaceful intentions the Fuehrer gave to you and to the world in April have proved as worthless as his words at the Sportpalast last September when he said – 'We have no more territorial claims to make in Europe.'

Never has a Government ordered subjects to their death with less excuse. This war is utterly unnecessary. Germany was in no way threatened or deprived of justice. Was she not allowed to re-enter the Rhineland, to achieve the Anschluss, and to take back the Sudeten Germans in peace? Neither we nor any other nation would have sought to limit her advance, so long as she did not violate independent non-German peoples.

Every German ambition – just to others – might have been satisfied through friendly negotiation.

President Roosevelt offered you both peace with honour and the prospect of prosperity. Instead your rulers have condemned you to the massacre, miseries and privations of a war they cannot even hope to win.

It is not us, but you they have deceived. For years **their iron censorship has kept you from truths that even uncivilised peoples know.** It has imprisoned your minds in, as it were, a concentration camp. Otherwise they would not have dared to misrepresent the combination of peaceful peoples to secure peace as hostile encirclement. We had no enmity against you, the German people.

This censorship has also concealed from you that you have not the means to sustain protracted warfare. **Despite crushing taxation you are on the verge of bankruptcy.** Our resources and those of our allies in men, arms and supplies are immense. **We are too strong to break by blows, and we could wear you down inexorably.**

You, the German people, can if you will, insist on peace at any time. We also desire peace and are prepared to conclude it with any peace-loving Government in Germany.

Nickel **273**

for No. 3 Group comprising the area of Dorum–Bergstedt–Wusterhaven–Wolfenbuttel–Lemgo–Dorum. These so-called 'reconnaissances' over Germany were in effect bombing missions but without the bombs! They were used to acquire a wealth of information on air-to-ground visibility, navigation, meteorological conditions, the effect of moonlight and searchlights on identifying targets, and so on. It was estimated that an average crew should be able to get within 10 miles of its target using DR (Deduced Reckoning) navigation techniques but once within this 'box' they would have to be able to identify ground features in order to make accurate attacks on the industrial targets against which they were likely to be tasked.

Meanwhile, February 1940 had seen the introduction to service of the first of the truly great Wellington variants, the IC, when 9 Squadron at Honington received the variant in place of its IAs. (A Wellington IB had also been proposed but was not put into production.) Some 2,685 of this Mark IC variant were eventually produced and it soldiered on – in the training role late on – until the end of the war. The aircraft was the result of design changes in the light of experience gained with the other variants. One of the major changes was the removal of the ventral turret and its replacement with Vickers 0.303 beam guns (beam guns, of Vickers K type, having been trialled in Wellington IA P9211 at Boscombe Down by the A&AEE). The Wellington IC was powered by the reliable Pegasus XVIII but incorporated new hydraulic and electrical systems.

The AFDE continued its trials work at an increased pace after the outbreak of war, a number of these trials involving the bomber force. AFC report 83 dealt with 'Bomber tactics to counter beam attacks'.

Specification – Wellington IC	
ENGINES	Two Bristol Pegasus XVIII
DIMENSIONS	Span 86ft 2in (26.26m); length 64ft 7in (19.68m)
PERFORMANCE	Max. speed 235mph (376km/h); ceiling 18,000ft (5,454m)
ARMAMENT	6 × 0.303in guns, 4,500lb (2,000kg) bombs
FIRST FLIGHT	23 December 1937
NUMBER BUILT	2,685

Wellington IA P2517 was one of eighteen aircraft delivered in January 1940, this one going initially to 37 Squadron but seen here with 149 Squadron. Ken Delve Collection

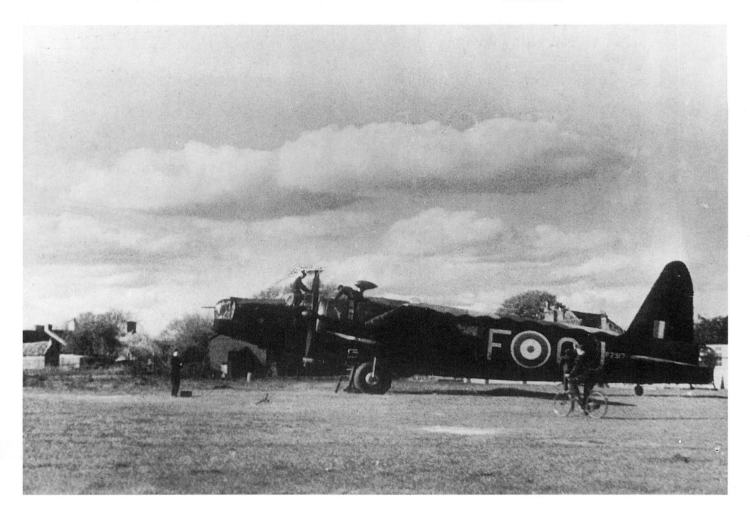

The first of the truly great variants, the Mark IC.
FlyPast Collection

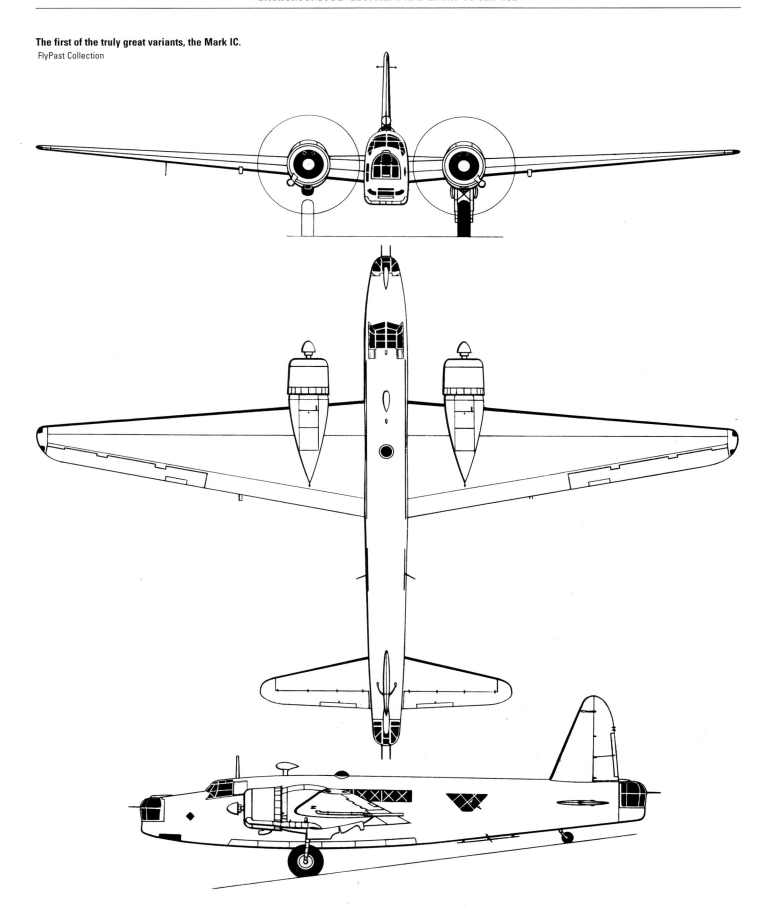

(Above) **A 99 Squadron Wellington IA on a wet day in 1940; the gun turrets of the IA were an improvement over the early Wellingtons, but the bomber was still by no means well defended.**
Peter Green Collection

Wellington IA N2895 of 75 Squadron at Stradishall in May 1940. Andy Thomas Collection

This trial in March 1940 involved seven aircraft from 37 Squadron working with Defiants of 264 squadron and Spitfires of 65 Squadron, and was intended to, ascertain the best form of defence to be taken by bombers against beam attacks as carried out by the German Me 110 ... The Wellingtons flew in a box of six, in two sections of three, the rear section being stepped up. Beam guns were not used as trials with these are not yet complete. The report concluded that,

> ... it appears that the Me 110 has an excess of speed over the Wellington of at least 160mph and it is therefore obvious that with this great excess the fighter can practically pick its time and position for an attack at will. Thus the Wellington with its lack of a sufficiently high speed and poor formation flying qualities in speed, range and acceleration is forced to rely entirely on its defensive armament. It therefore

appears that the only sure way to drive off such an attack is to have a really effective defensive armament i.e one in which the bomber has practically no blind spot. The Wellington field of fire is blind close on the beam and above and it is therefore considered that the beam guns as suggested by 37 Squadron, which cover quite a large proportion of this blind area, offered the best solution. It is understood that the addition of this extra gun has not been approved at present. It is suggested that for formations of four, or multiples of four, the '37 Formation' is used and for formations of six, or multiples of six, the '99 Formation' is used.

On 16 March, Air Chief Marshal Sir Charles Portal became C-in-C of Bomber Command and on the 19th the command undertook its first planned attack on a land target in Germany when a force of Hampdens and Whitleys attacked the seaplane base at Hornum, Sylt. However, this

was seen as a 'one-off' reprisal for a German attack on the Orkney Islands, and so the Wellingtons continued to drop their loads of propaganda 'bumpf' over Europe. All this was to change in April.

On April 9 the Germans invaded Denmark and Norway, the latter being an area of great concern to British Prime Minister Winston Churchill, who saw it as of vital strategic import to Britain. A Wellington detachment, from 9 and 115 Squadrons, had been present at Lossiemouth since the beginning of the month, preparing for operations over Norway, and on the 7th a strong force of Wellingtons took off on a shipping search. They failed to find the enemy convoy but were intercepted by a force of Bf 110s; two of 115 Squadron's aircraft were shot down and others damaged.

Then, on 11 April, Sqn Ldr du Boulay of 115 Squadron led the RAF's first intentional bombing attack on a mainland

Wellington ORBAT, April 1940	
No. 3 Gp	
Honington	9, 215 Sqns
Feltwell	37, 214 Sqns
Marham	38, 115 Sqns
Stradishall	75, 148 Sqns
Mildenhall	99, 149 Sqns
No. 16 Gp	
Bircham Newton	2 GRU (forming)
Manston	1 GRU
OTUs	
11 OTU	Bassingbourn
15 OTU	Harwell

European target, six Wellingtons being tasked to 'bomb runways, aircraft and aerodrome installations' on the now German-held airfield at Stavanger-Sola. The aircraft were loaded with 500lb SAP bombs; take-off was timed for 1810. Attacks were to be delivered from 1,000ft to ensure accuracy; the first section of three made their attacks with little opposition but the second section, led by Plt Off Barber, met heavy *Flak*. Barber's P9284 was shot down and one other aircraft so badly damaged

that it had to force-land at Kinloss. The following day a force of Wellingtons and Hampdens, out on armed shipping reconnaissance near Stavanger, ran into heavy fighter opposition which pursued the bombers out to sea; six Hampdens and three Wellingtons were shot down, although the bombers claimed to have shot down five fighters.

This was the last major daylight raid undertaken by the Wellingtons at this stage of the war in Europe. Operations over Norway, attacks on airfields and anti-shipping work, remained the primary task for the rest of April but the rapid German fighter build-up made the unescorted raids hazardous.

In April Portal had been given a new operational directive which, in the event of 'general air action' being implemented, would bring into force the provisions of pre-war strategic plan WA8 authorizing attacks on:

1. Identifiable oil plants;
2. Identifiable electricity plants, coking plants and gas ovens;
3. Self-illuminating objectives vulnerable to air attack;
4. Main German ports in the Baltic.

This was still far short of the all-out industrial and economic offensive that many bomber theorists desired, and even then

was conditional on the political will to initiate such a strategy. In April 1940 this still seemed unlikely and so the bomber force, and especially the Wellingtons, was left with no real mission. (The Whitleys were heavily engaged on leaflet dropping and assorted other operations and the Hampdens had found a new mission with minelaying, code-named 'Gardening' during which they planted *vegetables* – mines.) However, there was second element to the directive which, in the event of a German attack in the west, authorized attacks on 'vital objectives in Germany, starting in the Ruhr, to cause the maximum dislocation to lines of communication of the German advance through the Low Countries.' The primary target groups under this plan were troop concentrations, communications in the Ruhr (especially marshalling yards, the use of rail for mass military transport being seen as a key factor and one that would be easy to disrupt), and oil plants in the Ruhr.

Strategic Bombing Begins

The German attack in the west, launched on 10 May, was soon making spectacular advances and air power was used by the Allies in an attempt to stem the enemy advance. Then, on 15 May, Churchill at last authorized Bomber Command to bomb

An atmospheric night shot of Wellingtons at Marham; the night bomber offensive really began in May 1940 when Churchill authorized attacks on targets in Germany. Ken Delve Collection

targets east of the Rhine, thus clearing the way for attacks on many of the old Western Air (WA) series of targets. On the night of 15–16 May Bomber Command launched ninety-nine bombers (including thirty-nine Wellingtons) to attack various targets in the Ruhr: the RAF's strategic bombing offensive (SBO) had begun. Although none of the bombers was lost to enemy action, a 115 Squadron aircraft (P9229, Flt Lt A. Pringle and crew) crashed near Rouen and was thus the first casualty of the SBO.

Most nights throughout the remainder of May saw the bombers in action against industrial or battlefield targets, attacking communications or troop concentrations. Typical of the night raids being carried out by Bomber Command 'heavies' against tactical targets was that recorded by 37 Squadron for 7 June:

Operations – Somme. Bois de Boulers and Bois de Baileux. Ten aircraft were ordered to carry out operations on the night of 7–8 June. One aircraft was unable to take off owing to engine trouble. Eight aircraft were detailed to attack bridges across the River Somme and enemy movements on roads leading towards them. The other two aircraft were detailed to attack the area of Bois de Boulers and Bois de Baileux. Weather over the target was making identification difficult. Most of the crews, however, were able to pick up the line of the Somme, giving them a lead to their objectives. Attacks on the Somme bridges were sustained from 2315 hours to 0100 hours; aircraft were despatched at half hourly intervals to attack each target. All crews carried out high level bombing attacks with the exception of Sgt Watt who made shallow dive attacks from 9–6,000ft. Direct hits were made on the woods and extensive fires, accompanied by heavy explosions, resulted. Of the aircraft attacking communications and bridges, two definitely claimed to have straddled the bridges. Hits were also claimed on road junction at St Valery and on Flak and searchlight positions. All aircraft returned safely.

The last British troops left French soil on 18 June and as the summer progressed, so the bombers turned their attention to a new threat: that of invasion. The Germans were gathering barges and merchant shipping in various ports, the situation being summed up by a Bomber Command report:

The invasion ports face us in a crescent, centred on Calais, some of the world's greatest cargo and passenger installations; in fact, if the enemy had

---

Operations Against Italy

When Italy entered the war on 10 June it was considered essential that an early bombing raid be made against industrial targets in northern Italy to show that these were not safe from attack. Because of the distances involved it was decided to operate from southern France, and *Haddock Force* was formed with Wellingtons being deployed to Salon, near Marseilles. The planned attack on Milan had to be cancelled when the French authorities objected; by the time of this political wrangling the first attack on Italy had been made by the Whitleys of No. 4 Group. The Wellingtons soon joined in, making attacks on 15–16 June (Genoa) and 16–17 June (Genoa and Milan). On the first operation only one of the eight bombers claimed to have bombed the target; twenty-two aircraft went out the second night and fourteen claimed to have attacked the targets.

---

built the ports himself for the express purpose of invading this country he could hardly have improved their actual layout – Amsterdam, Rotterdam, Flushing, Bruges, Zeebrugge, Ostend, Antwerp, Dunkirk, Calais, Boulogne, Dieppe, Le Havre and Cherbourg, plus all those on the 'flanks' of this crescent.

Whilst the Blenheims of No. 2 Group were particularly heavily engaged against these targets, and against shipping in general, the heavy squadrons soon joined the fray. This was especially so in September and early October when the majority of Bomber Command's effort was expended against the invasion ports.

However, throughout the late summer and autumn the command continued to divide its resources by attacking several kinds of target with, apparently, little attempt at any strategic concentration, even though as early as 13 July the Air Staff had concluded that operations had been too dispersed and that for the coming moonlight period effort should be concentrated on a limited number of targets; this was duly reflected in a new directive which gave fifteen primary targets. The strategic offensive against targets within Germany was still considered to be paramount and Berlin was attacked for the first time on 25–26 August in retaliation for attacks on London; the target was covered in cloud and few bombs actually fell anywhere near the city. However, from now on the 'Big City' was to become a frequent target for Bomber Command. George Bury was in a

115 Squadron Wellington that attacked Berlin on 28 August:

The target was Klingenberg Electric and, having been warned that the area was very heavily defended, we decided to fly at 15,000ft, that was 5,000ft higher than our normal height, just what we expected to achieve by this I am not sure, maybe the benefit was more psychological than practical and after flying for eight hours at this height we reverted to our normal height for future flights. On our very first operational flight we had flown at 15,000ft and it is essential to use oxygen all the time, but after a few hours the masks became wet and uncomfortable to use, and if taken off, frequent movement is very tiring, not so at 10,000ft.

The bombers also targeted German crops and forests as part of the 'economic war' and for this task special 'fire raising' devices were used, known as *Razzles* and *Deckers*. These weapons consisted of small phosphorous pellets in celluloid strips, 3 × 1in (75 × 25mm) for *Razzle* and 4 × 4in (100 × 100mm) for *Decker*; the idea being that they would ignite as they dried out and so set fire to their surroundings (including, in a few reported cases, the pockets of those who had collected them as souvenirs!). These 'incendiary leaves' were stored in tins of alcohol and water, about 500 to a tin, the idea being to put them down the flare chute when the time came. It appears that they caused little damage to the Germans, but they did cause concern in some of the attacking aircraft as leaves stuck on the aircraft, dried out and then caught fire! The first such raid took place on the night of 30 June but the first of the specific forest attacks was carried out by thirty Wellingtons on the night of 2–3 September, the target being the Black Forest and the Thuringian forests.

The *Luftwaffe* was fully aware of the locations of the main aircraft factories in the UK and on Wednesday 4 September it was the Wellington production line at Weybridge that was hit in a low-level daylight attack. A group of about twenty Bf 110s of V.(*Zerstörer*)/LG1, equipped with 500kg bombs on fuselage racks had been briefed to attack the Hawker factory at Brooklands. Despite a determined attack by the Hurricanes of 253 Squadron, the bombers reached the target area; however, it was the Wellington sheds that received hits, at least six bombs falling on the machine shops and assembly sheds causing hundreds of casualties, with eighty-eight workers being killed. Although dispersal plans were already in hand, this attack caused them to be implemented much more quickly, component manufacture being dispersed to a variety of locations in the area, although final assembly still took place at Brooklands.

Whilst Portal as AOC Bomber Command was pushing for an offensive strategy, he was constrained by the need to attack invasion targets and other targets aimed at 'reducing the scale of air attack on the UK.' Nevertheless, Churchill, in a memo to the War Cabinet made it clear that Bomber

the Wellington was, for the next two years, to be the prime instrument. Expansion in 1940 was, however, to prove very slow; although fourteen squadrons formed or re-equipped with Wellingtons during the year, most of these did so in the last three months of the year.

The winter weather over Europe was one of the greatest enemies that the bomber crews had to face, and the Wellington was no better equipped to handle the problems than any of the other types. The usual operating heights of 10–15,000ft meant that the aircraft could

aircraft, the Wellington was all too often unable to maintain flying height; furthermore, ice build-up on propellers usually resulted in chunks of ice being thrown off the props and into the side of the aircraft, this tending, fortunately, to be rather more noisy than dangerous. The extreme cold also made life very uncomfortable for the crew, as George Bury recalls:

It was a very cold night and the captain, who had been flying the aircraft for over three hours, handed over to the second pilot and came back to the navigator/wireless compartment and

August 1940 and a Wellington II engine test. Note the fully-feathered right-hand propeller. FlyPast Collection

Command had a key role to play. 'The Navy can lose us the war, but only the Air Force can win it ... the bombers alone are our salvation. We must therefore develop the power to carry an increasing volume of explosives to Germany.' Expansion of the bomber force was to be a key element of air strategy for the remainder of the war and

rarely climb clear of any bad weather that was encountered; the risks inherent in trying to fly below the weather made this option equally unattractive. However, when flying through freezing cloud the aircraft soon became covered in ice; with thick build-up of ice on wings and other surfaces adding dangerous weight to the

squatted on the floor to warm up a bit. Hot air from the engines was ducted to the cockpit but it had very little effect, whereas the navigation compartment, having a door between it and the main fuselage, was almost warm.

The bomber crews were being called upon to navigate to, find and then attack

A classic picture of the sturdy nature of the Wellington's geodetic structure; the tail turret has gone and the fabric has burnt away, as well as severe damage to the tail surfaces – but the aircraft made it back.
Ken Delve Collection

small(ish) industrial targets, sometimes located in major cities, a type of mission that had seemed perfectly feasible in the pre-war period and for which the pre-war bomber crews had been trained – by day. Since the lesson had been hammered home the previous year that daylight medium bomber operations in the face of enemy fighter opposition were not viable, the command had simply resorted to seeking the cover of night whilst giving little real consideration to how crews were going to achieve their task. Enemy air opposition had, it is true, been all but removed from the equation by taking to the night skies – although this was soon to change – and the *Flak* defences, whilst strong in certain areas, where still on a rel-

atively small scale. But if the bombs could not be delivered to their targets, then what was the point of going at all? In the absence of bomb run photography, cameras being fitted in only a small number of aircraft at this stage, and with limited photo-reconnaissance resources to carry out post-attack reconnaissance, the command was to some extent in ignorance of what it was or was not achieving.

The basic navigation technique was that of the 'airplot', whereby the navigator kept track of the aircraft's position by plotting the heading and speed of the aircraft from a known point (commencing with the overhead of the airfield from which the aircraft had departed). Every time the aircraft changed heading or speed this was

reflected in the air plot. The major effect upon this position was that caused by the wind; hence the effect of the wind had to be applied in order to arrive at a position of the aircraft over the ground. The initial information regarding the wind was obtained from the meteorological briefing at base and so reliance had to be placed on the accuracy of this forecast – all too often it proved wildly inaccurate. Having commenced the air plot, it was then updated by taking fixes, ideally from a visual pinpoint (a recognizable feature) over which the aircraft passed – a headland, island, or lake, for example. The airplot could then be updated and started again from this new ground position and a more accurate wind calculated. Without regular fixes the

airplot became ever more prone to errors introduced through inaccurate wind forecasts, compass and other instrument errors and it was quite possible for the aircraft to end up more than 100 miles 'off track'. The only electronic aid available in this early part of the war was Direction Finding (D/F), whereby the aircraft could receive a signal from a ground station: this indicated the line of sight from the aircraft to the station, the aircraft being somewhere along that line. If two or more lines could be made to cross, then the position at which they did so would indicate the position of the aircraft. At best this was only a general aid; it was far more useful as a homing aid whereby the aircraft could follow the signal from, and thus arrive at, its base. Position lines could also be obtained using astro 'star shots' if the sky was clear, but all too often the weather intervened and the Wellington was seldom capable of climbing above the cloud into clear air.

Having arrived in the area in which the target was calculated to be, and even having identified the area to be bombed, the

(Above) **Re-arming the rear turret of a Wellington; at this stage the turret is only fitted with two 0.303 Brownings and yet it was thought that close formation and mutual firepower would enable Wellingtons to operate by day.** Ken Delve Collection

Two sergeant air gunners take great care with the re-arming of their aircraft; the early Wellingtons suffered problems with the turrets. Ken Delve Collection

problems of bombing accuracy were not over, as George Bury recalled:

> Bombing from a Wellington of a night time was not easy using the Course Setting Bomb Sight and I think that the use of this instrument introduced great errors, in fact I have often felt that the World War One practice of the pilot throwing the bombs over the side by hand might have been an improvement on the use of the CSBS! The instrument consisted of a compass bowl on the front of which was an arm with two parallel wires and a foresight, at right angles to this and above the compass was a height bar together with a back sight. Upon approaching the target area the wind speed and direction would be set on the CSBS and the height being flown above ground set on the height bar. When the target was sighted the pilot would be directed to turn on to it and the compass on the CSBS would be set to coincide with that of the pilot. It was then necessary to direct the pilot, 'left, left, steady, right, steady' etc. in order to keep the target within the drift wires on the front of the compass bowl but as each turn was made the compass had to be rotated so that it was showing the actual course being flown. Reasonably easy except that neither the compass, drift wires, foresight or backsight were illuminated. There was a small light above the compass but the use of white light reflected from the Perspex viewing window and greatly affected night vision.

Another variant entered service in the latter part of the year when, in November, 12 Squadron received its Merlin-powered Wellington IIs, replacing its Fairey Battles. The aircraft had its origins in early 1938 as part of the policy of using the most powerful engine type available or likely to be available. The prototype, L4250, first flew on 3 March 1939 with Merlin Xs, and it incorporated a number of features that were also working their way into other Wellington designs, such as the use of Frazer-Nash turrets and a 24v electrical system. The aircraft was also fitted with an astrodome, astro navigation being an important technique in the absence of radio aids, as well as cabin heating. Initial flight tests were not promising and a degree of redesign on the fin and engine nacelles was required. With these and other changes the Mark II was, by late 1939, seen to be superior in overall performance to the IC and by spring 1940 series production had commenced. Numerous weapon developments were taking place around the same time and it was decided to

modify a Wellington II to take a 4,000lb (1,800kg) bomb; three aircraft (W5389, W5399 and W5400) were converted and used for trials, and despite a number of problems, mainly with the bomb rather than the aircraft installation, it was cleared for operational use early in 1941.

Specification – Wellington II	
ENGINES	Two Rolls-Royce Merlin X
DIMENSIONS	Span 86ft 2in (26.26m); length 60ft 10in (18.54m)
PERFORMANCE	Max. speed 270mph (432km/h); ceiling 23,500ft (7,121m)
ARMAMENT	6–8 × 0.303in guns, 4,500lb (2,000kg) bombs
FIRST FLIGHT	3 March 1939
NUMBER BUILT	400

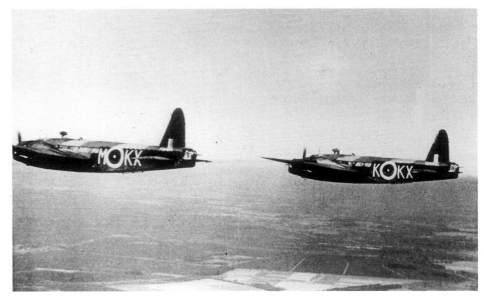

The sole Czech bomber squadron, 311 Squadron, formed at Honington in July 1940 and was soon taking part in Bomber Command's night offensive; the unit was transferred to Coastal Command in April 1942. Ken Delve Collection

Six other squadrons formed or re-equipped with Wellingtons in October–November: 103 and 150 at Newton, 300 at Hemswell, 142 at Binbrook, 301 at Swinderby, 304 and 305 at Bramcote; the four Polish units (all in the 300-series of numbering given to Allied squadrons) contained a high proportion of experienced aircrew and two of them had already seen operational service with Fairey Battles. (The first of these Allied

squadrons had been 311 Squadron, a Czech unit formed in July 1940.)

November brought a major expansion of Wellington strength with four more squadrons receiving the type within No. 3 Group: 15 Squadron (Wyton), 40 Squadron (Wyton), 57 Squadron (Wyton, but moved to Feltwell the same month) and 218 Squadron (Oakington and then to Marham the same month) all receiving Mark ICs. This gave the Group a strength of eleven Wellington squadrons.

The bomber war was hotting up on both sides and, following a series of *Luftwaffe* attacks on British cities (the so-called *Baedekker* raids), Bomber Command was authorized to carry out a major attack against a German city. Under Operation *Abigail Rachel*, some 200 bombers were tasked against Mannheim, although with the Motorenwerke Mannheim AG facto-

ry as a notional aiming point; this was very much the first of the area attacks against enemy cities. The strike force was subsequently cut as the weather forecast at certain airfields was poor; the final attack on 15–16 December was carried out by a force of 134 aircraft, including sixty-one Wellingtons and eight of these, flown by experienced crews, opened the attack, the idea being that they would

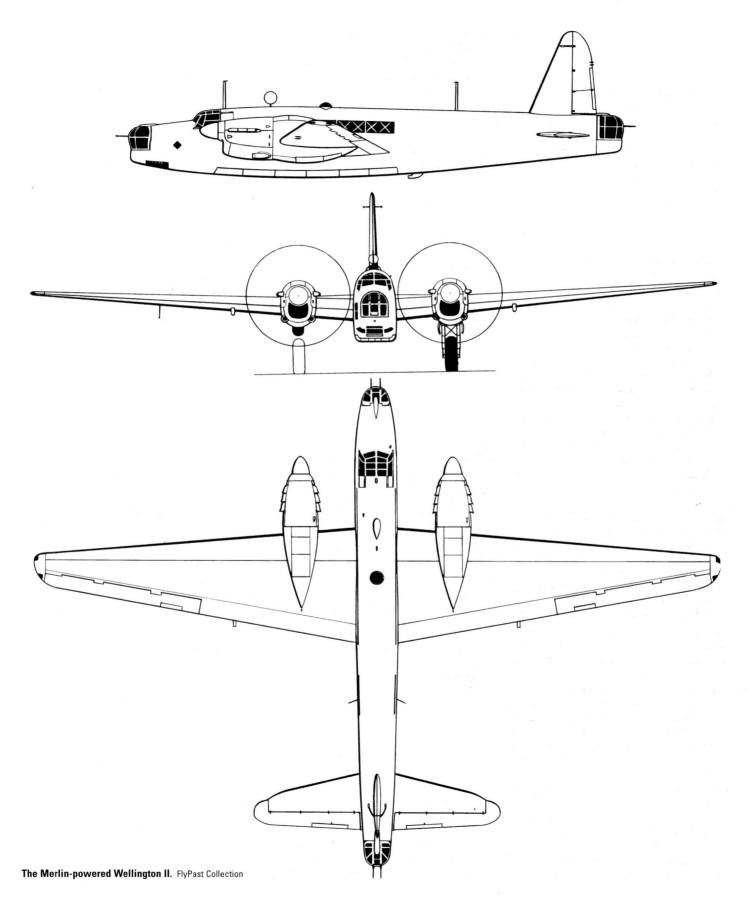

The Merlin-powered Wellington II. FlyPast Collection

The first of the Polish bomber squadrons, 300 Squadron, re-equipped with Wellingtons at Hemswell in October 1940. Ken Delve Collection

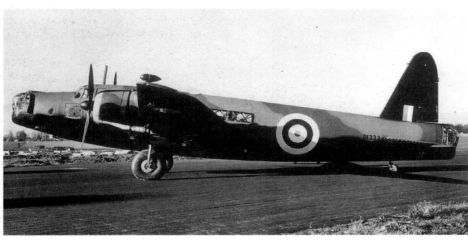

Wellington IC R1333 'The Broughton Wellington', 7 November 1940. This was a presentation aircraft that went to 99 Squadron; it had a short life as it hit the Devil's Dyke on take-off from Newmarket on 18 December. via Gerry Tyack

start enough fires at the target to act as a beacon for the following bombers. These aircraft dropped their loads away from the centre of the target and the main weight of the attack fell on residential areas. Nevertheless, it was considered to have been a success. No Wellingtons were lost over Germany, but three crashed in England with the loss of three crewmen in T2577 of 311 Squadron.

In December the Wellingtons of No. 3 Group formally took over the task of bombing Italy and the first attack was made on 4–5 December, the target being the Royal Arsenal at Turin.

Special Duties

By mid-1940 it had been confirmed that the Germans were using radio beams to help their bombers navigate to their tar-gets and the attempts to learn more about this, and to counter its effectiveness, led to the creation of the RAF's Radio Counter Measures (RCM) organization. The Wellington was one of the earliest types to be involved and by late 1940 it formed part of the BATDU (Blind Approach Training and Development Unit) – a cover name to hide its real purpose – at Boscombe Down; the unit had reformed in June equipped primarily with Ansons and in October it was renamed the Wireless Intelligence Development Unit (WIDU). The main task for the unit was to discover more about the German *Knickebein* navigation beams by investigating their signature and pattern. On the night of 13 October a Wellington carried out the first actual bombing attack on a transmitter site, having flown down the beam to its point of origin. Such attacks continued into 1941, but with mixed results. 10 December saw

the unit become 109 Squadron, still at Boscombe Down; during 1941 its workload would continue to increase.

December also saw the Germans acquire their first complete Wellington, T2501 of 99 Squadron having to force-land in enemy territory whilst on a raid to Düsseldorf (on 4–5 December). The aircraft was handed over to the Experimental and Test Centre at Rechlin.

Training Duties

In a 1938 report Air Chief Marshal Ludlow-Hewitt stated, 'One of the chief results of the year's experience is that the work of the members of the crew of a modern bomber requires a very much higher standard of training and specialization than has hitherto been contemplated.' The Wellington was very much a case in

The Germans 'acquired' a Wellington in December 1940 when T2501 force-landed in enemy-held territory. The aircraft is seen here with 99 Squadron and then in Luftwaffe markings. John Hamlin

point as it was the most complex of all the bombers then in service. There is no space in this study to look at all aspects of the training of bomber crewmen, but it is important to cover the pre-squadron stage, one in which the Wellington was to play a significant role.

In November 1938 Air Marshal Welsh put forward a proposal to the Expansion Progress Meeting for the establishment of one Advanced Flying Training Centre for each operational group to '... provide each operational Group with a reservoir or pool from which replacement crews can be drawn [and] to train the output of the Flying Training Schools up to an operational standard before it passes to the operational

squadrons.' It was considered that six Bomber Pool squadrons would feed the seventy-three bomber squadrons and as a temporary measure this role, for bomber pilots, should be taken on by the non-mobilizable squadrons. The first to take on the role was 75 Squadron on 1 March 1939, equipped with Harrows (although it re-equipped with Wellingtons in July) at Honington. By June 1939 there were nine such group pool squadrons, equipped with a variety of types; the first Wellington unit to take on the role was 148 Squadron at Honington, on 1 June.

Ludlow-Hewitt later commented, 'It is most uneconomical in practice, even in peacetime, to make operational squadrons

undertake the initial operational training of pilots and crews coming direct from the elementary training schools, and it would be quite impossible in wartime. It is necessary, therefore, to consider the extent of the training organization required to undertake the whole of this initial operational training.' At this stage the pre-squadron course was notionally fourteen weeks long with sixty-two hours of flying, twenty-four hours being by night (at this period the concept of bomber operations was for daylight missions) and it was suggested that units with 16+8 aircraft would be able to train twenty-two pilots per course. On 16 September it was agreed that the group pool squadrons should be concentrated in a separate group, No. 6 Group, under Air Commodore Macneece-Foster. The Wellington component, providing crews for No. 3 Group, comprised 75 and 148 Squadrons at Harwell, and 215 at Bassingbourn.

The syllabus for those destined for Wellington squadrons comprised fifty-five flying hours and there were to be eleven crews per course. The aircraft establishment was set at only twelve aircraft, 50 per cent of which were to be Ansons (later changed to 25 per cent, and even this ratio was not achieved due to a shortage of Ansons). In addition, a number of reserve squadrons, including 214 Squadron with Wellingtons at Methwold, were to act as holding units for trained aircrew leaving the group pool units and keep them in flying practice pending their postings to operational squadrons.

The outbreak of war, the expansion plans and a host of other factors led to frequent changes of plan and a conference on 4 December agreed that the output of the training schools fell short of operational standards and the group pools needed to bring them up to an operational standard rather than rely on the first-line squadrons to take on this training task; thus, it was decided to give the units a more appropriate role (and name) by turning them into Operational Training Units (OTUs):

Operational training needed operational types of aircraft, but operational aircraft were not abundant, and the fewer that were locked up in training, the more there would be for expanding the first line. It was a compromise between economics of aircraft and the need for satisfactory training, it would permit satisfactory training if the standard of school (i.e. SFTS) output were considerably raised, and it would provide enough trained men to expand the first-line if the wastage rates were kept down. (AHB *Narrative*, Aircrew Training)

Wastage rates refers to the loss rates on the first-line squadrons. The overall dilemma was one that would haunt Bomber Command for much of the war, although the increasing use of Wellingtons in the OTUs

Courses were established for 180 pupils: sixty pilots, thirty observers and ninety air gunners.

On 4 February 1940, Ludlow-Hewitt had defined the role of these units:

> The proper role of the OTU is to convert otherwise fully-trained pilots, air observers and air gunners to the type of aircraft in which they will

need for 1,350 pilots. The flow of pilots could be increased only by either cutting the length of the course, with a reduction in quality, or forming new OTUs, but where were the aircraft and instructors to come from? Two more OTUs were formed in June, including the Wellington-equipped 20 OTU at Lossiemouth, although this was only a half-size OTU for some time. At this time the course was still of six weeks' duration. The following month a second training group, No. 7 Group, was formed.

Jack Wetherly joined a course at 15 OTU and made his first flight in a Wellington (L4233) on 30 July 1940 under the guidance of Sgt Gibbs of C Flight:

> Here Jack assembled a crew comprising a second pilot, navigator, wireless-operator and two air gunners. In the next ten days they flew nearly thirty-six hours, practising single-engined flying, forced landings and instrument flying, before progressing to formation bombing practice, dropping dummy bombs on the Odstone ranges, and air firing at Aberystwyth ... In their five weeks at Harwell, Jack and his crew flew 120 hours on Wellingtons. Their last flight, on 2 September, was to practise live bombing and air firing at night over the Irish Sea. They also practised the new technique of taking a flash photograph to record the fall of their bombs. (*Portrait of a bomber pilot*, Christopher Jary, Sydney Jary Ltd, 1990)

August 1940 and Flt Lt Turner and Plt Off Le Bas of 149 Squadron pose with three Free French aircrew attached to the squadron – Lt Jacob, Sgt Morel and Lt Roques.
Ken Delve Collection

as they were replaced by four-engined bombers in the operational units was to ease one of the problems.

By April 1940 Bomber Command's training organization had undergone major development and the basic course for all types had been set at six weeks and some fifty-five flying hours. A Bomber Command report of 11 April states that two of the eight 'new' (i.e renamed) OTUs were Wellington equipped: 11 OTU at Bassingbourn and 15 OTU at Harwell. Each unit had an establishment of fifty-three Wellingtons plus seventeen Ansons – although neither actually achieved this strength for some time – and the plan was for one primary airfield plus one satellite.

be required to operate and to give them sufficient operational training to fit them to take their place in operational squadrons. Obviously the first essential is to teach the new pilots how to fly a service type by day and night, which entails a considerable amount of local flying. Once a pilot has mastered the new type he has to be trained in advanced instrument flying, and long-distance flying by day and night, but to enable him to do this the rest of the crew must have reached a satisfactory standard in wireless and navigation. Finally, the complete crew must be taught bombing and air firing.

The OTU organization was, notionally, able to provide 930 pilots a year – but Bomber Command was already predicting a

On 16 July Bomber Command approved the use of OTU aircraft for *Nickel* operations, although they were not to operate beyond a line Lille–Amiens–Rouen–Brest (extended in October to Lille–Paris–Brest). 18 July saw three OTU aircraft from No. 6 Group take part in a *Nickel* operation as part of the Bomber Command operational plan for the night, their first such involvement. The following month, No. 7 Group aircraft joined in.

The employment of OTU aircraft in operational missions was to become standard policy for Bomber Command, the theory being that sending student crews to 'easy' targets was a means of increasing their experience. It was, as we shall see, a philosophy that was to cause much argument and dissent. (The first operational loss of an 11 OTU aircraft was on 27–28 July when N3002 crashed at Clophill, near Bedford, when returning from such a mission.) The growing threat of a German invasion led to the development of the *Banquet* plan creating a 'second line' bombing force from the OTUs; on 20 November the Wellington

OTUs were recorded as having 136 aircraft available for such employment.

By November the OTU course had been lengthened to ten weeks, with ninety hours of flying, in response to two cuts in the length of the SFTS course. To make this work a further four OTUs would be needed; as part of this process 18 (Polish) OTU moved to Bramcote in November and re-equipped as a half-size Wellington OTU. This was the situation at the close of 1940; Bomber Command now had ten OTUs but further expansion and the re-equipment of some of the existing units was now essential.

Maritime War

One of the most effective weapons in the maritime war was the mine and the Germans began a comprehensive minelaying campaign, often laying at night by aircraft, of British estuaries and shipping lanes soon after the outbreak of war. Amongst the counters to this threat (which by the end of 1939 had accounted for over 250,000 tons of Allied shipping) was a very strange modification to the Wellington and the creation of a special unit. No. 1 GRU (General Reconnaissance Unit) was formed at Manston on 15 December 1939 under Sqn Ldr John Chaplin, equipped with the so-called DWI Wellington. The DWI stood for Directional Wireless Installation, which, of course, it was not, the name being a cover for the true nature of the aircraft.

The combination of fears over the losses to German magnetic mines and the recovery of a mine from the mud flats at Shoeburyness provided the necessary impetus and Vickers were instructed to modify a Wellington to carry a coil that could be used to trigger the mines. Design and installation were carried out in less than a month under the leadership of George Edwards, the prototype aircraft being P2518 which was, in due course, test flown by 'Mutt' Summers, the first flight taking place on 21 December. The prototype went to Boscombe Down for the installation of generating equipment and in early January 1940 flew trial sorties over the firing unit from the captured mine, this being wired to a flash so that the position of the aircraft at the moment of 'detonation' could be noted. The prototype aircraft joined the GRU at Manston on 4 January and four days later was tasked to destroy a mine near the Tongue Lightship, north of Margate:

> The Wellington was airborne at 1420 hours and was soon headed towards the lightship with the three Blenheims as escort. Several runs were completed on various parts of the mined area without success when, just as we were beginning to abandon hope, a mine detonated. (Rear Admiral A. S. Bolt in *Air Pictorial*, April 1979)

Four Wellington IAs were converted on behalf of the Admiralty to become the first Wellington DWI Mk Is.

> The DWI installation consisted of a 48ft diameter horizontal air-cooled coil of 153 turns of aluminium alloy strip about 2in wide and ½in thick. The coil was housed in an aluminium outer casing, which was supported on the aircraft at four points. The power leads entered the coil at the rear attachment point with the fuselage. The coil was cooled by means of three air chutes with the air outlet at the rear. At an engine speed of 2,100rpm and a voltage of about 450, a current of 170–190 amps was passed through the coil. A strong vertical magnetic field was set up by this coil, all aircraft having been fitted with a change-over coil for reversing polarity in the air. The amperage of the current was maintained by a hand-operated rheostat controlled by the DWI operator.

The maximum period of operation of sweeping was governed entirely by the temperature of the coil, which increased as the current was passed through it. From experiments carried out, the limiting temperature was laid down as 90°C as after that point the minimum amperage of 160 could no longer be maintained. The cooling of the coil naturally depended on external air temperature and for a maximum day temperature of 40°C, the period during which current could be passed was about twenty minutes. [NB. these notes were written by Philip Dawson in relation to operations by the GRU in the Middle East.]

Ground speed is an essential factor in sweeping. If the ground speed is too slow it will endanger the aircraft, if too fast the period of influence of the magnetic force is reduced, thus impairing the efficiency of the sweep. The distance astern of the centre of the aircraft coil at which a mine will explode is determined by the relation between the force applied and the time over which it is applied and the distance the aircraft travels is the time of delay. For example, if an aircraft flies at 140ft at a ground speed of 120kt, a mine with a setting of 0.04 Gauss will explode approximately 80ft astern of the centre of the coil.

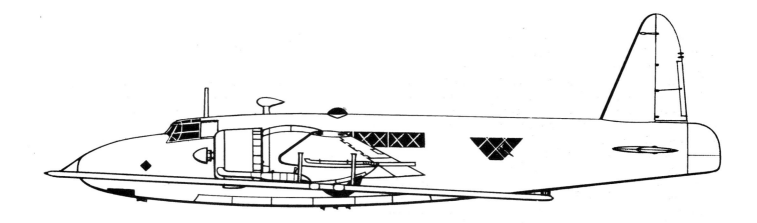

The unique DWI Mark I with its distinctive circular 'mine-exploding' ring under the fuselage. FlyPast Collection

The following regulations must be adhered to when sweeping:

a. sweeping never to be carried out in water depths of less than six fathoms.

b. Ground speed never to be less than 150mph, this allowing for a margin of safety.

c. Height of aircraft above mine not less than 120ft.

By February the GRU had three DWI aircraft on strength (soon joined by a fourth) and after a few frustrating weeks, successes were soon being registered, the unit developing a tactic whereby three aircraft flew in close formation to give better cover and thus a higher chance of success. The fourth aircraft, L4356, had a high-powered generator and this was soon proving to be more effective. The earlier aircraft, along with eleven Wellingtons Is withdrawn from service for conversion to DWI, were in due course upgraded with the installation, by Rollasons of Croydon, of Gypsy Six auxiliary power units to become Wellington DWI Mk IIs. By 31 March, the GRU had exploded fourteen mines and the technique was well established; in the period 11–16 April, Sqn Ldr Chaplin led a number of formation sweeps that exploded seven mines. The work continued and on 10 May a standard sweep by three aircraft was made to sweep the Ijmuiden area to make it safe for a naval evacuation of the Dutch Royal family. However, a week later it was confirmed that the GRU was to move to the Middle East.

Middle East

When Italy declared war on 10 June 1940, the RAF's air strength in the Mediterranean, Middle East and Africa was small and largely equipped with outdated types – especially when one considers the huge geographic area that it had to cover. The theatre had no true strategic air element and in due course Wellingtons arrived to carry out this role.

However, the Wellington also played a vital role in minesweeping and in May 1940 the special Wellingtons of 1 GRU arrived in Ismailia from the UK. Five aircraft, led by Sqn Ldr Chaplin, had set out from Manston but one crashed on take-off from Marseilles and was, no doubt, subsequently inspected by the Germans after the collapse of France – indeed, did it serve as a model for the German minesweeping types such as the Ju 52s with their Wellington-like rings? By 23 May the remaining

four aircraft were settling in at Ismailia, although they were soon required to operate from other airfields, such as Amriya, in order to carry out their duties on behalf of the Navy. The first operational sorties were flown on 11 June when a formation of three Wellingtons swept the Great Pass approach to Alexandria Harbour. Further sorties were flown over the next few days, covering parts of the Suez Canal and the approaches to Port Said; however, there was, as yet, no magnetic mine threat to be countered in this theatre.

The first bomber Wellingtons began to arrive in the theatre in September to replace the Valentias which equipped 70 Squadron at Kabrit in the Suez Canal Zone of Egypt; the first six (T2730 to T2735) departed the UK for Heliopolis on 1 September, the unit subsequently moving to Kabrit on the 9th and coming under No. 202 Group for operational tasks. With an offensive spirit that it was to maintain for its four years of Wellington operations, 70 Squadron flew its first Wellington mission in the early hours of 18 September:

The squadron attacked three targets in the Dodecanese Islands:
1. T2735 (Sgt Brooks) and T2733 (Fg Off Wells) – hangars, barracks and slipways in Portolago Bay, Leros Island.
2. T2734 (Flt Sgt Mirfin) and T2732 (Fg Off Ridgeway) – hangars and buildings at Maritza, Rhodes.
3. T2731 – dispersed aircraft and fuel stores at Callato, Rhodes.

For the second operation, on the night of 19–20 September, four aircraft deployed to Fuka and from there attacked shipping in Benghazi harbour – a target that was to become almost a 'bread-and-butter' one for the squadron. Benghazi was hit again the following night…

T2730 Fg Off Wells – this aircraft was over the target at 0346 and dropped ten 250lb in two sticks. One bomb was observed to fall on the pier and several near misses were registered on ships. On the return journey the hydraulic system was found to be u/s. The emergency hand-operated system was also found u/s. The aircraft was landed on its belly. Repairs were made with parts taken off other aircraft and this aircraft was flown to Abu Sueir for permanent repair on 27.9.40. (70 Squadron ORB)

Air power in the Middle East certainly needed increasing and, despite a continu-

ing shortage of aircraft, efforts were made to improve matters:

Air Ministry policy now turned towards a bombing programme as the best contribution to resolving the situation in our favour. The Blenheims were operating at extreme range and at the beginning of October there were only fifteen Wellingtons available. It was a heartening signal from the Chiefs of Staff on 11 October which informed Middle East commanders that immediate steps were being taken to accelerate and increase Wellington reinforcements. In a reversal of policy it was decided to exploit Malta's offensive potential by letting Wellington Middle East reinforcement stay on the island to carry out a few sorties against ports before proceeding; the aim was to have sixteen Wellingtons always available on Malta. The first targets were Naples and Brindisi in order to interfere with the flow of enemy reinforcements to Albania. In the first eleven days of November, twenty Wellington sorties were flown from Malta. (AHB *Narrative*, 'RAF in the Maritime War')

Malta was operating Wellingtons on a somewhat *ad hoc* basis and this began to cause problems:

For a few weeks the Wellington unit in Malta operated without any identity and no commanding officer. After their first few operations a series of accidents occurred at Luqa which lowered morale in the unit, and it was some time before the pilots regained confidence in this aerodrome as suitable for Wellingtons … AOC Malta to Air Ministry, 3 December: in spite of commendable effort by individuals, Wellington unit lacks cohesion and verve, while lack of squadron spirit is marked and in my view detrimental to success of operations.

The response was rapid and on 1 December the various Wellington elements on Malta were combined to form 148 Squadron, the squadron's first operation, an attack on Naples, taking place the following day.

Having left the UK, the Wellingtons of 37 Squadron had spent a few days operating out of Malta in November before moving on to Egypt, initially to Fayid but in December to Shalluffa. Further reinforcements arrived in December with 38 Squadron, again via Malta, moving into Shallufa by the middle of the month, although the first operations had been flown, in company with 37 Squadron, from Fayid on 8 December with an attack on the airfield at Benina.

Malta was to play a significant role in the war in the Mediterranean and North Africa, and Wellingtons units were involved from 1940 onwards. Squadrons en route **to the Middle East often spent a few days at Malta carrying out bombing sorties, but Luqa also 'acquired' its own Wellington flight, Wellington IC T2818 being one such aircraft.** Peter Green Collection

With attacks on the supply organization, particularly ports and airfields, the medium bombers were destined, in concert with the Blenheim squadrons, to have a major impact on the desert campaign. The Wellington I, however, was not an ideal aircraft for the hot climes of the Middle East:

My first flight in the aircraft was hardly auspicious. I had just completed two tours on day fighter duties with Spitfires and Hurricanes and was accustomed to that performance. The Wellington flight took place from Abu Sueir in a Mark IC captained by Flt Lt Clarke [later to become CO of 37 Squadron]. After take-off there was little sense of climb, only evidenced by an occasional movement of the altimeter. Flt Lt Clarke leant over towards me in the second pilot's seat and shouted 'when we get to 5,000ft, you'll find she starts to climb a bit slowly.' Good grief, I thought, what have I come into! (C. Mount)

November, however, had brought a major change in the, up to that point, successful operations of the British forces in the Middle East. The Axis invasion of Greece led to Churchill's demand for British air and ground participation in support of the Greeks. A Wellington detachment of 70 Squadron moved to Eleusis on 6 November and the following day flew a daylight attack on Valona:

A daylight raid was made upon the harbour and aerodromes at Valona, Albania. Clouds obscured the journey out but cleared over the target where they were engaged by enemy fighters – Breda 65s and CR.42s. T2734 (Sgt Brooks) exploded in mid-air and T2731 (Flt Lt Brian) went down in flames. The remainder dropped

Wellingtons ICs of 37 Squadron take off from Shallufa. The squadron moved to the Middle East in November 1940, arriving at Shallufa on 17 December to become part of the Middle East strategic bombing force. Peter Green Collection

70 Squadron in the Western Desert. This was the first Middle East bomber squadron to operate Wellingtons. Andy Thomas Collection

(Below) **Vickers-Armstrong advert carried in** Flight **magazine for 24 October 1940.** Ken Delve Collection

their bombs, registering hits on aircraft and ships. T2813 and T2826 were severely damaged. One CR.42 and one Breda 65 believed shot down. Bombs dropped, 54 × 250lb and 39 × 120lb. (70 Squadron ORB)

Once again the vulnerability of daylight medium bombers had been shown and future attacks were flown at night. In common with other air resources, further bomber reinforcements were fed into the Greek theatre of operations. This first detachment by 70 Squadron ended on 24 November, all surviving aircraft returning to Egypt. The squadron had flown the following missions, all except the initial Valona raid being by night :

7 November – six aircraft to Valona; two lost.
11–12 November – four aircraft to Durazzo; two to Valona.
12–13 November – one aircraft to Bari, two each to Durazzo and Valona.
14–15 November – two aircraft to Bari.
15–16 November – four aircraft to Brindisi.
17–18 November – three aircraft to Valona and three to Durazzo; one crashed on return.
19–20 November – two aircraft to Durazzo and one to Tirana; plus supply dropping to a Greek column.

As the campaign in Greece continued to unfold, further air assets, including Wellington detachments, were fed in; for example, the next 70 Squadron detachment moved to Greece on 4 December.

Nevertheless, as 1940 ended the Wellington squadrons in the Middle East could be fairly happy with their record to date and now with four squadrons on strength the prospects for an effective 'strategic campaign' in 1941 looked good.

"WELLINGTON" (BRISTOL PEGASUS ENGINES) DESIGNED AND CONSTRUCTED BY
VICKERS-ARMSTRONGS
LIMITED
Head Office : VICKERS HOUSE · BROADWAY · LONDON · S · W · 1

CHAPTER TWO

1941: Germany, U-Boats, Students and Deserts

Bomber Command Main Force

As 1941 opened, the Wellington strength of Bomber Command comprised twenty-two squadrons, plus OTUs; an increasing number of Merlin-engined Wellington IIs were joining the squadrons, although many units received only a small number of the new variant to supplement the existing Wellington ICs. The new variant was generally well liked by the pilots, as recalled by John Gee of 99 Squadron:

The extra power from the Merlins made it faster and more manoeuvrable than the Wellington IC, but it was a bit of a handful on take-off. The Merlin engines stuck out further from the leading edge of the wings; in addition, the propellers revolved in the opposite direction to those of the Pegasus engine. As a result it had a tendency to swing sharply to the left immediately take-off was commenced. To counter this, the pilot had to lead with the port throttle so that the port engine was developing greater power than the starboard engine. He could then control the swing until the tail came up off the runway and

there was enough airflow over the rudder to give directional control. Whilst this was good fun and rather exhilarating on unladen practice flights, it was a bit worrying when taking-off on an operation sitting on top of a 4,000lb bomb. The prospect of a swing and a broken undercarriage was not particularly attractive, but I loved the Mk II Wellington, and W5458/Z-Zola became my favourite aeroplane.

The reduced rate of Bomber Command operations that had been evident since the previous October saw few raids of more

Excellent shot of 149 Squadron. Note the nose art on the first two aircraft; this unit, like the growing number of Wellington squadrons, was flying an increasing number of missions by 1941 and suffering rising losses as German defences improved. Ken Delve Collection

than a hundred aircraft take place; in January the command only operated in any major way on six nights, the targets being Bremen, Brest, Gelsenkirchen and Wilhemshaven. On 15 January the command had received yet another new directive, this time instructing that oil targets should be the priority. This, of course, was easier said than done as these targets required precision bombing and there was little evidence to date that such accuracy was being achieved – indeed, 1941 was to see a damning report published on bombing accuracy.

The attack of 15–16 January by ninety-six bombers against Wilhemshaven had been fairly effective and so the command tried to repeat it the next night, eighty-one bombers being sent out. These were still the days when crews acted as individuals, so in effect eighty-one independent aircraft made their way to and from the target; the concepts of streaming and concentration had not yet been put into force. Amongst the aircraft operating that night was T2622 of 150 Squadron (which sent five aircraft, each carrying two 500lb GP bombs and two containers of incendiaries), and a typical entry from the squadron ORB reads:

Sqn Ldr H. R. McD. Beall and crew took off at 1742 making a landfall between the towns of Egmond and Schoorl on the Dutch coast. Flying at 15,000ft, the rail junction on the Kusten Kanal and the river Ems were located and from this point the target was easily located. The results of the 2x500lb bombs were not observed but on leaving the target four distinct fires, two of them large ones, were seen to have been started by the two containers of incendiaries. An intense barrage followed the aircraft away from the target, and flying in a westerly direction they were picked up and held for approximately five minutes by six searchlights. Flying back to base on the same route as on the outward journey, a landfall was made at Boston where at 2245 hours, flying at 3,400ft, the port engine suddenly cut out and as height could not be maintained the pilot landed his aircraft in a large field that was picked out three miles west of Cranwell. This was done without mishap to either aircraft or crew.

In common with most other units, 150 Squadron had increased its UE (Unit Establishment) of aircraft from eight to sixteen in January, although the ORB records that by February it had sixteen Mark ICs on strength plus 'one dual Wellington'. It was rare for squadrons to

Nose art carried on R1210; the aircraft crashed on 12 February 1941 after it had run out of fuel. Ken Delve Collection

have a strength that reflected the notional establishment: frequently there were more aircraft on charge and invariably they were not all of the stated mark.

Few major raids were mounted in February, although the night of 10–11 saw the command make its biggest effort to date when 222 bombers (including 112 Wellingtons, of which two were lost) attacked Hannover. A further forty-three aircraft attacked oil storage tanks at Rotterdam, this latter raid being notable as the first operational outing of the first of the

new four-engined heavy bombers, the Short Stirling (three aircraft from 7 Squadron). The night was also marked by the fact that No. 3 Group had contributed 119 Wellingtons to the night's efforts, the first time that a single group had put up more than a hundred aircraft.

The following month certain squadrons received a new warning instruction:

Recently instructions were issued by 1 Group that bombing by day is likely to be carried out by Bomber Command in the near future. To prepare for this, formation flying in threes is to be carried out as a practice but aircraft are not to take off or land in formation. The unit has also been instructed to practise flying the twin-engined Wellington with one engine only for experience in dealing with contingencies when one engine cuts out. (150 Squadron ORB, 4 March 1941)

Two weeks later the ORB compiler recorded another Bomber Command milestone:

A special scheme was initiated today whereby members of air crews who carry out 200 hours in continuous operational service are to be rested by being transferred as instructors to other units. The datum line of 200 hours is to be slightly elastic in that more robust persons may continue for more than 200 hours and less robust, either physically or temperamentally, may be taken off operational flying under the scheme, before they have done 200 hours. The CO will decide in each case.

This was an aspect of operational flying and morale that Bomber Command wrestled with throughout its existence. The transfer to an OTU was, however, certainly no guarantee of survival: training losses in Bomber Command were to remain high throughout the war.

The reason behind this latest instruction regarding daylight operations was that the command was about to join the Battle of the Atlantic: German U-boats and surface warships had achieved a virtual stranglehold on Britain's vital sea supply lanes, 350,000 tons of shipping having been sunk in February and 500,000 tons in March. It was a life-and-death struggle and every available resource had to be used to counter the threat. A new directive of 9 March listed targets that would, it was considered, have a decisive effect on the enemy's capability; Brest was added to the target list when it was discovered that the battlecruisers *Gneisenau* and *Scharnhorst* had arrived there. Indeed, this target, and these two ships, were to occupy an enormous amount of Bomber Command's effort over the next few months (the ships were nicknamed 'Gluckstein' and 'Salmon' by the aircrew). The Wellingtons were not called upon to make daylight raids at this point, the series of attacks on Brest launched in late March and April all being night sorties. Nigel Walker recalled one 214 Squadron attack on Brest:

We were given specific instructions that we were not to drop our bombs unless we could see the target, on account of endangering the lives of friendly French civilians ... We were greatly disappointed but not altogether surprised to find that the weather experts were right and that heavy cloud covered the whole area for miles in every direction. In accordance with instructions we headed out to sea and dropped our heavy bombload safe in a position which we estimated to be well clear of land.

As we were flying above cloud in bright moonlight I decided to practise astro-sights and took up my position in the astrodome. Having done so I went back to my navigation table and plotted the position on my chart. I discovered that, according to the fix I had obtained, I was more than 100 miles south of my estimated posi-

tion and I dismissed the result as inaccurate after recording it in my log (adding that I suspected that the sextant was unserviceable). I then settled down to a cup of hot coffee from my flask and a taste of raisins and chocolate from my flying rations. After this I made one more attempt to establish my position by the sextant, but still obtained the same result and recorded that the sextant was definitely unserviceable and dismissed the matter from my mind.

Shortly afterwards, after we had been flying blind for about five hours, I agreed to the captain's suggestion to break cloud to investigate our position by visual means at a point which I estimated to be in the vicinity of Oxford. The peaceful atmosphere in A for Apple changed in a flash as four people shouted at once that we were still over the sea, and changed to a state of consternation when I failed to answer immediately whether we were over the English Channel, the North Sea or the Atlantic Ocean. I made a rapid check of my navigation and could find no clue as to my error, except the two astro-sights which suggested we must be over the English Channel. Accordingly I suggested that we altered course to the north in the hope that the south coast would appear before our rapidly diminishing supply of petrol ran out.

Almost immediately we spotted Beachy Head and altered course for Manston, where we landed without incident. As navigator, I was naturally feeling worried and rather depressed ... I was surprised and more than relieved to see two other aircraft from our squadron parked on the tarmac, and soon afterwards learned that the squadron aircraft were dispersed between Exeter and Dover and that no single aircraft had reached their own aerodrome.

Wellington showing Donald Duck nose art plus an 'OPSDUN' tally. Ken Delve Collection

The fault lay in a an error on the wind forecast by the Met Office, the actual wind being much stronger than that forecast. We will never know how many of Bomber Command's Wellington (and other) losses resulted from such navigation problems; how many crews 'missed' the UK and ended up over the Atlantic and, when out of petrol, ditched with little hope of rescue. Winter weather and lack of navigation aids continued to be a major drawback to Bomber Command operations, as Ian Lawson of 214 squadron recalled:

At this stage of the war there were no satisfactory aids to navigation or target location. If the ground was cloud-covered or one had to fly in cloud – and very often one did – navigation was very much by dead reckoning. Apart from pinpoints on the coast and drifts obtained by the rear gunners from flares dropped in the sea, the navigator had nothing to help him on the way to the target. The return from the target usually meant the navigator asking the W/T operator for QDMs – a bearing on a W/T station – to try to get a fix, and for all the crew to try to get a pinpoint on crossing the enemy coast on the return leg. The ability of the W/T system to provide a service for navigation was very limited.

The old GP set was not very powerful, limiting the range considerably over which such assistance could be obtained. At this time, however, the new Marconi set was just coming in. If you were lucky enough to have an aircraft fitted with one of these sets your operator was able to blast his way through those operators using GP sets! I remember on quite a few occasions looking back down the cabin to see the W/T set in bits on the cabin floor while the W/T operator worked frantically to fix a snag.

Radio Navigation

The 'powers that be' had, however, realized that navigation was the key to success and to reducing losses of valuable aircraft and crews, and various developments were in hand. A letter of 4 February from the Air Ministry to the AOC, Air Vice-Marshal Baldwin, had as one of its themes the advent of a navigation aid, TR.1335 (code-named 'Gee'), which, it was suggested, would '... confer upon your forces the ability to concentrate their effort to an extent which has not hitherto been possible under the operational conditions with which you are faced ... [and] will enable results to be obtained of a much more effective nature.'

(Above) **Polish Wellington crew express their opinion! The Polish squadrons carried the red/white checkerboard – and in this case an interesting dwarf-like figure.** Ken Delve Collection

Yet another rugged Wellington makes it back. The rear gunner was certainly lucky and inspects damage to the lower part of his turret. Ken Delve Collection

The concept of TR.1335 was fairly simple and relied on the reception of signals from a series of ground stations. The ground organization comprised three stations: a master (A) and two slaves (B and C) set along a 200-mile (320km) base line; each slave station was locked to the master. The time difference for signals A/B and B/C to reach the aircraft was measured and displayed on a display unit (a cathode ray tube) in the aircraft. In essence, this gave the operator two position lines, the Gee co-ordinates, and, using a special Gee chart, he could plot the intersection of the lines and so obtain a fix of the aircraft's ground position. The theoretical accuracy was ½–5 miles (800–8,000m), far better than anything else then in service. The system's main advantages were ease of operation and speed, less than one minute to obtain a fix. However, the system also had severe limitations, including range (line of sight to a maximum of around 400 miles) and reliability. Ron Tettenborn, an observer with 9 Squadron, was among the first to use Gee on operations:

First impressions were of staggering accuracy: on practice use in the UK you could say to the pilot 'we should hit the south-west corner of the airfield in *n* minutes' – and we did, to the astonishment of the crew! The rest of the crew knew nothing about this highly secret gadget, full of detonators, so we were told. Gee charts also had to be destroyed in the event of an emergency, but I doubt if this would have been possible with the rather clumsy equipment provided – rather like an explosive umbrella, just to the right of the nav. table.

A series of experimental flights were flown to determine the accuracy and potential range of the system. These *Crackers* I and *Crackers* II trials by No. 1418 Experimental Flight looked promising and so the system went into development. In July 1941 the Wellingtons of 115 Squadron were fitted with Gee sets in order to conduct operational trials. On the night of 11–12 August, a force of twenty-nine Wellingtons, including two Gee aircraft, attacked Mönchengladbach. This trial, and two others on subsequent nights, appeared to have been a success, the navigators having no trouble obtaining Gee fixes for most of the route. It was then decided to halt the experiment until sufficient sets were available to equip at least 300 bombers; the risk of losing a set over Germany was considered too great until the system was fully operational on a scale at which it would have a significant effect.

Indeed, the electronic war, commonly referred to as Radio Counter Measures (RCM), had begun to play an increasing role for both the RAF and *Luftwaffe*, although the former soon took a decisive lead in this important military development. Following the earlier Wireless Intelligence Development Unit (WIDU) work, Wellington involvement came about in January 1941 when the first four of a promised eight

A 1941 cartoon stresses the durable nature of the Wellington – crewmen, drinking coffee, chat over the missing middle part if their aircraft! Ken Delve Collection

Wellingtons arrived at Boscombe Down to join 109 Squadron and replace the Whitleys of that unit. The first four aircraft, T2513, T2552, T2556 and T2884 were received from 8 MU on 4 January and began operations that month. The intention was for the unit, with its specially equipped aircraft, to attack the German *Y-Gerät*, *X-Gerät* (codenamed *Ruffian*) and *Knickebein* beam transmitters in the Cherbourg area. One of the most frequent targets was the *Ruffian* transmitter at Morlaix and a typical Squadron attack was that of 11 May against this target during which the four bombers approached the target on different bearings:

Sqn Ldr Bufton – approach bearing 180
Fg Off Grant – approach bearing 360
Fg Off Sommerville – approach
                    bearing 060
Fg Off Cundall – approach bearing 315

The attack was considered to be a success and it seems that the beam was off the air for a number of weeks. This four-aircraft multiangle tactic was the standard one employed by the unit; however, such offensive work was only one of the duties carried out by the Wellingtons and other tasks included HF Meaconing tests (sending a false signal to decoy the user), operations for the Y Service and aircraft Meaconing, as well as 'routine' investigation flights over and around occupied Europe listening to and recording radar and radio information for analysis.

Another significant event of this first half of the year took place on the night of 31 March when a number of Wellingtons dropped 4,000lb (1,800kg) HC (High Capacity) bombs, usually referred to as 'cookies', as part of the attack on Emden; only six aircraft were involved and one each from 9 Squadron (Plt Off Franks) and 149 Squadron (Sqn Ldr Wass) dropped the weapons. In late 1940 a requirement had been placed for a 4,000lb HC bomb, partly as a result of the German use of parachute mines which had proved effective in the destruction of British buildings. A similar weapon of 1,650lb had been introduced in 1918 to equip the Independent Force to attack German industry; the requirement in 1941 was the same. The intention was to provide a cylindrical casing to contain the maximum amount of explosives, blast effect rather than penetration being the destructive medium. Development was rapid and in due course the weapon appeared in 2,000lb, 4,000lb, 8,000lb and even 12,000lb versions.

Wellington ORBAT, May 1941	
No. 1 Gp	
Binbrook	12, 142 Sqns
Newton	103, 150 Sqns
Swinderby	300, 301 Sqns
Syerston	304, 305 Sqns
No. 2 Gp	
West Raynham	101 Sqn
No. 3 Gp	
Feltwell	57, 75 Sqns
Honington	9, 311 Sqns
Marham	115, 218 Sqns
Mildenhall	149 Sqn
Oakington	3 PRU
Stradishall	214 Sqn
Wyton	15, 40 Sqns
Waterbeach	99 Sqn
No. 4 Gp	
Driffield	104, 405 Sqns
No. 6 Gp	
Bassingbourn	11 OTU
Benson	12 OTU
Bramcote	18 OTU
Harwell	15 OTU
Lossiemouth	20 OTU
Moreton-in-Marsh	21 OTU
Pershore	23 OTU
No. 15 Gp	
Limavady	221 Sqn
No. 18 Gp	
Leuchars	10 BATF (forming)
Thornaby	9 BATF (forming)
Middle East Command	
Kabrit	70, 148 Sqns
Shallufa	37, 38 Sqns (257 Wing)
Sollum	1 GRU
Fuka	dets of 38, 70, 148 Sqns

Expansion

Expansion of the Wellington force continued throughout the year. Having come from 22 OTU with its worn-out Wellington ICs, Philip Dawson found the relatively new Wellington IIs of 104 Squadron a great improvement when he joined that unit in July 1941 at Driffield, the squadron having only formed in April, the first of the new Wellington units for 1941. 'The II was a good aircraft, the extra power made all the difference, as did the feathering prop. Having arrived on the squadron new pilots flew about six trips of circuits and bumps in order to become familiar with the new aircraft – the swing on take-off was, off course, in the opposite direction on the Merlin-powered Mark IIs.'

Having re-equipped with Wellington IIs the previous October, 12 Squadron was one of the new medium bomber units entering the fray in early 1941, its first operation taking place on the night of 9–10 April with four aircraft taking part in an attack on Emden. It was a tragic start to the unit's operations as the squadron Commander, Wg Cdr V. Q. Blackden, flying W5375, failed to return. A few days later, Sgt Walsh's crew recorded their frustration at reaching the target, Boulogne, only to suffer a malfunction of the bombing system. 'The distributor on the bomb panel failed to work and the eight 250lb GP and two SBCs of 4lb incendiaries had to be manually released, thus making accurate bomb aiming difficult.'

Having given up its Blenheims in favour of Wellingtons in April (although the last Blenheim operation took place on 9 May), 101 Squadron moved to Oakington in July to join No. 3 Group. The next few months saw air and ground crews undergoing intensive lectures on aircraft systems, and crews flying familiarization sorties. The first operational sortie took place on 11 June and was recorded in the ORB, 'Today was the first day that 101 Squadron operated with Wellington IC aircraft, and two aircraft successfully attacked the docks at Rotterdam, both returned safely. Sqn Ldr Jones was captain of aircraft W5716 and Sgt Cawnt was captain of aircraft R1780. A total of 6,000lb of HE bombs were dropped in 500lb GP bombs.' April also saw the first Canadian bomber squadron 'join the ranks' with the formation, at Driffield on 23 April, of 405 Vancouver Squadron. Although Canadian aircrew were already serving in significant numbers, the decision had been taken to bring

Wellington II W5461 of 104 Squadron; the unit re-formed in April 1941 at Driffield.
John Hamlin

them together – especially in view of the expansion in their numbers – into RCAF units (and eventually into an RCAF bomber group). After an intensive training period this first Canadian unit undertook the first RCAF bomber mission on 12 June, sending four aircraft (in company with eighty Whitleys) to attack the rail yards at Schwerte. The first Australian bomber squadron also formed with Wellingtons, 458 Squadron receiving Wellington IVs when it formed at Holme-on-Spalding-Moor on 25 August (although it was October before this unit flew its first operation).

John Gee had joined 99 Squadron at Waterbeach in May 1942; the squadron had been one of the first Wellington units, having re-equipped from Heyfords in October 1938, and had operated from a number of bases, moving to Waterbeach in March 1941:

I was feeling very nervous and anticipated my first operational flight with dread, but at the same time wanted to get it over. I was crewed up with Plt Off Rendall and his crew as second pilot on 17 May when the squadron stood by for operations and was included in the order of battle. I remember us checking the aeroplane and flight testing it in the morning and then nervously awaiting the briefing. In the late afternoon we went to the Briefing Room wondering where the target would be ... a ribbon showed the route to Cologne. The Intelligence Officer pointed out a bend on the Rhine which should be useful as a landmark to help locate the target; this landmark was to be a regular feature in the

coming months and became legendary as the 'sign of the Pendulous Tit'. After briefing we returned to the mess to sleep, but I found this quite impossible. In due course we were called and went into the dining room for a pre-operational meal before going out to the aircraft. We then proceeded to collect parachutes, escape material, such as foreign currency, and maps of Europe printed on silk handkerchiefs, and Thermos flasks of tea and some sweets to help sustain us in the long hours over enemy territory. I climbed into the crew bus along with other crews and off we went to the aeroplanes at dispersal around the perimeter track. In a few minutes we arrived at Wellington IC N2856. The six-hour sortie went without any problems and after debrief and a meal of bacon and eggs it was back to the mess to sleep. (John Gee, *ibid.*)

The Wellington IIs were grounded in June, as recorded by 12 Squadron. 'Information was received of a defect in the engine nacelles of Wellington IIs and aircraft were grounded until checked; seven aircraft were found to be affected. Vickers Armstrongs personnel started work to rectify the problem, as Mod 988, on 11 June but work was still ongoing at the end of the month with two aircraft yet to finish.' Such minor problems were a continual headache but had little overall operational effect.

The Wellington was re-categorized as a medium bomber in June 1941 to reflect the introduction of the first of the true four-engined 'heavies' (the Short Stirling having made its operational debut on 10–11 February and the Handley Page

Halifax on 10–11 March). Of the thirty-three medium squadrons within the command, twenty-one were equipped with various marks of the Wellington, the majority being in No. 1 and No. 3 Groups. The continued expansion of the command was, however, under threat and the plan to achieve a Target Force of one hundred medium/heavy bomber squadrons by mid-1942 looked increasingly unachievable. Operational bombers were lasting an average of 11½ sorties, against a prediction of twice that, despite a policy of conservation that had been in place over the previous winter. The projected requirement was for 22,000 bombers to be delivered between July 1941 and July 1943, but the latest forecast suggested that only 11,000 would be available from home production; whilst some of the shortfall could be made up by increasing orders from America, other measures would also have to be taken, including keeping, and even expanding, the Wellington strength longer than had been originally envisaged. There was also a shortage of crews and with the Wellington bearing the majority of the OTU training task, there was a call upon the type to be transferred from operational units to the training groups – and not only for the OTUs. 'One cause of the decline in Wellington numbers was the need to divert operational types for specific training purposes, notably for gunnery training flights. The intention was to equip these flights with Whitleys, but few were forthcoming, and Wellingtons were supplied, to be replaced when practicable by Whitleys.' (AHB *Narrative*, 'The RAF in the Bombing Offensive against Germany'.) The comment referred to the reduction in medium bomber squadron strength from 40½ squadrons in July (against a plan for 46 squadrons) to 37½ squadrons in January 1942 (against a plan for 77 squadrons). At a time when Bomber Command was hoping to increase its striking power it was, in fact, in decline.

the prime targets, whilst a list of secondary (city) targets was added for those occasions when the primaries were unsuitable.

The renewed offensive had, in fact, begun even before the directive was issued, with 114 Wellingtons attacking Cologne on the night of 7–8 July, losing three of their number, in what was a heavy and effective raid, whilst other bomber forces went to Osnabrück, Munster and Mönchengladbach, Wellingtons being

the fuselage, and with a broken fuel pipe feeding fuel to the flames and thus putting the whole aircraft in imminent danger, James Ward decided that the only chance lay in crawling out onto the wing in an attempt to smother the fire using a cockpit cover. The VC citation (Air Ministry Bulletin 4667 dated 5 August 1941) included details of the incident: '... the flight home had been made possible by the gallant action of Sgt Ward in extinguishing the fire

T2961 of 15 Squadron at Wyton in 1941. Andy Thomas Collection

By the summer of 1941 Bomber Command had reduced the scale of its anti-shipping offensive so that it could return to its offensive against Germany. The major night offensive against shipping ended with an attack on 6–7 July and two days later, on 9 July, a new directive was issued calling for a mix of precision and area attacks:

It is accepted as a principle of this plan that the successful attack of a specific target can only be undertaken in clear moonlight. It follows, therefore, that for approximately three-quarters of each month it is only possible to obtain satisfactory results by heavy, concentrated and continuous attacks on large working-class and industrial areas in carefully selected towns.

The Railway Research Service was called on to help draw up a list of suitable targets; the nine locations they nominated became

involved in all except the last of these. The night was also memorable for Sgt J. A. Ward of 75 (NZ) Squadron for it was on this night that he was to earn the Victoria Cross – the only VC awarded to a Wellington crewman.

James Ward was second pilot to Sqn Ldr Reuben Widdowson in Wellington L7818. The crew had made a good attack and were on the homebound route, approaching the Zuider Zee, when they were hit by a Bf 110 night fighter which attacked from below and in a devastating initial attack caused major damage to the Wellington. The starboard engine was badly hit, hydraulic systems damaged (the bomb doors fell open), the cockpit filled with smoke and fumes and the intercom went dead. Fire then broke out in the starboard wing and the captain ordered the crew to prepare to bale out if nothing could be done to stem the fire. Unable to control the fire from inside

on the wing in circumstances of the greatest difficulty and at the risk of his life'; it also included an account by Ward himself:

First I had to hang on to the astro-hatch while I worked out how I was going to do it, then I hopped out on the wing. I kicked holes down the side of the fuselage which exposed the geodetics and gave me my foot-hold. I held on with one hand until I had two good foot-holds on the wing. Fire and blast from the cannon shells had stripped part of the covering from the wing and that helped. Then I caught hold of some of the sections of the wing with the other hand and managed to get down flat on the wing with my feet well dug in and hanging on with both hands. Once I could not get enough hold and the wind lifted me partly off the wing and sent me against the fuselage again. But I still had my feet twisted in, and I managed to get hold of the edge of the astro-hatch and worked myself back on to the wing again.

It was just a matter of getting somewhere to hang on to. It was like being in a terrific gale, only much worse than any gale I've ever known. As I got along the wing I was behind the airscrew, so I was in the slipstream as well. Once or twice I thought I was going. I had the cover tucked underneath me, and as I lay flat on the wing I tried to push the cover down through the hole in the wing onto the leaking pipe, where the fire was coming from. But the parachute on my chest prevented me from getting down close enough to the wing, and the wing kept lifting me up.

The cover nearly dragged me off. I stuffed it down through the hole but as soon as I took my hand away the terrific wind blew it out again. My arms were getting tired and I had to try a new hold. I was hanging on with my left arm when, as soon as I moved my right hand the cover blew out of the hole again and was gone before I could grab it. The rear gunner told me afterwards he saw it go past his turret.

After that there was nothing to do but to get back again. The navigator kept a strain on the rope and I pulled myself back along the wing and up the side of the fuselage to the astro-hatch, holding on as tight as I could. Getting back was worse than going out, and by this time

I was pretty well all in. The hardest part of the lot was getting my right leg in. In the end the navigator reached out and pulled me in.

For this amazingly heroic deed James Ward received the Victoria Cross (Widdowson was awarded the DFC and the rear gunner, Sgt Box, the DFM); sadly, Ward was killed on a raid during September.

The German night fighter force had undergone significant development during 1941 and was rapidly becoming a potent force, more and more encounters being reported by aircrew. Likewise, German targets were defended by an ever-increasing amount of anti-aircraft guns and *Flak*, combined with radar-laid searchlights, began to claim more victims. The weather, however, remained one of the chief dangers faced by Wellington crews; the experience of John Gee during a mission to Bremen was not untypical:

We set off for Bremen only to encounter severe electrical storms and bad icing conditions. The wings of the Wellington became heavily iced up and we suffered loss of engine power through ice forming in the carburettors. We had to

descend to try and clear the ice and regain power. After juggling with the hot air controls we succeeded in clearing the engines and tried to find a way round the storm clouds, but eventually gave it up as a bad job and decided to return to Waterbeach.

More often than not the only option in severe cold was to let nature provide the solution by descending to lower levels and hoping that the warmer air would free the ice.

New Variants

Three more marks of Wellington appeared during the year; two of these entered service in the summer, the Mark III joining 9 Squadron in July and the Mark IV joining 300 Squadron the following month. The prototype Wellington III, L4251, had first flown on 16 May 1939, detailed design having commenced the previous year. However, initial results using the Bristol HEISM two-stage supercharged engines were disappointing (the Bristol Hercules being the specified engine for the variant) and the prototype was sent to Bristols for

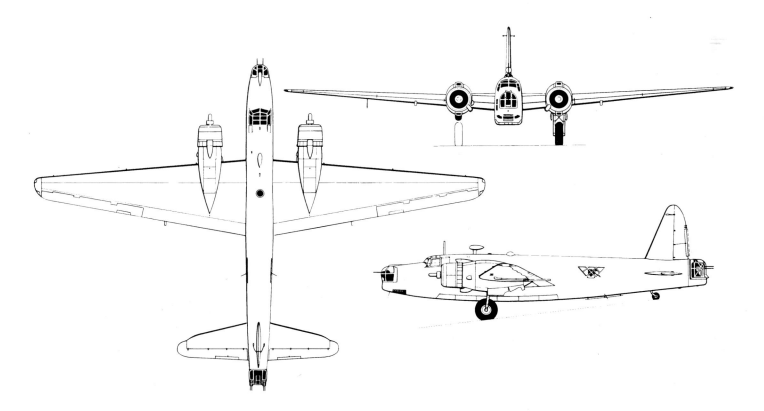

The Wellington III, powered by two Bristol Hercules IIIs; this variant entered service in July 1941.
FlyPast Collection

Specification – Wellington III	
ENGINES	Two Bristol Hercules III
DIMENSIONS	Span 86ft 2in (26.26m); length 64ft 7in (19.68m)
PERFORMANCE	Max. speed 255mph (408km/h); ceiling 19,000ft (5,758m)
ARMAMENT	8 × 0.303in guns, 4,500lb (2,000kg) bombs
FIRST FLIGHT	16 May 1939
NUMBER BUILT	1,519

further trials and development. In due course Wellington IC P9328 was fitted with the Hercules III; this aircraft made its first flight in January 1941 and was essentially the first production Mark III. A great many operational improvements were incorporated as a result of hard-won operational experience: cable cutters were fitted to wing leading edges; a reasonably effective de-icing system was installed; and windscreen wipers were provided, as was a direct vision windscreen. All of these were most welcome to the operational crews and helped overcome some of the problems of winter operations that had beset Bomber Command since the winter of 1939–40. The question of armament had also been addressed and having trialled, and rejected, a cannon-armed rear turret, the decision was taken to fit the Frazer-Nash 20A with its four 0.303in Brownings.

Just over 1,500 Wellington IIIs were produced and the type became the mainstay of

Bomber Command from late 1941 through to the large-scale introduction of the four-engined 'heavies'. The new variant was well-received by the squadrons, 150 Squadron (who re-equipped the following April) commenting 'The Wellington IC is undoubtedly a very wonderful aircraft but it is the opinion of pilots in this squadron that after the IC the Mark III is a revelation.'

The Wellington IV was a direct result of the shortage of British engines following the outbreak of war, especially when fighter aircraft were given priority for liquid-cooled engines. There was little option but to look overseas for a source of suitable powerplants, and the choice fell upon the Pratt & Whitney Twin Wasp. A contract was placed in late September 1939 for a Wellington prototype fitted with the Twin Wasp SC3-9; however, despite some initial design work, and an American agree-

Specification – Wellington IV	
ENGINES	Two Pratt & Whitney Twin Wasp R-1830-S3C4G
DIMENSIONS	Span 86ft 2in (26.26m); length 64ft 7in (19.68)
PERFORMANCE	Max. speed 229mph (366km/h); ceiling 20,000ft (6,060m)
ARMAMENT	6 × 0.303in guns, 4,500lb (2,000kg) bombsFirst flight: December 1940
FIRST FLIGHT	December 1940
NUMBER BUILT	220

ment to make the Pratt & Whitney R-2800 available, nothing came of the plan. However, the project was resurrected in July 1940 and it was decided to go ahead with an installation of two Twin Wasp R-1830s, with a designation for the new variant of Wellington IV. The prototype, R1220, first flew in December 1940 in the hands of Mike Hare, from Chester. There were few development problems and the type entered production at Chester, some 220 eventually being built. Various trial installations were put forward, some of which looked promising, but in essence the type became a standard bomber.

On the night of 14 July, 9 Squadron sent nine aircraft as part of the No. 3 Group contribution to attacks on Bremen and Hannover:

All aircraft returned safely, except Wellington T2619 (Sgt Saich and crew), which crashed on return. Whilst over the target area they were held in a cone of searchlights and fired at, but not hit. During violent evasive action they lost height from 13,000 to 11,000ft, when they were again caught in searchlights and sustained a number of hits in the fuselage and main planes. The aircraft was set on fire in the rear portion of the fuselage and on the fin. The forced landing flare in the port main plane was set on fire. The pilot, thinking that the port engine was on fire, switched off the petrol to that engine and switched the engine off, but the fire eventually went out so he turned on the petrol and restarted the engine. It was then found that the bomb doors were open, the hydraulics having been shot away. The navigator succeeded in extinguishing the fire in the fuselage. They had only

Wellington IV R1220; the Mark IV entered service in August 1941. Peter Green Collection

R1410 of 311 Squadron; the aircraft went on to serve with 12 OTU, finally being lost when it ditched off the Frisian Islands on the way back from Bremen on 26 June 1942.
Ken Delve Collection

been able to drop one bomb and the rest, consisting of six 500lb bombs, they were unable to drop by any means. Three members of the crew were hit by shrapnel but only slightly injured.

The captain set course for base but owing to the bombload still being on and the bomb doors open, his airspeed was very low, and the pilot was using as little throttle as possible to conserve his petrol, as he did not know if he had been hit in the tanks. There was a shell hole in the starboard main plane, which was blanking off the aileron and which made the aircraft difficult to fly. Two fixes were obtained from this aircraft, one over the Dutch coast south of Texel, and the other just off the English coast. Just after this latter fix, the aircraft obtained homing bearings from Newmarket H/F D/F Station.

About this time, the captain, being satisfied that he was going to reach land before running out of fuel, decided to test his undercarriage, which he lowered, thus detracting still further from the aircraft's airspeed. He was, however, unable to bring it up again as the main hydraulic system had been shot away. On reaching the coast and his petrol gauges having shown nothing for some time, he thought that he was about to run out of fuel and decided to force land immediately rather than attempt to make an aerodrome. He selected a large field where he could land into wind. In the half light of dawn the pilot had not noticed that the field was obstructed by poles and ropes. He struck two of these poles prior to touching down, which were carried away successfully. On touching down the starboard oleo leg collapsed and the aircraft, striking another pole, swung around and broke in two forward of the main rear member. All the crew

returned to Honington with the exception of the rear gunner, who was taken to Norwich Hospital.

High Altitude Wellingtons

However, the most specialized of this trio of new variants was the Wellington VI. This variant was to fulfil Specification B.23/39 for a bomber designed to operate above the level of *Flak* and fighters, for which it would need to be pressurised. A high altitude Wellington had its origins as early as 1938 when the Air Staff asked Vickers to look at an aircraft with a ceiling of 40,000ft (12,000m), for which it would need a pressurized cabin. To achieve this a pressure cabin had to be constructed and attached to the geodetic structure of the main fuselage. The outline requirement called for a crew of three, a bomb load of only 1,000lb and an endurance of just under ten hours. In addition to the problems of the pressure cabin – which was required to maintain a cabin altitude equivalent to 10,000 feet – was that of finding a suitable engine. It was intended to use the Hercules HE8MS then under development but as was so often the case at this period, the development of the engine was running behind schedule and, in June 1940, it was decided to use the lower performance Hercules III for the initial trials. The prototype, R3298, of what at this stage was the Wellington V first flew in early autumn and on 21 October made the first of its high-altitude test flights. Two flights suffered problems of ice forming on

canopies and windows, but this problem was solved by blowing warm air over these areas and on the fourth flight, on 31 October, the aircraft achieved a height of 30,000ft (9,000m). There were still problems, such as the need to provide a remote position (within the pressure cabin) from which the rear guns could be operated, but the basic principles appeared sound. A second prototype, R3299, fitted with Hercules VIIIs, joined the test programme but it was already evident that the Bristol engines were not really suitable and design work was carried out with a view to installing the Merlin 60. This latter design was given the designation Wellington VI and superseded the Mark V such that the latter never entered production, and this in due course became the production Wellington Mark VI, in which the Hercules engines gave way to 1,600hp Merlin 60s.

Specification – Wellington VI	
ENGINES	Two Rolls-Royce Merlin 60 or 62
DIMENSIONS	Span 86ft 2in (26.26m); length 61ft 9in (18.82m)
PERFORMANCE	Max. speed 300mph (480km/h); ceiling 38,500ft (11,667m)
ARMAMENT	4 × 0.303in guns, 4,500lb (2,000kg) bombs
FIRST FLIGHT	1941
NUMBER BUILT	63

R3298, one of a pair of Wellington V prototypes. The variant was not proceeded with and the Wellington VI was developed as the high level bomber. FlyPast Collection

Specification 17/40/V was issued on 31 October 1940 for a 'Pressure Cabin Wellington Aircraft' and, in part, it stated that:

1. The aircraft shall be constructed in strict accordance with the drawings and schedules defining the prototype pressure cabin Wellington, R3298 and R3299, as accepted by the Director of Technical Developments (DTD), except as modified to meet the requirements of this specification, or the detail alterations made to facilitate production.

II. Special requirements:

5. The auw of the fully-loaded aircraft shall not exceed 32,000lb.
6. A crew of three shall be carried, consisting of two pilot/navigators and a WOP/AG.
7. Adequate fuel and oil tankage shall be provided for an effective range, at maximum power for economic cruising at 35,000ft, of 2,200 miles when carrying 1,500lb of bombs, or of 1,500 miles when carrying 4,500lb of bombs.

18. The aircraft shall be camouflaged iaw ADM No. 332, Issue II except that the top surfaces of the cabin shall be finished to the satisfaction of the DTD. The undersurfaces shall be finished in duck-egg blue (Sky Type S).
22. The aircraft shall be fitted with two Hercules VIII MAS engines.
26. Provision shall be made for de-icing the pilot's dome and the bomb aimer's window.

An amendment was added in February 1941, but this only affected the navigation and communications fit.

The design now incorporated a crew of four – pilot, navigator, bomb-aimer (to use the American Sperry bombsight) and wireless operator – and a much-improved, and more operationally valid, bomb load of 4,500lb, a ceiling of 40,000ft and a range with full load of 1,590 miles. The only defensive armament was to be a four-gun rear turret with remote operation from the pressure cabin when the aircraft was operating at height. The entire front end of the

aircraft was very different from that of a standard Wellington, the pressure cabin incorporating the minimum number of vision windows in order to keep its integrity; the pilot was provided with a plastic dome perched on top of the fuselage, whilst the bomb-aimer was given an inclined, optically flat panel below the nose of the cabin area. A number of rectangular windows on top of the fuselage allowed the navigator to take his astro readings. Hot air was passed over these surfaces to prevent icing and misting. A number of other problems, such as the need to keep the hydraulic fluid thin enough to be effective – achieved by using a mixture of paraffin and non-freezing oil –also had to be overcome as Vickers carried out much groundbreaking work into the problems of high-altitude operations. A limited number of aircraft joined 109 Squadron in March 1942, though this was a short-lived experiment lasting only a few months. Only sixty-three production aircraft were built and in the event the type was not employed for its intended purpose, the de Havilland Mosquito having been adapted for high level work.

Battleships and the Big Cities

The scale of the bombing offensive continued to build and it was fairly standard practice during this period of the offensive for one major raid, of around a hundred bombers, to be 'supported' by a number of other smaller attacks, usually by thirty or forty aircraft on other targets. However, the command had barely got back into its night offensive when a major effort was called for once more against German capital ships, it being reported that the *Scharnhorst* had moved to La Pallice.

Therefore, a major daylight raid was planned in order to attack her at her new location, and *Gneisenau* at Brest. On 24 July, a small force of Halifaxes attacked *Scharnhorst*, whilst a hundred other bombers, including seventy-nine Wellingtons of Nos. 1 and 3 Groups, went to Brest. There was no fighter escort available for the Wellingtons and the German fighter opposition proved heavier than predicted; ten Wellingtons and two Hampdens were lost either to fighters or to the heavy concentrations of *Flak* around the port.

Nevertheless, the majority of the command's effort remained concentrated against targets in Germany, including Berlin, even though the German capital was not amongst the priority targets. One thing that was become increasingly evi-

dent was the growing strength of the enemy night defences, both *Flak* and fighters. An attack on the 'Big City' was to be Philip Dawson's first operational mission with 104 Squadron, flying as second pilot with Sgt Watson. On the night of 12–13 August some seventy bombers, including forty Wellingtons, attacked Berlin:

The weather was really bad and the searchlight belt really vicious; only about twenty-five aircraft found the target; we saw buildings through a gap in the clouds and dropped our bombs. On the way home we drifted well north of track and ended up over Hamburg or Bremen, one of the most heavily-defended parts of Germany. Flying at 10,000ft, we were held by searchlights and then the *Flak* opened up ... suddenly it stopped and we knew that a night fighter must be

Although the Wellington VI entered service in early 1942 with 109 Squadron, it did not fulfil its promise and the need for a high-level bomber went instead to the Mosquito. FlyPast Collection

around; within a minute a stream of tracer shot over the top of the aircraft; we took evasive action and put the aircraft into a steep dive – at one point I noticed 320mph on the ASI and it took both of us to pull the aircraft out of its dive. Meanwhile, the rear gunner had been hammering away at the Bf 110 fighter and claimed to have shot it down, seeing an explosion on the ground. By the time the engagement was over we were certainly lost and when we crossed the coast could not recognize any pinpoints; after some time flying over the water I noticed an ident. beacon and recognized it as AK for Acklington – a long way north of Driffield!

This dramatic start was followed by trips to Magdeburg and Cologne and then, whilst changing into his kit for his fourth mission, Philip Dawson was told by the deputy Flight Commander, Bob Doherty, to stand down: he wanted Sgt Watson to fly as he had only one trip to go. The aircraft failed to return – such were the twists of fate.

The Wellingtons were not without their technical problems; the 150 Squadron diarist recorded that on 2 September an aircraft crash-landed at Kenley 'because of the loss of the starboard airscrew – this is the fifth case of failure of the reduction gear on the Pegasus XVIII.' The Bristol Pegasus XVIII was the first of the two-speed versions of the long line of Pegasus engines and was, in general, a sturdy and reliable powerplant, although the Pilots' Notes warned that RPMs between 2,250 and 2,550 were to be avoided because of vibration.

Expansion brought a proliferation of specialist units and organizations, one of the most important being the Bomber Command Operational Research Section (ORS) which formed in September under Dr B. G. Dickins. The organization was given four main areas to study:

(Above) **405 Squadron's W5537 at Pocklington; this was the first of the Canadian bomber squadrons, and had formed in April 1941.** Ken Delve Collection

Six crewmen about to board their 311 Squadron Wellington. Ken Delve Collection

1. Bomber losses;
2. Success of bomber operations;
3. Vulnerability of bombers;
4. Radio and radar problems.

Although targets in Germany received most attention, the RAF's UK-based bombers did from time to time venture to the industrial cities of northern Italy, usually to attack aircraft factories. These were always difficult trips; on the night of 28–29 September a force of thirty-nine Wellingtons and two Stirlings was tasked against Genoa, a mission from which three of the Wellingtons failed to return. John Gee was one of the 99 Squadron pilots taking part:

This time we were flying a Wellington IC fitted with long-range tanks in the bomb bay, which reduced our bomb load to three 500lb bombs. We had to climb to maximum height to avoid the mountains of the Alps and even then had little height to spare. We duly arrived over Genoa and dropped our bombs in the target area ... the flight home seemed endless, but we eventually arrived in the Waterbeach area, only to encounter low cloud down to 300ft. To land was impossible and we were diverted to Honington, where we had to pump the undercarriage down by hand as the hydraulic power had failed. After practically ten hours in a Wellington we were glad to stretch our legs.

(Above) **Aircraft being recovered; the wings have been removed and a crane lifts a very sick-looking fuselage. The work of the recovery gangs and the RSUs (Repair and Salvage Units) was an important one and many aircraft, or at least bits of them, were returned to service.** Ken Delve Collection

(Right) **Interior of the Wellington, looking forward,** and (far right) **interior looking aft; the flare chute is on the left-hand side.**
Ken Delve Collection

The latter part of the year saw a number of other Wellington units join the strength of Bomber Command. On 15 November 'C' Flight of 458 Squadron was used to form the basis of the second RAAF bomber squadron, 460 Squadron. Two others formed in December: 215 Squadron at Newmarket on the 9th and 419 'Moose' Squadron RCAF at Mildenhall on the 15th. None of these units were operational until the early part of 1942, partly due to a slow rate of delivery of aircraft and partly through the requirement for the squadrons to carry out operational training.

bombers were lost. Of the 400 bombers despatched that night, 169 went to the 'Big City', which claimed twenty-one crews, whilst sixteen crews were lost over Mannheim, Cologne and less important targets. It was a night of foul weather out over the North Sea and the weather forecast spoke of very strong headwinds for the return. I attended the briefing and, in common with most of the Canadian crews, I expected a cancellation – but it didn't happen.

Each Wellington of 405 Squadron carried a 4,000lb bomb and at that loading the maximum range was 1,400 statute miles. Berlin lies some

'All went well on the outward bound flight until we climbed out of the overcast, after which we were on dead reckoning. When we reached a point where we believed, and hoped, Berlin was, we dropped our bombs and turned for home. It didn't take long before we realized we were in trouble, as the winds had increased. As soon as it was safe to do so I dropped down to sea level for two reasons: firstly, to avoid ice and thus save fuel and, secondly, I hoped we might experience less of a head wind.

'I have seen the North Sea in many moods, but I have never seen it in a more ferocious mood before or since that night ... After what

Superb, atmospheric shot of 218 Squadron's R1448. Ken Delve Collection

John Searby (later Air Commodore John Searby DSO DFC and a renowned Master Bomber) flew a number of missions with 405 Squadron in late 1941; in his book *Everlasting Arms*, he recalled one particular operation, on the night of 7 November:

This was the night when attacks were made on a number of targets and some thirty-seven

600 miles from the Yorkshire bomber bases; thus under normal conditions a safety margin of one hour was available. Well, these were not average or normal conditions and here lay the cause, I believe, of most of the losses. Sqn Ldr John Fauquier commanded one of the flight of 405 Squadron and was none too happy about the weather forecast we both heard that evening. This is what he wrote to me years later.

seemed like hours I realized that we were going to be forced to ditch as I had little or no fuel left. I told the crew to take up ditching stations. However, shortly after this I saw one of those wonderful homing lights and made a bee line for it. I crossed the coast of England with all gauges knocking on zero. A few moments later I flew over Driffield which was non-operational at that time. I could just make out the runway as it

57 Squadron Wellington at Feltwell in April 1941; the mascot nose art is a Daily Mirror cartoon character. D. Whitney via Gerry Tyack

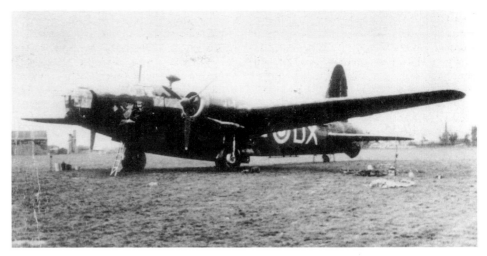

T2739 of 99 Squadron in April 1941; the top of the fin was shot away by a nightfighter.
Ken Delve Collection

was early dawn and, realizing that I could never make Pocklington, I slapped down the wheels and flaps whilst I still had power – only to find when I was at about a hundred feet that some silly so-and-so had erected pylons all down the runway. Of course, they forgot to put anything on the grass between the runways! In any event I swerved to port and did a little damage to the wing and cut off the starboard tail-plane. All in all we were very lucky and no one was hurt, thank God.'

The losses had been so severe that the new Bomber Command Operational Research Section was tasked to prepare a report. They examined three raids, Berlin, Mannheim and 'other minor raids/*Rovers* in the Ruhr area', and tabulated the losses. The Wellington statistics were:

Target	Group	A/C Sent	A/C Lost
Berlin	1	22	nil
	3	69	9
	4	10	1
Mannheim	1	46	7
	3	7	nil
Rovers	3	9	2

It was the Mannheim attack that attracted particular attention:

Forty-six Wellingtons of No. 1 Group set out to attack Mannheim: seven of these are missing, twenty-one landed at coastal aerodromes away from base, three of the sorties were abortive. The reason for landing at the coastal aerodromes was almost always lack of petrol; two of the missing aircraft sent out SOS's saying that they were landing owing to petrol shortage. The aircraft attacking Mannheim had a very high following wind and probably reached their targets quickly without realizing the difficulties they would have on their return journey. Icing conditions were prevalent and they probably used their superchargers to climb, using up more petrol. Again there seems no doubt that the reason for the high losses was petrol shortage. In this case the petrol-carrying capacity of the Wellington was ample, but having regard to the extremely adverse weather conditions, it seems that insufficient was carried.

decline. For much of the year the command had been in deficit on its Wellington strength to establishment of over a hundred aircraft, partly with 'blockages' at MUs and repair units but also due to a loss rate that averaged 3.5 per cent for much of the year (and 4.5 per cent in November, the worst month); however, the overall loss rate averaged out at 2.6 per cent, which was the lowest for any Bomber Command type: Whitley, 4 per cent; Hampden, 2.8 per cent; Stirling, 3.9 per cent; Halifax, 5.2 per cent; and Manchester, 4.2 per cent.

OTU organization be expanded. It was predicted that twenty such units would be required, along with 600 instructor pilots – at a time when there were only 1,120 pilots in the first-line units. This mismatch of requirements was to exist until late 1944 and was to cause major headaches for the training organization. In the interim, it was decided in March to reduce the course once more to eight weeks (and fifty-five hours); as Portal said, 'It is of vital importance to obtain a greater output from the OTUs, since if we do not do so I do not see

215 Squadron was amongst the early users of the Wellington, equipping in July 1939 and playing a full part in the bomber offensive until February 1942 when it departed for India, still to operate Wellingtons.
Peter Green Collection

The peak of Bomber Command (available) Wellington strength was reached at the end of 1941, the figures for December showing 266 aircraft available, with 246 crews (*see* Appendix III for table of aircraft and crew availability). Although the type was to remain an important element of Bomber Command's Main Force for much of 1942, it was, especially as a percentage of total 'bomb lift', to see a significant

Training

The changes made in the latter part of 1940 had the net effect that by early 1941 the OTUs were incapable of producing enough crews for the planned expansion of the front line in 1941. The expected flow of pilots from the overseas SFTSs was expected to put an additional strain on the OTUs; it was, therefore, essential that the

how we are to produce the crews for our expansion and at the same time keep up our pressure on Germany.' The reduced course would mean that a pilot would arrive on his squadron having flown 177 hours (fifty at EFTS, seventy-two at SFTS and fifty-five at OTU) over a period of twenty-four weeks. Two more OTUs were formed in March but it was still not enough, and in April Portal agreed that

'The course should be radically cut, that trainees should go to squadrons for a short period as second pilots.' On 12 April the command agreed to a thirty-hour course (six weeks), but only for a trial period and only in a small number of OTUs. By June three more OTUs had formed, giving a total of sixteen, of which nine were equipped with Wellingtons (11, 12, 15, 18, 20, 21, 22, 23 and 27); indeed, some 40 per cent of UK-based Wellingtons were in the training units.

One of the new units in 1941 was 21 OTU which formed at Moreton-in-Marsh in January, although the first three Wellington ICs did not arrive until late February and No. 1 Course did not start training until 1 March (graduating on 14 April). The unit comprised operational, bombing and navigational flights. Build-up of aircraft strength was slow and various changes were made to the syllabus as the OTUs were called upon to react to the perceived requirements of the front-line. By early summer, 21 OTU had thirty-seven Wellingtons and six Ansons on strength and had formed a second conversion flight in response to a syllabus change in June.

John Gee flew his first dual sortie at 11 OTU, Bassingbourn, on 7 April 1941:

In the early months of 1941 the system of training at OTU was not the scientific procedure of the later war years and many of the instructors had not taken a flying instructors' course. In addition, the aeroplanes were not fitted with a full set of dual controls; all of this made the first few hours rather tricky and a bit frightening, particularly for a pilot without any previous twin-engined experience. Some of our flying, particularly 'circuits and bumps' was done at a satellite aerodrome at Steeple Morden. After five hours of dual instruction I was allowed to go solo on 17 April; I remember taxying round the perimeter and praying that I had completed all the cockpit checks in correct sequence. After lining up on the runway I opened the throttles and took off, climbing straight ahead to 1,000ft. I then did a circuit to port and approached to land. I had put the wheels down on the downwind leg and slowed down and put 10 degrees of flap. Then as I turned into wind and lined up for the touch down, I applied full flap. Over the boundary of the aerodrome I came and held off. I must have been a bit high or my speed was a bit low for suddenly we dropped, hit the runway and bounced back high into the air then fell back on to the runway with a resounding bang. I thought I had at least broken the undercarriage, but to my amazement there I was rolling merrily down the runway. The bumpy landing had caused the top escape hatch of the canopy to fly open and it was that which had made the loud bang ... when I got out of the aeroplane I gave it a good looking over as I expected to find some damage and I was surprised to find that the wings were not bent. The Wellington had clearly been built to withstand the efforts of heavy-handed sprog pilots.

Philip Dawson arrived at 22 OTU, Wellesbourne Mountford, in May 1941 and was soon introduced to the Wellington ICs with which the unit was equipped:

The aircraft were generally pretty clapped out having been taken from operational units. The first part of the course was general flying, circuits and bumps and familiarity with the aircraft. The second phase was the more 'advanced' elements with navigation and bombing; the longest sorties were about five hours which often included visiting the ranges at the Isle of Man to bomb smoke floats. A crew on the course ahead of us were killed in a flying accident and so we were 'accelerated' to join this course, this meant flying eight trips day and night in one 24-hour period. At the end of the course, in July, four of us were posted to 104 Squadron at Driffield.

At Harwell, 15 OTU was primarily responsible for training bomber crews for the Middle East; indeed, a major part of the unit task was despatching reinforcement aircraft (and crews) to the Middle East – this task being undertaken by the Middle East Despatch Flight. This latter unit moved to the satellite airfield at Hampstead Norris in late July, as the main airfield was becoming somewhat crowded, and later became the Ferry Training Unit. This despatch task had commenced in May 1941 when three aircraft left Harwell; in the period up to the end of December the total number of aircraft despatched in this way was 218 (162 Wellington ICs and 56 Wellington IIs), the majority via Gibraltar as it was considered

Hendon, September 1941 and in the 140 Squadron photo album this picture is titled '1416 Flight say farewell to Hendon on the move to Benson to become 140 Squadron.' Peter Green Collection

too hazardous, especially in periods of poor weather, to send inexperienced crews on the direct route over France. December was a record month with fifty-three aircraft making the trip.

Nevertheless, training of crews was the primary task of the unit and typical of the entries in the ORB for this unit, and for most other OTUs, were the following two general reports:

General Report on 36 Course, passing out 1 July 1941. The general standard of all crews on this course was average, with the exception of one crew whose keenness and proficiency was well above average. This crew is one of the best which has been trained in this flight. All captains had experience in flying in bad weather conditions by day and night. With the exception of two crews, the course successfully completed a Nickel solo operational exercise. One crew crashed during a training flight in the Welsh mountains due to engine trouble, three members of the crew being killed. [This aircraft was R1286 and it crashed whilst attempting a force-landing, the port engine having failed, near Pontrhydfendigaid.]

General Report on 37 Course, passing out 8 July 1941. This course was characterized by great keenness and cheerfulness on the part of the whole course. The pilots were of high quality and showed a fine capacity for really hard work. The observers were also of the same high standard. The wireless operators were good and the air gunners, though inexperienced at first and tending to make mistakes in their turret drill, came up to standard.

Three actors pose in full flying kit for their lead roles in the 1941 film One of Our Aircraft is Missing; l–r: Bernard Miles, Eric Portman and Hugh Burden. Gerry Tyack

July was a typical month for the unit with some 3,316 hours being flown; 205 pupils arrived for training and 132 passed out, twenty complete crews being despatched to the Middle East and two to other operational stations. In November the OTU was re-organized ... 'each flight will now convert pupil pilots to Wellingtons prior to the same flight training them with their whole crew for operational work.' Prior to this a separate conversion flight had undertaken the basic pilot conversion to type. A, B and C Flights remained based at Harwell whilst D and E Flights, along with the Middle East Despatch Flight, operated from Hampstead Norris.

In November 21 OTU had also started to train crews for the Middle East, which required a few minor changes to the syllabus, the first crews graduating on 14 December and flying aircraft to the Middle East in January.

By early August it was obvious that the shorter course was not working and that not only were the OTUs unable to complete the training in the allotted time, but the squadrons were not capable of providing the 'top up' training, partly through a shortage of dual-control Wellingtons at unit level. It was also considered that poor quality SFTS output was hampering the experiment. The net result was a reduction in operational effectiveness of the first-line squadrons.

In October the old eight-week course was re-instituted, although Bomber Command wanted a twelve-week course over the winter period because of the problems of completing the night flying elements in the poorer weather. The command had also reached the point at which there were too many new crews on the squadrons, many of whom were receiving little or no flying. Bomber Command requested that the flow of crews be slowed. Air Marshal Peirse stated that,

In my opinion a dangerous situation has arisen which, if allowed to continue, may well become disastrous ... The standard and experience of airmanship necessary to enable a pilot to handle a modern medium or heavy bomber in the face of the enemy and the extremely exacting hazards of the weather is something far in excess of what we have today. We are deluding ourselves and expecting the impossible, with the net result that the dividend we earn in damage to the enemy is not commensurate with the wastage in men, material and labour expended. In present circumstances it is no exaggeration to say that by the time the best pilots become reliable captains they are due to leave their operational squadrons.

The proposed solution was what was known as the 'New Deal', in which it was agreed that first-line operational effectiveness depended on a general raising of training standards. The Air Ministry decided to lengthen pilot training to 216–290 hours

L4250 in October 1940 with a Vickers S turret and the original single fin configuration *(above)* **and twin fin configuration** *(below)*. **The Wellington was used by a number of organizations for trials duties.**
Ken Delve Collection

pre-OTU and 300–350 hours pre-squadron, and to make corresponding increases in the training of other aircrew trades. This lengthening of the training routine was to be introduced gradually – it remained to be seen if this admirable concept could be put into place in the face of pressures for first-line expansion. The increased pace of operations did serve to provide a reasonable flow of 'screened' aircrew (i.e. those who had completed their operational tour) for instructional duties.

stuck on here and there, all doped – all odd colours. Somehow, between lectures, training on the link trainer and learning the rudiments of bombing theoretical hell out of the Germans, we learned, after a while, to fly as a crew ... The Wellington growled and whined, lumbered off the ground, wallowed in flight, and squatted heavily on landing.

The course proceeded and gradually the sorties became more complex; on 26 October a night cross-country and bombing

singly and in sticks, before returning to Hampstead Norris. The dropping of a stick of bombs was controlled by a clockwork Mickey Mouse, something like a clockwork timer. A small arm would traverse the face of eighteen contacts, at the press of a button, so releasing the bombs from the bomb bay in a regular sequence. The speed of the arm could be altered to adjust the spacing between each bomb. The wireless operator, under the watchful eye of an experienced 'sparks', would need to take bearings from radio beacons.

The groundcrew on the bomber squadrons performed marvels to keep the numbers of serviceable aircraft at 'acceptable' levels; this was also true at the OTUs where 'operationally tired' aircraft were often the main equipment of the unit; this shot may be 27 OTU. Ken Delve Collection

Eric Barfoot, a sergeant pilot, arrived at 15 OTU, Harwell in the latter part of 1941:

Our first introduction to the Wellington IA took place at Hampstead Norris, a satellite airfield. Our first walk around the Wimpey did not install confidence. The two huge tyres looked very vulnerable; ballooned and spongy and without any tread. Oil seemed to drip from the engines, hydraulic oil from the undercarriage. In a wind the fabric covering seemed to flap against odd parts of the structure. Patches were

exercise was detailed and Eric and his crew were on the roster:

All crews were briefed to undertake an exercise, a night cross country flight, flying from beacon to beacon, to the north of Scotland, returning down the Irish Sea. There we were to drop a flame float for the rear gunner to take a drift. The navigator would calculate a wind velocity and the gunners would proceed to shoot out the flame. Thereafter we were to return to the bombing range, drop a few practice bombs,

Came the time to start up. I can only liken the noise of the 'Peggies' to a thousand old-fashioned cast iron mangles operated by as many fit Chinese in a laundry. Certainly the noise was not a healthy one, the engines sounded very worn ... The thousand mangles were replaced by five thousand as the engines strained to enable the plane to reach 80mph before the end of the runway was reached. The brakes were released and the fabric-covered motorized Meccano set stirred and lurched forward. At 45mph the tail responded to forward pressure on the control column ...

A sweep around the field, climbing, then on course. The engines had to be synchronized frequently to obliterate the beat, and Lance and I took turns at the controls, the other keeping a watchful eye on the instruments, and handling the fuel controls in the fuselage. Spare engine oil was carried in a tank on the starboard side of the fuselage, and frequent pumps had to be made to the handle supplying lubrication to the engines. The driving needed considerable attention and, as we climbed into the blackness, the exercise became one of dead-reckoning navigation ... We let down over the Irish Sea; at 800ft we saw it, foaming white in no light. We dropped our flame float and Robbie took drifts on it with his rear guns, reading the drift from a scale inside of his turret. Then the gunners tried to extinguish the float with several bursts ... We changed course for the bombing range and dropped singles and sticks on the circle of goosenecks.

Having landed and entered debriefing the crew were amazed to find that everyone else had landed long before – the weather forecast had led to a recall message being sent out.

By the end of the year Bomber Command was complaining of 'inexperienced crews resulting from too great a shortening of the OTU course'. This was expressed in a forcible memo in December:

> I am under the impression that when it was agreed to reduce the OTU course it was agreed by all concerned that the reduced course would be adequate to produce the necessary training. I understand that the course is being lengthened once more and I fully support this, but there arises out of these ideas a point upon which we must insist most firmly. It is the responsibility of Bomber Command, its group and station commanders to ensure that no crew is normally sent on an operation if they are considered to be insufficiently trained ... It is vitally important that the command should not relax the standard required for operations simply because the Air Ministry have cut down the training course.

This was, of course, easy to say but far harder to implement at squadron level, the primary pressure being for squadrons to fulfil their operational commitment, a task made harder if they had to take on a significant training task to 'top up' the experience level of the new crews from the OTUs.

Maritime War

As part of the expansion of anti-submarine capability, 221 Squadron had reformed in November 1940 at Bircham Newton with Wellington ICs, primarily flying convoy escort as well as a series of anti-submarine patrol lines. In January the squadron received the first of its ASV-equipped Wellingtons; the distinctive four aerials on the upper fuselage of the Wellington earning it the name 'Stickleback' (or, by the crews, 'Goofington'). The first operations with the new aircraft were flown in March, the primary task being ASV search for enemy shipping off the Dutch coast.

The changing nature of the maritime war led to a re-disposition of units and as part of this, in May, 221 Squadron moved to Limavady in Northern Ireland, though a detachment had been operating at this airfield for some time. The squadron was soon very busy on day and night patrols, the standard load being three 450lb DC bombs for day patrols and five 250lb AS bombs for night patrols. The situation continued to change and in August the

A somewhat fogged photo, but one full of atmosphere as bombs arrive and preparations take place for another operational sortie. Ken Delve Collection

July 1941 and a close-up of the ASV aerials array on the starboard wing of a Wellington.
FlyPast Collection

squadron sent a detachment to Reykjavik, Iceland, the first patrols being flown from there on the 11th. The following month it was decided to move the whole squadron to Iceland and from there the routine of convoy patrols and AS-patrols continued, Flt Lt Starling making the first attack on a U-boat on 11 October, although with no result. This deployment lasted until December and when the squadron returned to Limavady, AOC Iceland sent the following signal:

I should like before they leave to express my appreciation of the very fine performance of 221 Squadron both in the protection of convoys and in giving assistance and guidance when needed

to escort vessels and merchant vessels. Also to congratulate them on their sustained offensive against enemy submarines in spite of weather conditions as bad as anywhere in the world.

In autumn the Air Ministry had at last approved Coastal Command's request for Wellingtons to be equipped with the Leigh Light system (explained in detail on p.94); six aircraft being authorized. The original prototype aircraft and system was used for further demonstrations in November, following which the AOC requested thirty-six sets to be provided in order to equip the Wellington ICs of 221 Squadron, this unit at that time operating from Reykjavik. This was refused on the grounds that the system had to be proven

operationally before any increase could be agreed.

However, following completion in December of trials by the Coastal Command Development Unit, a request was once more submitted for more equipment, in this instance for thirty Wellingtons to be fitted out. The trials had been carried out on two nights in mid December against a surfaced submarine that was underway in Lough Foyle and, despite poor weather conditions, had proved very satisfactory. The Air Ministry approved a further twenty sets of lights and radar but held to its argument that further increase depended upon operational success. The first Leigh Light unit, 1471 Flight, formed at Chivenor in January 1942.

221 Squadron flew convoy and anti-submarine patrols from Reykjavik, Iceland from August to December 1941; here W5674 is at the squadron dispersal. Peter Green Collection

Middle East

As 1941 opened the Wellingtons, except for 148 Squadron still at Luqa on Crete (until March, when it moved to Kabrit, although even then it maintained a detachment on the beleaguered island), were concentrated in the Canal Zone area from where they continued their attacks against Italian targets in North Africa.

The attacks made by 37 Squadron were typical of those being undertaken by 257 Wing's bomber units; the squadron was fairly active during January, although operations were somewhat curtailed in the last week of the month by poor weather:

Date		Target	Aircraft
Jan	2–3	Bardia	4
	3–4	Tobruk	2
	4–5	Tobruk	2
	5–6	Tobruk	7
	7–8	Benghazi	8
	8–9	Benghazi	8
	10–11	Benina airfield	3
	10–11	Berca airfield	4
	13–14	Benghazi	7
	14–15	Benghazi	1
	15–16	Maritza airfield	4
	17–18	Tobruk	8
	20–21	Tobruk	5
	21–22	Derna	3
	22–23	Maritza airfield	2

The 70 Squadron diarist recorded the rationale behind the run of attacks on air-fields, for all the Wellington units were attacking such targets 'for the purpose of rendering enemy aerodromes unservice-able. Delayed Action bombing was used as it was believed that the enemy do not use their aerodromes for seventy-two hours after being bombed by DA bombs.'

The airfield at Maritza on the island of Rhodes was attacked by 37 Squadron again on the night of 4–5 February, six Wellingtons taking off at around 1700 to fly direct to Rhodes; three of the aircraft returned early with engine trouble but the other three found the target and,

> ... carried out level attacks from heights between 5,000–7,500ft. Sgt Paul who was first over the target dropped his bombs in one stick which fell from the north end of the runway to the barracks and workshops. A mass of red flames shot up immediately and the fire was still burning when Plt Off Ford made his attack. He dropped two sticks among the hangars and in the vicinity of the petrol dump, causing two fires. Plt Off Thomas also dropped two sticks; the first on the aerodrome and the second close to the hangars. He then descended to 600ft and made a machine gun attack on the hangars and buildings, the front and rear gunners both firing 1,000 rounds of ammunition.

In January the first German forces began to arrive and although attacks on ports were increased, the build-up continued and, with the arrival of General Rommel, the first combined Axis offensive was launched in March, British forces being driven back towards Tobruk. With Ger-man ground forces also came the *Luftwaffe* and the air situation was dramatically changed.

In February it was 37 Squadron's turn to send a detachment to Greece in support of Allied forces operating against the Ital-ians; six aircraft moved to Menidi on 12 February and were in action the same night, attacking Durazzo and Tirana. A few days later five aircraft moved to Paramythia in order to 'operate against Albania with a full bomb load'; however, poor weather caused this mission to be cancelled. On 20 February two aircraft were detailed,

> ... for the unfamiliar role of operating by day-light in close proximity to the front lines. In company with a Ju 52 their task was to drop five tons of supplies for the Greek troops. Two air-craft, captains Flt Lt Baird-Smith and Sgt Spiller, each carrying 1½ tons of supplies, took-off from Menidi at 1235 and proceeded to Paramythia LG where they landed at 1400 hours. At 1445 the aircraft left Paramythia and climbed to 3,000ft flying in vic, escorted by fif-teen Gladiators flying 1,000ft above. The exact location for the supplies was indicated by ground strips ... descended to 100ft above ground level and began dropping supplies through the mid-under hatch. This operation lasted half an hour during which an enemy fighter patrol arrived and was engaged by Glad-iators, who shot down four of them.

The detachment returned to Shallufa on 22 February but, like other units, returned over the next few months, the first occasion being 7–23 March. The situation in Greece had reached crisis point when German forces, with decisive air support, swept through the country in April 1941, Germany having declared war on Yugoslavia and Greece on 6 April. Two days before, 37 Squadron had returned to Greece on the third of its major detachments, except that this time eleven aircraft moved to Menidi. On the night of 6–7 April they flew their first raid over Bulgaria, six aircraft attacking the marshalling yards at Sofia. The Wellingtons were only a small part of the Allied air effort in Greece, but like the others they were overwhelmed by the *Luftwaffe* in the air and on the ground. In an effort to

stem the German advance, additional detachments were sent from Egypt, including 38 Squadron on 11 April; before being sent back to Egypt on the 17th, the Wellingtons flew a number of attacks on communications routes and troop concentrations, but it was impossible to stem the tide of the German advance and in mid-April the Wellingtons of 37 Squadron returned to Shallufa.

Two weeks later, however, a detachment of ten aircraft from the squadron was sent to Aqir to 'await operations'. On 2 May, they moved to Shaibah and that same afternoon flew their first operation over Iraq, four aircraft being sent to attack Iraqi

gun positions, MT and armour to the south of the RAF station at Habbaniya. 'Level and shallow dive attacks were made from 4,000–1,000ft and the only opposition from the ground was rifle and some machine gun fire' (37 Squadron ORB). In late April the Iraqi leader, Raschid Ali, had, under German 'encouragement' decided to remove the British – and free airfields such as Basrah and Habbaniya for German use. As a flying training station, Habbaniya had a variety of non-operational types and these would be put to good use as 'light bombers' but the Wellingtons, promised by Air Marshal Tedder on 1 May, would be the main strike force. Dawn the

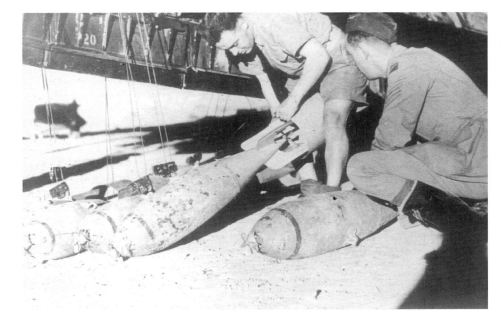

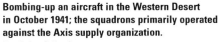

Bombing-up an aircraft in the Western Desert in October 1941; the squadrons primarily operated against the Axis supply organization.
Ken Delve Collection

Kitting-up for another sortie over North Africa; the desert conditions played havoc with the aircraft and the early marks of Wellington were underpowered for the hot climate.
Ken Delve Collection

following day saw three bombers attack the petrol and ammunition dumps at Raschid airfield, Baghdad, whilst a fourth Wellington flew a 'security patrol' to attack Iraq positions around Habbaniya. Raschid was attacked by eight aircraft on 3 May, while two other aircraft rotated on three-hour security patrol over Habbaniya. Similar missions were flown up to 8 May when the Wellingtons attacked Sharnaban and Ba'quba airfields in search of the remaining Iraqi aircraft. It had been intended that ten Wellingtons would operate from Habbaniya but this had to be limited to four as re-arming and handling facilities were inadequate. The final missions were flown on 10 May; the four aircraft attacking barracks at Mosul. By 12 May, Wg Cdr Collard had led the detachment back to Shallufa.

Since early February, 70 Squadron had maintained a forward detachment at El Adem; the diarist recorded the chaos prevailing in April:

> During the period 6–15 April the detachment was on the move all the time, evacuating its personnel from each base as it moved back. On April 6 El Adem was evacuated to Sidi Azuz about 70 miles east; each aircraft flew a double trip in order to get as many men and as much equipment as possible away.

The Battle for Crete

By 14 April the squadron was back at its old base at El Adem – dropping bombs on its new occupants!

April also brought something of a crisis in the Western Desert: Allied forces, including air power, weakened by diversions such as Greece, were unable to stand against a determined German-Italian attack. Meanwhile, the situation in Greece had further deteriorated and by 1 May the last Allied troops had been evacuated from southern Greece (under Operation *Demon*); Crete was now the main Allied 'stronghold', but a German attack on that island was thought to be imminent. On 20 May the Germans launched their air assault against the island, this being the last major airborne operation undertaken by the élite German paratroop forces. The airfield at Maleme was one of the key targets and despite fierce fighting it was soon in German hands.

Strategic bombing from bases in Egypt was an essential element of overstretched Allied air power, although the Wellingtons also flew other missions, such as on the night of 22–23 May when three aircraft of 70 Squadron dropped supplies at low level to troops at Candia, Heraklion and Retimo. The following night, 37 Squadron sent six aircraft to attack Maleme airfield and various beach sites. One aircraft turned back early and three failed to return; of these, L7866 (Sgt Faulkner) crash-landed at Heraklion, the crew being taken prisoner; T2875 (Sgt Harris) ditched near a British warship off North Africa, the crew being rescued; and of T2895 (Sgt Mew) nothing was known. A further four Wellingtons from 38 Squadron were also over Crete that night, the main target being Maleme. Intensive operations by 257 Wing's Wellingtons over and around Crete continued throughout the latter part of May, airfields being primary targets in an attempt to restrict the German air effort that was causing havoc to Allied naval operations around Crete. Despite heavy naval losses, the evacuation of Allied forces from Crete was a success, the Wellingtons, as well as other types, having provided essential air support up to the last minute. The supply-dropping role continued right up until the last minute:

> Wellington 2951, Fg Off Sewell, took supplies to army forces awaiting evacuation on the beaches near Sphakia, Crete. The aircraft located the approximate position where supplies were to be dropped, fired a two-star cartridge upon which an Aldis lamp flashing SOS was seen. This light was pinpointed and a 310lb box of supplies dropped. After patrolling the coast to see if there were any bonfires, the aircraft returned to where the Aldis lamp was flashing and dropped five more cases of supplies. The captain then flew up to the high ground north of the beaches and dropped sixteen 60lb sacks of supplies. As the aircraft turned for home an Aldis lamp flashed 'Thank You'. (70 Squadron ORB for 2–3 June)

An indicator of the increasing use, and importance, of the Wellington units comes from 37 Squadron when it records that May saw a record number of operational hours flown by the unit – 781 hours, as against 330 hours in April. (The record was soon broken as in August the squadron recorded 1,102 operational hours!)

Expansion

Effective air power was already seen as an essential requirement for campaigns in the Western Desert, both in its tactical sense with direct support of the land forces and in its strategic role of destroying the enemy's logistics system. In mid-1941 the Defence Committee approved a programme of reinforcements for Middle East Command aimed at raising strength to 40 1/2 squadrons by 15 July, this force structure to include five Wellington bomber squadrons each with twenty aircraft. Although the programme was increased to 62 1/2 squadrons after the failure of the June *Battleaxe* offensive, this did not affect the number of Wellington units. It was further stated that,

> Provided that delivery of Wellingtons by air via Gibraltar and Malta continued to be practicable it was thought possible to achieve and keep up the proposed force of five squadrons. It was necessary, however, to introduce the Wellington II as far as possible as the Wellington I had not proved altogether satisfactory under summer conditions in the Middle East. Supplies of Wellington IIs for the Middle East would for some months be limited as Bomber Command had first claim on these aircraft. (AHB *Narrative*, Middle East Campaigns)

The increase in strength brought its own problems, not least that of crew training as most multi-engine aircrew arriving in the Middle East were straight from SFTSs in Iraq, Africa or Australia; an Operational Training Flight (OTF) for Wellingtons had been formed at Kabrit in early 1941 but this was unable to keep pace with the expansion. However, the Air Ministry

> ... refused to recognize the Wellington Flight at Kabrit as an OTU nucleus as replacement crews for heavy bomber and general reconnaissance aircraft were to be provided by crews flying out aircraft from the UK. Middle East found, however, that refresher courses were necessary for Wellington crews. To eliminate this need it was decided in April [1941] that 15 OTU in England was to be employed exclusively on training fresh Wellington crews for the Middle East. (AHB *Narrative*, Middle East Campaigns)

Mines and Canals

As with European operations, minelaying was considered to be a vital part of any campaign of attack on enemy ports and a number of Allied aircraft types undertook this work, including the Wellingtons from July onwards; the first such sortie was flown by 38 Squadron on 16 July when aircraft dropped mines in Benghazi harbour.

Meanwhile, the DWI Wellingtons of 1 GRU continued their minesweeping operations and on 1 February 1941 scored a spectacular success during a sweep of the Suez Canal, exploding an enemy mine just ahead of the 25,000-ton SS *Dominion Monarch*. Over the entire period of its operations, the unit exploded ten mines in the Suez Canal, two in Tobruk harbour and one in Tripoli harbour (the latter probably being British mines that had

With German control of Greece, the Corinth Canal became an important Axis waterway for supplies, being a short route between the Ionian and Aegean Seas – and as such it became a target for Allied bombing. On 8–9 August, 257 Wing bombers launched attacks on this target; the 37 Squadron ORB noting:

Ten aircraft of this squadron took part in an important operation against the Corinth Canal

Three heavy raids were mounted by the squadrons of 257 Wing, some eighty-nine effective sorties, against the entrances and banks of the canal and were reported to have blocked, or partially blocked, the waterway for considerable periods. With Axis ships having to route the longer way around the Pelopennese of Greece, they were more vulnerable to air attack by Beauforts and Wellingtons. The major effort against enemy sea logistics was

The DWI Wellingtons moved from the UK to the Middle East, forming No. 1 GRU.
FlyPast Collection

been laid in these harbours). The Axis forces made a number of determined efforts to mine the vital Suez Canal waterway and it was essential that it was swept at regular intervals to supplement the net defence that was in place; in due course a number of modified trawlers (known as LL Sweepers) were used in conjunction with the Wellington operations.

in conjunction with other aircraft of 257 Wing. A successful attempt was made to deny the enemy use of the canal by causing landslides to block it and by laying mines at its eastern entrance. Nine aircraft carried two 1,000lb bombs each and one had three 500lb bombs, the object being to drop these as near as possible to the edge of the canal banks at a point 3,000yd from its eastern end.

indeed directed against the ships themselves and in this Malta played a major part. The Wellington units joined their colleagues in the Blenheim and Beaufort units in taking every opportunity to attack Axis shipping on the routes from Italy to North Africa.

The end of the year was to see the Wellingtons trying out what was, for them,

(Above) **A DWI Wellington of 1 GRU making a low pass.** Philip Dawson

A Malta quarry claims a Wellington. W. D. Roberts

a new anti-shipping weapon – the torpedo, but more of that later. Bomber strength in the Middle East had, in the meantime, increased again in August with the formation, at Kabrit, of 108 Squadron, equipped, like all the other MEC squadrons with Wellington ICs.

Operations Continue

It is worth at this point highlighting the problems of aircraft supply. There are two aspects to be considered: firstly, the competing needs of the various operational theatres, priority being given to the UK – and in terms of bomber aircraft, to Bomber Command, with whom the Wellington was still the most important type; secondly, the problem of actually getting aircraft out to the Middle East in the face of enemy occupation of most of mainland Europe. The only 'route' was a long oversea journey around France and Spain to Gibraltar and then on to the Middle East, via Malta. Losses of aircraft *en route* were not insignificant. Additional aircraft were, however, urgently needed both to replace losses and to allow a build-up of strength in the face of growing Axis air and ground strength.

Again to stress the types of targets (and the scale of operations mounted against Benghazi), as well as the intense nature of operations for the Wellington units, it is worth highlighting a typical month, and this time we will look at August 1941 for 70 Squadron:

Date	Target	Aircraft
Aug 2–3	Benghazi	8
4–5	Benghazi	6
7–8	Benghazi	4
8–9	various (inc. Corinth Canal)	11
10–11	Benghazi	10
13–14	Corinth Canal	8
13–14	Heraklion	1
15–16	Benghazi	5
17–18	Benghazi	8
20–21	Benghazi	3
23–24	various	4
26–27	Benghazi–Derna	5
28–29	Menidi–Eleusis	11
30–31	Maritza	9

On the Menidi raid Wg Cdr Read 'flashed the V for Victory sign over Athens several times – until he had to commence nursing his starboard engine which gave trouble all the way back to Fuka.'

The Wellington II arrived in the Middle East in mid-1941 and was soon having problems:

The Wellington II was OK until it got to the desert and then overheating and low oil pressure problems caused great difficulties. The bench-life of a Merlin was only 6–10 hours and so this meant that one trip, one engine! As soon as the Mark X was available, we disposed of the Mark IIs; the extra 100hp gave us that extra edge and the X was a lovely aircraft, the best by far. (Philip Dawson)

The critical role that Malta played in the Allied war effort can never be overstated; not only in the value of its resistance in terms of morale but, increasingly, the offensive role that it played in combating Axis shipping plying between Europe and the desert war. Additional bomber reinforcements arrived in Malta in autumn 1941, 104 Squadron detaching Wellington IIs and crews to the island from October to January, 1942, and 40 Squadron doing likewise, although this unit remained on Malta until the following summer. The 40 Squadron ORB recorded the move on 16 October: 'Orders were received for the squadron as a whole to move to Malta for a two-month tour of special operations duties. The squadron, now reduced to nine fully trained and two freshmen crews was to be made up to sixteen operational flight crews.' On 23 October, Wg Cdr Stickly led the first eight aircraft from Alconbury, followed by a second eight on the 25th, although not all of these arrived in Malta.

Philip Dawson had just returned to flying after being in an aircraft crash and was one of those due to go to Malta:

We were told that the detachment would be for about three months and that we should be home by Christmas; the reason we were going was that the Wellington II had a greater bomb load than the ICs and a major effort was needed to support the Crusader offensive. Aircraft were flown to Heston in order to have beam guns fitted and

Trio of 37 Squadron aircraft, October 1941.
Ken Delve Collection

then we deployed to Stanton Harcourt as the starting point for a direct route to Malta. It was soon discovered that the take-off run at Stanton was insufficient for an overloaded Wellington – we had overload fuel tanks, extra guns, six air-crew, four groundcrew and spare parts on board; the solution was soon to hand when a swathe was cut through the offending trees thus giving us an acceptable run! Once airborne we set course over Brighton, flying between two searchlights being used as markers, and then off across France; it was easy to see when we crossed into Vichy France as all the lights were on as if it was peacetime. We arrived off Malta just before dawn and had to circle Filfla Island until it was day and we were able to land. I logged eight hours twenty-five minutes for that trip.

Indeed, 104 Squadron composed a little ditty about this period:

There came the much-feared rumour,
We were going overseas.
Then they packed us off the Malta
To scare the yellow Wops,
Across the sea to Italy
We mounted up the ops.
In the sky
Hear them roar,
That was when I'ties heared about the boys of 104.

We were told that after three months,
We would all be going back,
And although the rumour sounded true,
The outlook still looked black.
For meanwhile crafty Jerries
With their Junkers 88s,
Were coming over every night
And writing off our crates.
In the sky

And our thoughts are back in England
With the boys we left at Driff.
When this blasted war is over
And our enemies no more,
We will tell our kids the things we did
In Squadron 104.
In the sky
Hear them roar,
Victory planes that once belonged to all the boys of 104.

The squadron became operational immediately and was soon engaged against a variety of targets. The squadron was primarily engaged in anti-shipping work, either at sea or in port, although enemy airfields were also frequent targets.

In August a requirement had been put forward for heavier bombs for use against ports such as Tripoli and in due course the

104 Squadron sent a detachment to Luqa in October 1941 and operated from there until early 1942 when the squadron re-united in the Middle East. Philip Dawson

THE BOYS OF 104

On a station back in Blighty
They had Wimpeys by the score,
Then they got the finest bunch of chaps
Formed Squadron 104.
Each evening during summer
of 1941,
They loaded up those Wimpeys
And they bombed the blasted Hun.
In the sky
Hear them roar
There's another load for Jerry from the boys of 104.

As the winter nights came nearer
And our toes began to freeze,

Hear them roar,
Now's the time for us to beat it said the boys of 104.
We thought our troubles ended
And our hearts were full of cheer,
Overloads on boys said Chief
We're getting out of here.
But the pilots set the wrong course
As they circled round the drome.
And headed for the Middle East
Instead of going home.
In the sky
Hear them roar,
As those Wimpeys headed eastwards with the boys of 104.

Now we are here in Egypt,
Other squadrons bore us stiff,

Air Ministry sent twelve 4,000lb bombs to Malta by submarine and three specially-modified Wellingtons of 104 Squadron to drop them. It was Air Marshal Tedder's intention to use these against Naples and Benghazi and indeed it was Naples that was attacked first, on 21–22 October, when four of these weapons were dropped. The opportunity was also taken to drop a new leaflet on the population of Naples, which read as follows:

Neapolitans. We British, who have never been at war with you before, send you this message. We bombed Naples tonight. We did not want to bomb you Neapolitans. We have no quarrel with you. All we want is peace with you. But we are forced to bomb Naples because you let the

Perhaps one of the best of all Wellington photographs – you can almost step into this picture of 37 Squadron's T2505 at dispersal. The nose art is one of the most dramatic ever carried by a Wellington.
Peter Green Collection

Germans use your port. So long as ships continue to leave Naples with German arms and German supplies for the Germans in Libya your city will be bombed again. Tonight's bombing is only the first drop of the coming storm. Therefore if you want to save yourselves:

1. Your dockers must refuse to load ships for the Germans.
2. Your sailors must refuse to sail ships for the Germans.
3. You must go yourselves to the docks and scream at your dockers and sailors to cease work.

That same month Tedder issued a new set of operational instructions giving target priorities for the Malta Wellingtons:

1. Sustained light scale nuisance raids on Naples area, docks and shipping;
2. Sustained heavy raids on Tripoli;
3. One heavy attack on Castel Benito (to prevent the Italians moving aircraft east of that place).

The Wellingtons attacked Castel Benito twice in early November, on the nights of the 2nd–3rd and 5th–6th, claiming the destruction of twelve aircraft on the ground during the first mission.

In September three ASV-equipped Wellingtons had been sent to Malta to increase the effectiveness of the anti-shipping operations. Upon arrival they were designated as the Special Duties Flight (SDF) and tasked to:

1. Co-operate with RN forces based at Malta;
2. Co-operate with Fleet Air Arm Albacores;
3. Undertake night bomb attacks on, and night shadowing of, enemy shipping;
4. Carry out sweeps along the enemy's known shipping lanes.

The strategic reconnaissance unit, 69 Squadron, had been on Malta since January 1941, having been renumbered from 431 Flight, supplementing its Baltimores with Wellingtons from August 1942.

The only confirmed success that Philip Dawson had in the anti-shipping role came on the night of 31 October when, flying his usual Z8404, he was one of four Wellingtons tasked, in company with a flare-dropping aircraft of 69 Squadron, to attack a small convoy of three ships (one warship and two MVs) that had earlier been located by a 69 Squadron aircraft:

> We reached the rough area and then the flare-dropper began to do his stuff; it was a good moonlit night and I saw three ships in the moonpath and so set up for a run against the larger of the MVs. Having made three runs at 6,000ft it was impossible to make a good attack because of the evasive tactics of the ships. We tried again at 3,500ft, the minimum height for using the bombsight, but again had no luck. We then decided to make a diving attack, from 3,500ft down to about 150ft over the target. The warship seemed to have only one good gun on the stern and this kept shooting over our starboard wing. The bomb aimer had to guess the release – and got it right as two bombs struck the ship. Another of the Wellingtons also hit this target and when a reconnaissance sortie spotted the convoy the following day it was down to two ships.

One of the major problems faced by the offensive forces on Malta was shortage of munitions and fuel and this had an adverse effect on the scale of operations; the commonest weapon being dropped by the Wellingtons was the 250lb GP bomb (or 250lb SAP); no special anti-shipping bombs were available and a number of weapons that dated back to the latter part of World War One were also called into service. Many of these bombs could only be tail-fuzed and so reliance was placed on the weapon actually penetrating the deck of the target as without nose fuzing they would not go off on impact.

Whilst Malta-based units hunted shipping, their colleagues from Egypt were frequently tasked against the main logistics depots, and of these Benghazi was one of the most important as it was the chief port in Cyrenaica and had a capacity of handling 30,000 tons of supplies a month. In the period from June to October the bomber units kept up an almost nightly offensive against this port, recording 102 raids (578 effective sorties) as part of the overriding Allied air strategy of cutting the enemy supply routes and depriving him of an offensive capability. Counter-air operations remained another prong of the air strategy. Although most of the airfield attacks were carried out at medium level, there were occasions when the crews went in at low level; one such was 2 November, a fine moonlit evening when

sixteen Wellingtons from Malta bombed and strafed Castel Benito. Philip Dawson was still flying his favourite Z8404:

> We went over the airfield with all guns blazing, our front gunner saw a truck moving over the airfield and opened fire on it. One poor Italian aircraft arrived in the area with its lights on and a number of Wellington gunners latched onto him and let rip. The airfield was very poorly defended, we had the impression that it had one machine gun in each corner and that was about it.

ELINT

Meanwhile, the Egypt-based Wellington force also expanded with the arrival, in October, of a flight from 109 Squadron (in January the flight was renumbered becoming the 'Signals Squadron', until its new numberplate, 162 Squadron, was confirmed). The 'Signals Squadron' designation indicated the unusual role of these particular Wellingtons: all were equipped for the RCM role, and in particular for electronic intelligence gathering (ELINT). The AHB *Narrative* records this move:

> In order to hinder the enemy control of his tank forces plans were activated for the employment of Wellington ICs especially equipped for jamming inter-tank radio communications. The specialist equipment had been developed by 109 Squadron in conjunction with a number of technical experts from 80 Wing and the TRE (Telecommunications Research Establishment) ... With the use of a *Hoover* motor it was eventually found possible to convert a general purpose transmitter to emit musical jamming tones over 28–34 MCS wavebands; the power came from an ASV alternator specially fitted into the aircraft. (AIR 26/850)

Flight trials had been conducted by 109 Squadron and in due course six of these aircraft had been flown out from England in October; experiments were subsequently carried out in Palestine with captured German tank radio sets. CAS reported to the Prime Minister that

> We should be able to jam out completely, from about 20–30 miles range, all German inter-tank signals between units 2 miles apart and perhaps less. The Wellingtons will have to fly by day and near the battle area and may, therefore, require some fighter escort, but they will not be flying all the time as the intention is to put them up only when the situation is considered opportune.

Each of the special aircraft trailed a 9ft aerial and with its transmitters was able to jam communications in the 27–35MHz band – but this story belongs to the early part of 1942 and so will be picked up in the next chapter.

Before the arrival of this unit aircraft of 148 Squadron had conducted ELINT sorties in conjunction with their standard bombing role and during the summer of 1941 a number of aircraft had been fitted with special receiving equipment, and an extra crew member. It was noticed that these special aircraft appeared to attract more than the usual amount of *Flak* and it was thought that this might be due to the aerial producing a better radar signature for the Germans! In response the squadron decided to drop aluminium foil of the same size (18in x 1in) in an effort to produce a false target. This was tried on the next sortie to Benghazi but proved of no value and so was not tried again. (True 'Window' decoy aluminium strips would have to wait until the Hamburg raid of 1942.)

Operation Crusader

The five Wellington squadrons of 257 Wing were the main strategic bombing asset available to the commanders and

> To control the five squadrons in the Middle East, No. 205 (Heavy Bomber) Group was formed with effect from 23 October at RAF Shallufa in place of 257 (HB) Wing; it remained under the command of Gp Capt L. L. Maclean. The group was not placed under the jurisdiction AHQ Egypt but remained directly under the hand of the AOC-in-C. Operational control could be granted to the AOC Western Desert when the situation demanded it. (AHB Narrative, Middle East Campaigns)

Throughout the latter part of 1941 the range of roles for the Wellingtons had been increasing, but from November the maximum effort was once more directed against land targets as all available air power was thrown in to support the *Crusader* offensive launched on 18 November. The air campaign had commenced in October with anti-shipping and anti-air sorties designed to achieve a measure of control in these aspects before the ground offensive opened. The tactical aircraft of the newly created Desert Air Force (DAF) played a part in the softening-up process and then gave close support to the advancing ground forces whilst the strategic elements, such as the Wellingtons, attacked longer-range targets.

The Wellington ORBAT for Middle East Command during *Crusader* (11 November) was:

	Unit	Base	Aircraft
250 Wing	1 GRU	Ismailia	7 Wellington I
205 Gp	37 Sqn	Shallufa	18 Wellington IC
	38 Sqn	Shallufa	21 Wellington IC
	70 Sqn	Kabrit	18 Wellington IC
	148 Sqn	Kabrit	8 Wellington IC
			+23 Wellington II
	108 Sqn	Fayid	19 Wellington IC
201 Gp	Sea Rescue		
	Flt	LG152	4 Wellington IC
HQ Malta	40 Sqn det	LuqA	Wellington IC

The 40 Squadron detachment (sixteen aircraft) arrived on Malta from Alconbury on 31 October, along with a detachment of 104 Squadron (fifteen aircraft had arrived in mid-October but are not mentioned in the MEC ORBAT), the intention being to strengthen the bombing campaign against Sicily and Italy as part of the overall strategy of denying the Axis forces their essential supply lane across the Mediterranean.

The *Crusader* Air Plan was complex. Within it,

> The heavy bombers of 257 Wing [205 Group by this time] were to continue their pressure on shipping and port facilities at Benghazi by night

and attack such other strategic targets as might be decided on from time to time. It was decided that the Wellingtons should operate at maximum effort from the night of 5–6 November onwards … In their constant effort by night the Wellingtons of 257 Wing flew a total of 144 effective sorties, dropping nearly 184 short tons of bombs – including during the last week of the phase [i.e the preparatory phase] a proportion of 4,000 pounders. The targets attacked included the moles, shipping, petrol storage, stores, and marshalling yards. There were no losses due to enemy action. On the night of 1–2 November, however, heavy losses were caused through a fog developing 'suddenly four hours before the Met expected'. Of the Wellingtons operating on that occasion seven of 148 Squadron attacked petrol dumps at Coefia, north-east of Benghazi. These aircraft were routed to alternative landing grounds as soon as the fog started to form, but all the Western Desert landing grounds were quickly obscured. Five of 148 Squadron's aircraft crash-landed, four being destroyed. Five crew members were seriously injured.

Although the intensified Wellington effort resulted in further damage to port facilities and virtually stopped off-loading at night, the attempt to hit shipping at night proved the most difficult task. (AHB Narrative, Middle East Campaigns)

The Wellington units made use of a number of ALGs for certain of the missions, LG60, LG104 and LG106 being particularly favoured. During Phase II of the operation, and still pre D-Day (the ground forces opening their advance on 18 November), the Wellingtons concentrated on further

weakening of enemy logistics to prevent supplies reaching the battle area and also attacks on enemy airfields as part of the air superiority strategy. On many of the night missions the Albacores of 826 Squadron, Fleet Air Arm, were used as flare droppers to illuminate the target, thus ensuring that the Wellingtons could apply maximum effort to the actual bombing rather than, as previously (and subsequently), providing their own illumination aircraft.

The armoured battle was joined in earnest on the 19th and most air effort, including that of the Wellingtons, was addressed to neutralizing the enemy air force; on the three nights of 18–20 November, the 205 Group units flew 104 effective sorties against Derna, Gazala, Martuba and Tmimi, the prime targets being dispersed aircraft. The major effort was then switched to direct support of the battlefield. 20 November saw the first use of the special Wellingtons (often referred to as 'Winston's Wellingtons' due to the Prime Minister's direct interest in such operations); a report from advanced HQ the following day stated 'Preliminary reports from prisoners indicate tank jamming most effective causing breakdown in their communications.' Later analysis showed this to have been somewhat over-optimistic although the unit flew twenty missions during *Crusader* (for the loss of two of its six aircraft).

The Malta squadrons were making their contribution to *Crusader* by bombing supply centres in Italy, particularly the docks and rail facilities at Naples and Brindisi, as well as targets in Libya. By late November the Axis supply situation was becoming critical and an attempt was made to use Ju 52s to fly fuel from Eleusis (Greece) to Derna; a concentrated series of attacks on Derna destroyed many of these Ju 52s.

By mid-December the enemy had been forced back almost 1,000 miles, but then the offensive petered out, defeated by lack of supplies and support facilities.

Although the units in Malta were still playing a vital role, life on the island had become almost intolerable; although 104 Squadron had 'commandeered' every Wellington II to pass through the island, the losses being suffered, primarily on the ground as a result of enemy air strikes, meant that by the end of the year they were down to eight aircraft (having 'used up' thirty Wellingtons in three months). However, they were not destined to be home by Christmas, instead, they moved further away – to Egypt.

The Sea Rescue Flight

The Sea Rescue Flight was formed on 13 August 1941 under the operational control of No. 201 Group:

> The first aircraft supplied were three operationally-tired Wellington ICs fitted with long-range tanks which increased their endurance to fourteen hours. The choice of the Wellington was a good one in view of the hazardous nature of the work. The plan of action was for the aircraft to drop supplies, and rubber dinghies if required, and then to shadow them until they were rescued by surface craft or amphibian. On 15 September the unit moved to Burg-el-Arab but there was a delay in getting the ground equipment into place and the unit was not operational until the 26th. The time was occupied in changing the camouflage of the Wellingtons from that of a bomber to that resembling the blue, grey and silver scheme adopted by flying boats. (RAF Middle East Review April–June 1943).

The unit kept an aircraft on standby day and night, complete with rescue kit. In the first four months they carried out ten searches with three successes. The second success came on 25 November when a report came in of a dinghy with three occupants 30 miles north of Sollum:

> Following a signal from the sea rescue aircraft giving position, a Walrus was despatched to pick up the dinghy's occupants, but after landing it was unable to take off with the overload so, shadowed until dusk by the Wellington, it taxied ashore. During the return flight to base, the petrol filler on the port wing of the sea rescue Wellington broke off causing that wing to have a higher stalling speed than normal, and in consequence while making a left-hand circuit preparatory to landing in the dark the aircraft slipped in on its final turn and hit the ground, immediately bursting into flames. The second pilot was thrown clear but the remaining five members of the crew were killed. An unhappy ending to a good day's work.

CHAPTER THREE

1942: Bomber Command Demonstrates its Power

Bomber Command

The most significant event during the first part of 1942 in respect of the strategic bombing offensive was the appointment in February of Sir Arthur Harris as C-in-C Bomber Command. With a fervent conviction of the power of the bomber weapon and a determination to take the war to the enemy, he re-vitalized the fortunes of the command. 1942 was also to be the year in which the Wellington began to relinquish its pre-eminent role in the bomber force as the new four-engined 'heavies' began to enter operational service in significant numbers; it was also, however, the year in which the aircraft took an ever-increasing role in the training of bomber aircrews.

The primary target in the first half of January had been the capital ships at Brest, the Wellingtons flying almost nightly attacks. In the second half of the month German cities were once again on the target list, but by early February Brest was again the priority.

RAF air power, and Bomber Command in particular, had expended great effort trying to destroy the ships in Brest, but with only limited success, though they had been damaged and repairs were proving impossible to complete in the face of such air attacks. The Admiralty's fear was that the ships would break out into the Atlantic and cause havoc amongst the convoy routes at a time when Britain was already under great pressure from shipping losses – the Battle of the Atlantic was not going well. The chiefs of the German Navy, however, determined

Wellington II of 12 Squadron at Binbrook. Peter Green Collection

that the ships needed to be moved to safer havens in order to complete their repairs and refits. The scene was set for one of the most dramatic events of early 1942, the so-called 'Channel Dash'. The Allies, through intensive reconnaissance sorties and other intelligence sources, were aware that the ships were likely to move in February and RAF and Fleet Air Arm air assets were put on standby for a maximum effort. Squadrons of Bomber Command, including the Wellington units, were put on alert for daylight operations; this is, typically, recorded in the 150 Squadron ORB for 5 February. 'At 0630 hours, twelve aircraft stood by for daylight operations. Petrol load was fixed at 650gal with a bomb load of six 500lb SAP bombs. The squadron stood down at dusk.' The same comments are made for the next few days on then on February 12 the diarist recorded as follows:

At 0800 hours nine aircraft and crews stood by for daylight operations. Nothing further was heard until 1230 hours when a tannoy broadcast called all crews to the squadron operations room. All available news concerning the position of the battleships *Scharnhorst* and *Gneisenau* and the battlecruiser *Prinz Eugen* was imparted to the crews who immediately left for their aircraft, where a complete take-off was made within forty-five minutes of the broadcast, a tribute to the work of both air and ground crews. The last position of the enemy squadron was given as 135 degrees South Foreland 10 miles, proceeding in a north-easterly direction, and it was on this information that the three sections of three aircraft set course. Climbing steadily over England to 8,000ft, our crews encountered ⁹/₁₀ths cloud, being from 2,000ft to 7,000ft. These conditions completely obliterating any landmarks on route. When ETA was reached a hole in the clouds enabled the squadron to descend safely to 3,000ft where a sweep was carried out in search of the enemy convoy. Visibility was down to 1,500yd with large amounts of cumulous cloud; this made an effective search extremely difficult. At this point sections split up making individual searches, but after flying for over two hours the search was forced to be abandoned owing to the impossible conditions.

Bomber Command had flown 242 sorties, ninety-two of these by the Wellingtons, who lost four aircraft, two from 419 Squadron, a Canadian unit that had only formed the previous December.

When Harris took charge he had an average strength of just under 400 service-

TABLE 1

Group	Hampden	Whitley	Wellington	4-engined types
1 Gp			10½	
3 Gp			12	4
4 Gp		5½	2	5
5 Gp	10			4
Total	10	5½	24½	13

TABLE 2

Group	Wellington	Halifax	Lancaster	Other
1 Gp	3½	4		
3 Gp	2			5
4 Gp	10	11		
5 Gp			10	
PFF	1½	1	1	1½
Total	17	16	11	6½

able bombers on a typical day, of which the majority were Wellingtons. With this force he was tasked to enforce the Air Ministry Directive of 14 February '... to focus attacks on the morale of the enemy civil population, and, in particular, of the industrial workers.' Harris saw three major problems that had to be overcome, 'lack of suitable aircraft in sufficient numbers, absence of effective navigational aids, and a serious deficiency of trained aircrew.' He promptly set about trying to correct all three.

On the same day that the directive was issued two more Wellington squadrons joined the ranks of Bomber Command, 156 Squadron forming at Alconbury and 158 Squadron at Driffield, the former with ICs and the latter with Mark IIs. Both flew their first operations within days of their formation as they had both been created out of experienced units. However, for 158 Squadron it was to be a fairly short association with the Wellington as the unit re-equipped with Halifax IIs in June.

It is worth at this point producing two tables that appeared in Sir Arthur Harris's post-war *Despatch on War Operations*. Table 1 showed Bomber Command's operational composition in February when Harris took over and Table 2 showed the position at the end of the year. In Table 1 the Wellington figures include nine non-operational units whilst Table 2 includes 10½ such units. The non-operational squadrons are those in the process of forming or re-equipping that have not at that point been declared as part of Main Force; it is interesting to note that at the end of the year the total number of operational squadrons had fallen from 37 to 32½. How-

ever, this was of course to some degree offset by the greater capability in terms of range and bombload of the four-engined types .The large number of non-operational Wellington squadrons in Table 2 reflected the formation in the last few weeks of the year of eight squadrons within No. 4 Group who were to form the basis of the Canadian bomber group.

No. 156 Squadron formed from a nucleus of 40 Squadron personnel at Alconbury on 14 February, the first aircraft, a Wellington III, arriving from Honington five days later. The first mission was flown on 17–18 February when Sqn Ldr McGillivray took Z8969 on a *Nickel* sortie to Lille; a few weeks later, 3–4 March, the squadron was able to send twelve aircraft on the attack – described below – against the Renault works.

Gee and 'Gardening'

The first part of the year also saw the first of the new electronic navigation aids being introduced to operational service. High hopes were expressed for Gee, it being hoped that it would '...confer upon your forces the ability to concentrate their effort to an extent which has not hitherto been possible under the operational conditions with which you are faced [and] will enable results to be obtained of a much more effective nature.' By 25 February the command had five Gee-equipped Wellington squadrons: 9, 57, 75, 101 and 115. Bomber Command drew up a list of German cities whose destruction, it was felt, would have a decisive effect upon the course of the war – Essen headed the list

P9299 of 115 Squadron; the aircraft served with each of the Marham squadrons during 1941 and then went to the Czech Training Unit (which became 1429 Czech Flight). Ken Delve Collection

and Berlin was included. New tactics were developed to make best use of the limited number of Gee-equipped aircraft available; the basic technique adopted was referred to as 'Shaker' and involved two waves of Gee-equipped aircraft, the first to drop flares over the target and the second to drop incendiaries and target markers, preceding the main bomber force. In the weeks following Harris's appointment the

lowest possible height. We gradually ran out of cloud and were able to see the sun set fairly soon after we started – then it began to get dark but the sky was quite clear and so we were able to identify landmarks quite well. On arrival over Beachy Head we immediately set course for Abbeville, at the mouth of the Somme. As we approached the French coast a terrific glow was visible in the sky on the starboard quarter which we immediately presumed to be Paris; later our presumption was

bend of the river was our guide to the target so we turned and followed the river in a south-westerly direction and, as we turned, it was possible to identify such world-famous places as the Eiffel Tower, Arc de Triomphe and Champs Elysees. Then we came to the actual target, brilliantly illuminated by a combination of moon, flares and a number of colossal fires.

We decided to run over the area once and then drop our bombs on the diesel engine shops,

419 Squadron Wellington III; the unit operated the type from February to November 1942 when it re-equipped with the Halifax. Ken Delve Collection

command flew few major raids; however, on 3–4 March a modified 'Shaker' technique (the flare technique but not using Gee) was used when 233 aircraft, including eighty-nine Wellingtons, attacked the Renault factory at Billancourt, near Paris. The raid was a major success. Sgt Saunders was observer in Wellington X9683 of 150 Squadron and he recorded his impressions of the attack:

At 1815 hours we took off in bright daylight and headed south towards Reading and Beachy Head. On reaching a height of 2,000ft we levelled out as this was to be a surprise attack delivered from the

proved to be right. We crossed the mouth of the Somme just south of Abbeville and turned on to our last course – to the target.

This was what we had been waiting for and everybody eagerly watched the glow drawing closer ... We passed close to the outskirts of the town and were able to identify Beauvois aerodrome, in fact, they fired a green Verey light to invite us to land! By this time I had taken my place at the bombing panel and had everything set and ready to bomb. As we passed over the River Seine for the first time the whole area was brilliantly illuminated by flares – this enabled me to pinpoint myself on the target map as being north and west of our objective. The third

making a run from north-west to south-east. On our first run over the target we were tossed about like a cork by the blast of other peoples' bombs exploding – at first it felt like *Flak* bursting below us. Then came our biggest moment, as we turned on and the pilot opened the bomb doors. I was just getting my sight lined up on one of the workshops when it simply disintegrated before my eyes – somebody had pulled a fast one and got in before us, so I shifted my line of sight to the next whole workshop. I was able to observe all the bombs in the stick burst directly across the diesel workshops and the air was absolutely filled with flying debris. The most impressive part of the whole raid from my point of view was that I did not see one bomb fall outside of the factory walls. The only way to describe the scene as we left was to say that the whole target area was absolutely devastated. The whole squadron returned quite safely and everybody said it was the most wonderful show they had ever seen.

Three waves of bombers had hit the factory, the whole attack taking less than two hours and only one Wellington being lost; there was no anti-aircraft defence at the actual factory and the low-level tactics and routing appears to have confused the night fighter defences. It appears that some 300 bombs fell within the factory area, destroying 40 per cent of the buildings and causing serious disruption in the production of lorries for the German army. However, despite the accurate low-level bombing, it is estimated that 400 French

civilians were killed. The same night was also significant for the future of Bomber Command as it saw the operational debut of the Avro Lancaster, aircraft of 44 Squadron undertaking 'Gardening' sorties.

The night of 2–3 March saw the first minelaying sortie by a Bomber Command Wellington, a task that up to this point had been largely undertaken by the Hampdens. The Wellington was able to carry two mines and it was a natural development that the squadrons would become involved in this work, especially after Harris had agreed to an Admiralty request to greatly increase the number of mines being laid. From March onwards the number of Wellington 'Gardening' sorties increased and they became a regular feature of squadron's operations, especially for freshmen crews.

Despite 'one-off' missions like that to Paris, 'Happy Valley' – the Ruhr – remained

the main target area for the command and Essen was the recipient of a number of raids during March and April. In a series of major attacks the Wellingtons bore the brunt of the offensive and loss rates averaged 6 per cent as the bombers battled against heavy *Flak* and concentrations of night fighters in this most heavily defended region of Germany; the attack on the night of 26–27 March cost ten of the 104 Wellingtons despatched. Two nights later the full 'Shaker' technique was used against the port of Lübeck, with 146 Wellingtons being included in the force of 234 bombers. The attack went as planned and was one of the most accurate to date with much of the city being destroyed. Late April saw Rostock under attack on four consecutive nights as part of a strategy to concentrate on one town until it was effectively 'destroyed'.

Extract from the 156 Sqn ORB for the precision attack on the Renault works, Paris, March 3–4 1942.

Wimpey the Wellington

In 1942 a booklet called *Wimpey the Wellington* was published; this told the story of Wimpey and his travels from Britain to the Mediterranean and India, and eventually, America. The booklet was illustrated with caricature Wellingtons and the extract below gives a good flavour of this amusing little publication.

Once upon a time a brand-new bomber came out the factory. His family name was Wellington, but they called him Wimpey for short.

He had a mottled jacket of green and brown, a smart black waistcoat, two big round engines and a lovely shiny nose that you could see through, and in which he wore two guns. But when he got to his aerodrome he began to feel shy like you did on your first day at school ... for there in a huge shed were lots of other Wellingtons all sitting around and chattering and telling the most amazing stories. In fact, they were 'shooting a line' (that's what aeroplanes call bragging), but Wimpey was too new to realize this, so he was very impressed. There was one Wellington called WimPeter, another called Wim-Paul, another called WimPatrick, and another called WimPercy. All of them had rows of little yellow bombs painted on their noses, one bomb for each trip they had been on.

WimPeter, who wore a bandage around his tail, was telling them all about search-lights and a place called Essen and how he came to have a bandage. He said it was flak that did it. (Wimpey did not know that flak was anti-aircraft guns, which just shows how new he was.)

Wimpey shyly edged himself round the door and said: 'Please I'm Wimpey and I've just come in and is this the right shed and what do I do please?' So Wimpey crawled into the darkest corner he could find. By and by a lot of men came and towed WimPaul, WimPatrick and WimPercy outside and gave them petrol to drink through long pipes, and other men brought big yellow bombs, opened their black waistcoats and hauled the bombs up inside, and polished their shiny noses and tested their engines.

And there was a lot of talk about places with funny names like Essen, and the Wellingtons grinned at Wimpey and said: 'Don't you wish you were coming? Still, you're only a new bloke!' And in climbed the crews and into the dusk, with a flip of their tails at poor Wimpey ... When Wimpey woke up it was morning and the Wellingtons were back chattering and having breakfast and shooting a line. WimPatrick had a big bit of sticking plaster on his wing and WimPercy a patch over one eye. And as the men painted one more yellow bomb on each of them Wimpey wished they'd send him on a trip so that he could shoot a line. The very next morning they woke Wimpey up very early and wheeled him out and filled him up (but only with petrol not bombs). And he heard a lot of talk about somewhere called the East, and then his crew came out carrying kitbags, and an electric fan and a mosquito net and, yes, sun helmets!

It was still a difficult period and the strain of the intensive operations of March and April was beginning to show on crews and aircraft; loss rates were at an unsustainable level and there was pressure on Harris to give up squadrons to Coastal Command for the Battle of the Atlantic – indeed, six squadrons, including two Wellington units (304 and 311 Squadrons) were duly transferred. From time to time particularly heavy blows fell on a single squadron; for example, on the 1–2 April attack on Hanau 57 and 214 Squadrons were badly hit, the former losing five aircraft (twenty-five aircrew killed) and the latter seven aircraft (forty-one aircrew killed).

Harris, however, was now more determined than ever to prove beyond all doubt the power and capability of his bomber weapon, and he conceived a dramatic demonstration.

Thousand Bombers

Perhaps the best-known events of 1942 were the 'thousand-bomber raids' made in late spring and early summer as a means of 'proving' the C-in-C's conviction that a suitable bomber force could be a devastating weapon; it must be recalled that there was a great deal of pressure on Bomber Command to produce results or risk losing resources to

Wellington ORBAT, April 1942	
No. 1 Gp	
Binbrook	12, 42 Sqns
Elsham Wolds	103 Sqn
Hemswell	300, 301 Sqns
Holme	460 Sqn
Lindholme	304, 305 Sqns
Snaith	150 Sqn
No. 3 Gp	
Feltwell	57, 75 Sqns
Honington	9, 311 Sqns
Marham	115, 218 Sqns
Mildenhall	149, 419 Sqns
Oakington	101 Sqn
Stradishall	214, 109 Sqns
Wyton	156 Sqn
No. 4 Gp	
Driffield	158 Sqn
Pocklington	405 Sqn
No. 6 Gp	
Bassingbourn	11 OTU
Bramcote	18 OTU
Chipping Warden	12 OTU
Harwell	15 OTU
Lichfield	27 OTU
Lossiemouth	20 OTU
Moreton-in-Marsh	21 OTU
Pershore	23 OTU
Wellesbourne Mountford	22 OTU
No. 7 Gp	
Finningley	25 OTU
Upper Heyford	16 OTU
Upwood	17 OTU
Wing	26 OTU
No. 19 Gp	
Chivenor	1417 Flt
Middle East Command	
Amriya	221 Sqn
Ismailia	1 GRU
Fayid	108 Sqn
Kabrit	104, 148 Sqns
El Dhaba	70 Sqn
Shallufa	37, 38, 40 Sqns

other critical areas. The first of these raids eventually took place on the night of 30–31 May; the force of 1,047 bombers sent against Cologne comprised:

No. 1 Group	156 Wellingtons
No. 3 Group	134 Wellingtons (88 Stirlings)
No. 4 Group	9 Wellingtons (131 Halifaxes, 7 Whitleys)
No. 5 Group	(73 Lancasters, 46 Manchesters, 34 Hampdens)
No. 91 Group	236 Wellingtons (21 Whitleys)
No. 92 Group	63 Wellingtons (45 Hampdens)
Flying Training Command	4 Wellingtons.

Thus no less than 602 of the bombers sent that night were Wellingtons, but of these over half came from training units. In many cases the latter were attached to operational squadrons; typical of this was the arrival on 25 May of ten Wellington ICs and crews from 21 OTU at Snaith to work with 150 Squadron (all ten took off for the attack on Cologne). Whilst it is not practicable to list all the Wellington units and their participation, it is instructive to

April 1942 and Wellington nose art is still present, although such decoration was not popular with most senior commanders within Bomber Command. Ken Delve Collection

(Below) **218 Squadron aircraft having a name applied following the unit's adoption as the Gold Coast squadron.** Ken Delve Collection

look at typical examples; 101 Squadron's ORB states:

The squadron despatched twelve Wellington IIIs and three Wellington ICs, the latter being detached from 23 OTU; of these, two returned to base early and two failed to return. Bomb loads were nine SBCs, each containing 540 × 4lb bomblets, and aircraft dropped from between 12,000 and 19,000ft.

Aircraft	Captain	Duration	
X3654/A	Sqn Ldr Watts	2255–0445	
X391	Flt Lt Harper	2300–0510	
X3973/S	Flt Lt Edwards	2315–0045	RTB early
X3668/G	Sgt Atwood	2300–0410	
X3669/H	Plt Off Callender	2305–0430	
X3754/R	Sgt Llewelyn	2305–0430	
X3670/F	Plt Off Gardner	2305–FTR	
X3694/U	Sgt Early	2305–0410	
X3634/T	Sgt Deimer	2305–0355	
Z1612/Z	Plt Off Read	2310–FTR	
X3648/M	Plt Off Kennedy	2310–0305	RTB early
X3657/Q	Flt Sgt Williams	2310–0420	
DV702/F2	Plt Off Tyrell	2310–0420	23 OTU
X9748/L2	Plt Off Atkinson	2315–0415	23 OTU
T2994/A2	Plt Off Goodwin	2315–0530	23 OTU

156 Squadron despatched sixteen aircraft, nine Mark ICs and seven Mark IIIs, from Alconbury, two aircraft being lost:

Aircraft	Captain	Duration	
DV813	Plt Off MacLachlan	2340–0505	
Z1108	Flt Sgt Shilleto	2345–0410	
DV786	Sgt Terris	2320–0710	
DV812	Sgt Thomson	2359–0525	
HF918	Sgt Powell	2353–0540	
DV715	Sgt Malin	2355–	FTR
DV814	Sgt Mayhew	0005–0510	
DV739	Flt Sgt Woof	2335–0450	
DV799	Sgt Owen	2330–0445	
X3598	Plt Off Bain	2315–	FTR
X3677	Plt Off Green	2320–0450	
X3471	Sgt Potts	2320–0400	
X3742	Sgt Kelham	2307–0327	
X3422	Sgt Bright	2305–0345	
X3339	Plt Off Smith	2325–0140	
X3728	Flt Lt Gilmour	2300–0340	

Fg Off Paul Moskwa was a navigator/bomb aimer with 300 Squadron airborne that night:

We knew that something special was planned because all communication with the outside world had been cut off; when we attended the briefing and the curtains were drawn back there was an elated response to the words of the briefing officer. On the route out to the target the gunners kept on calling out other aircraft passing close by and once or twice we had to take avoiding action. We could see the glow of the fires at Cologne when we were still over Holland – and also saw a number of bombers, or at least their incendiary bomb loads, burning on the ground and so knew that enemy night fighters were around. Our aircraft arrived over the target at 0200 and we were awe-struck at the sight of the burning city; I almost forgot to drop the bombs! I looked for a dark area to bomb and saw an area south-west of the cathedral and dropped there. When I checked a map later I saw that this was the marshalling yards. We could still see the glow

Lindholme, spring 1942 with Wellington II W5590 of 305 Squadron as the backdrop to a parade; note the Polish Air Force badge on the hangar door. Peter Green Collection

June 1942 and WAAFs service a Wellington in the hangar. Ken Delve Collection

when back over the North Sea and all the crew were elated that we had really hit the Germans.

All four of the Polish bomber squadrons had taken part in the raid, as had twenty-four crews from the Polish OTU, 18 OTU, and on 4 June Sir Archibald Sinclair sent the following message to General Sikorski:

> Polish crews to the number of 101 took part in the large-scale operations on Cologne and the Ruhr. The RAF has learnt to admire the valour, tenacity and efficiency of their Polish allies. In these operations again they have shown how admirable is their contribution in support of our common cause to the destruction of the war power of the enemy.

Two nights later the thousand-bomber force was in action again, 956 bombers (including 545 Wellingtons, which lost fifteen of their number) attacking Essen. For a variety of reasons the attack was not well concentrated and results were poor. For most of June the command sent smaller raids against German industrial cities but the thousand-bomber force was kept 'in existence' for one more attack. This took place on 25–26 June when 1,067 bombers (including 472 Wellingtons from Bomber Command plus others from Coastal Command) attacked Bremen. The raid was moderately successful and the overall loss rate was 5 per cent; the loss rate for No. 91 Group was, however, an horrendous 11.6 per cent, twenty-three of their 198 Wellingtons and Whitleys failing to

return. It was statistics such as these, and the damage being caused to training by disrupting the OTU programmes, that led to the dispersal of the thousand-bomber force. Whilst looking at loss rates it is interesting to note that a Bomber Command report of early 1942 claimed that some 2 per cent of Wellington losses during the winter period were probably due to 'the effects of adverse weather and, in particular, icing'. Bremen was attacked again on the night of 27–28 June, fifty-five Wellingtons being amongst the 144 bombers involved in the operation (four Wellingtons and five other aircraft being lost). The majority claimed to have bombed blind through the cloud using their Gee sets; the 150 Squadron ORB stated '...judging by the number of British aircraft seen in the target area, the raid was a success and was judged as successful as a test of the new TR equipment'. Two nights later against the same target, '... all crews were confident that their TR equipment had enabled them to navigate successfully to the target area and the glow of fires through the cloud was seen by all crews.'

Bomber Command was still aiming at Target Force E (2,000 bombers) but with a strength of only forty-four heavy and medium squadrons, this was well behind schedule. The major problem was shortage of labour and a marked under-production of Halifaxes; the net result was that the Wellington force continued to bear the operational brunt, but even here there were problems. 'Medium bomber output at

this time was almost up to schedule with the vital exception of the Wellington III, deliveries of which were held up during the summer months owing to a shortage of propellers and Constant Speed Units. This delay had considerable repercussions on the expansion programme.' The knock-on effect of this, and the detaching of two squadrons to Coastal Command – 311 Squadron in April and 304 Squadron in July, both becoming permanent transfers in December – caused a marked drop in the number of medium bomber squadrons available for the bombing offensive; furthermore, squadrons had to be re-issued with Wellington ICs in the absence of supplies of the Mark III and these were not Gee-equipped, thus slowing development of the Gee force. The last aspect was that aircraft that should have been available for the OTUs, and the planned expansion of the OTUs, were now required by the operational units. However, by August the situation had eased sufficiently for three of the medium bomber squadrons to re-equip.

Throughout the summer, the Wellington squadrons continued to make up over 50 per cent of the offensive strength of the command, and although some units had begun to re-equip, new units were still appearing with Wellingtons as their initial equipment. June saw the formation of 425 'Alouette' Squadron at Dishforth and August saw 420 'Snowy Owl' Squadron give up its aged Hampdens in favour of Wellington IIIs.

In mid-September the Wellington force within Bomber Command comprised

Z1657 of 115 Squadron near Ladywood, Marham late 1942. The aircraft went on to serve with the CGS and survived to May 1947. Ken Delve Collection

(Below) Martlesham Heath late 1942 (?) with Wellington IV Z1382 of 300 Squadron. Peter Green Collection

thirteen squadrons, a total strength of 191 aircraft – only twenty-five short of the planned establishment. However, the requirement for new aircraft was still high and in September, under pressure to increase production, the Ministry of Aircraft Production promised to provide 893 Wellingtons between September and November; this target was considered achievable as the ASUs held a reasonable stock of aircraft and the delivery of these could be speeded up. The aircraft were needed to equip the nine new Wellington units that were planned for October/November.

Pathfinders

Discussions had been underway at the Air Ministry since early spring as to the best solution for creating a 'target-finding force' for the 'Shaker' technique, and during the thousand-bomber raids the most experienced Wellington crews of No. 3 Group had been used as raid leaders for flare dropping and target marking. Harris had always been against the creation of a special élite organization, but in June had to give way to Air Ministry pressure; on 20 June he instructed No. 3 Group to set aside two Wellington and two Stirling squadrons to become the core of the new Pathfinder Force (PFF). In the event, only one Wellington unit, 156 Squadron (from No. 1 Group), was used as part of the initial five-squadron force when it formed on 11 August 1942 under the command of Gp Capt Don Bennett, this particular squadron moving to Warboys. The next few weeks were occupied with lectures, including some by Bennett himself, on the proposed role and tactical employment of the new force.

Commonwealth Squadrons

The decision to create a Canadian bomber group, a reflection of the numbers of RCAF aircrew within Bomber Command and the political desire to have an 'independent' group, led to the formation of No. 6 (RCAF) Group on 1 January 1943.

In the last months of 1942 nine more Wellington squadrons were formed, the majority being Canadian units that would, in January, become operational with the newly formed No. 6 (RCAF) Group:

Squadron	Base	Formation Date
466 (RAAF) Sqn	Driffield	Oct
424 'Tiger' Sqn	Topcliffe	Oct
426 'Thunderbird' Sqn	Dishforth	Oct
427 'Lion' Sqn	Croft	Nov
428 'Ghost' Sqn	Dalton	Nov
429 'Bison' Sqn	East Moor	Nov
196 Sqn	Driffield	Dec
199 Sqn	Blyton	Nov
431 'Iroquois' Sqn	Burn	Dec

Amongst the new units for No. 6 (RCAF) Group was 424 'Tiger' Squadron which formed at Topcliffe on 15 October under the command of Wg Cdr Carscallen; by the end of October the unit had eight Wellingtons on strength and had commenced an intensive work-up, the intention being that the squadron would be operational early in 1943. The work-up included intense ground activities for the aircrew:

Pilots from A and B Flights held a general discussion on future operations, Flt Lt W. Klassen giving points of interest from his previous operational experience. All bomb aimers practised ground training, cleaning guns, turret practice, radio positions, fixing Gee box, and Link training. There was also a visit to the bomb dump and they were shown and received information on everything from small arms and detonators to 8,000lb bombs.

January came and there was a distinct feeling of frustration being expressed in the ORB:

The last of the dinghies was fitted today, this item having been one of the most difficult to bring up to date. Special cartridges being very scarce and hard to obtain. Engines appear to be giving little trouble of late, apparently the maintenance crews must be improving. Trimming tabs are the riggers' nightmare on these machines, the elevator and rudder trim tab control box getting badly damaged due to the central setting not being made when flaps are lowered.

The various problems were soon overcome and the squadron flew its first operation on the night of 15 January, five aircraft attacking Lorient. No. 6 (RCAF) Group was to become a potent element of Bomber Command for the remainder of the war.

The formation of these units was not as straightforward as had been hoped; delivery of aircraft did not match the MAP promise, only 648 Wellingtons having been delivered by 27 November. The main hold-up was still at the ASUs where significant numbers of aircraft were still awaiting props and CSUs. By the time these problems had eased the bad weather had set in and squadron work-up was delayed, and it was early 1943 by the time that most became operational.

One of the last RAAF bomber squadrons to form within Bomber Command, 466 Squadron, received its first aircraft (Mark III X3790) at Driffield on 29 October, the aircraft being delivered from the MU by an ATA pilot. A few days later the ORB reported:

The lack of certain of the initial equipment of the squadron, including tool kits and engine and airframe publications, proved a serious handicap but groundcrews made improvisations and went to work with great keenness on the initial checks. The squadron possesses fourteen complete aircrews, who were busy carrying out

a ground training programme designed to supplement their OTU training. Of these crews, nine were trained on Wellington ICs, three had some flying experience in Wellington IIIs, but the remaining two were Hampden trained and presented their own particular problems.

More aircraft arrived, along with other equipment and the squadron soon painted its HD code letters on their aircraft. In mid-November a number of pilots flew second pilot operations with the Halifax-equipped 102 Squadron to targets in Italy.

Late 1942 Operations

The rugged nature of the Wellington was once more confirmed in dramatic fashion on the night of 4–5 September. Some 250 bombers (ninety-eight Wellingtons) attacked Bremen and amongst those taking part were Wellingtons of 300 Squadron. The ORB states:

The fourth aircraft, K1320, Z for Zosha, of Plt Off E. Machek was holed by *Flak* over the target area and set on fire. The pilot put the plane into a dive to extinguish the fire. The whole of the fabric from the trailing edge of the mainplane to the leading edge of the tailplane was burned away.

Other reports say that the damage was caused by a night fighter attack. This incident was included in the Bomber Command *Quarterly Review*:

A remarkable photograph appeared recently in the press, of a Wellington IV which returned home from Bremen with the fabric stripped off the fuselage the whole way from the trailing edge of the mainplane to the rear turret. Not the least remarkable feature of this incident is that the Polish crew, who belonged to No. 300 Squadron, flew their aircraft in this skeleton-like state a distance of some 400 miles and made a perfect landing at their base. The crew were uninjured and there was only slight structural damage to the Wellington. It happened over Bremen at 16,500ft amid heavy *Flak*. The wireless operator, who was near the flare chute, was suddenly blinded by a tremendous flash, and when he recovered his vision he found all the fabric gone. Apparently the trouble had started when a spent AA tracer entered the aircraft, damaging one of the geodetics and the wooden bulkhead of the rear D-frame and started the fabric smouldering. As the burned area of fabric grew larger the slipstream must have torn at it until the whole covering ripped off. There was a nasty moment over Holland when an enemy fighter was encountered, but engagement was avoided by evasive action – or perhaps Jerry just couldn't believe his eyes!

The same edition of the *Review* included two further stories highlighting the sturdy nature of the Wellington:

A similar experience befell Wellington III 'Y' of 150 Squadron returning from Cologne in April. The aircraft was near home when it happened,

ric had been burned and ripped off from the mainplane to tail. Nor was that all. Explosive incendiary bullets which struck the aircraft near the after end of the bomb beam had put out of action the hydraulic gear which operates the undercarriage and bomb doors and shattered numerous geodetics of the fuselage, and both main and tail-plane were damaged. After the attack the aircraft flew with port wing low, bomb doors open and without rudder control. Nevertheless the pilot brought his aircraft back to his base in Yorkshire and, being unable to

the rear fuselage of the Wellington but did not explode, and none of the crew was injured. The shell ... distorted the longeron, bending it upwards over about 1ft of its length. The corresponding geodetics attached to the longeron were also distorted. On the starboard side there was a large horizontal gash, also below the tail-plane, where the shell had exited. The longeron had apparently received a direct hit as, in addition to distortion over 4ft of its length, 1ft of it had been torn out completely and was missing. All the geodetics near the longeron were badly

1942, Bourn, and R1781 of 101 Squadron. After its operational period with this squadron it went on to serve a number of OTUs. Peter Green Collection

but the damage was more serious. Just after crossing the Dutch coast on the return to base an Me 110 approached and delivered an attack from the starboard quarter. It opened up at 350yd with three streams of tracer bullets, starting a fire in the Wellington. Our rear-gunner replied with a short burst, setting the enemy's port engine alight. What happened to the Me 110 is not known as the Wellington crew were busy putting out the fire in their own aircraft. They succeeded in this, but not before the fab-

lock down the undercarriage, made a good belly-landing. None of the crew was injured.

The final example related to Wellington III 'V' of 9 Squadron which had been coned by searchlights over Cologne on 28–29 July:

In the course of evasive action the aircraft lost height, coming down to 4,000ft before shaking off the searchlights. At some point in the descent a heavy AA shell passed clean through

damaged. The shell-hit had no appreciable effect on the performance of the aircraft. In fact, it was not until they reached base that the crew realized the nature of the damage and its cause.

In the latter part of the year the command flew a number of small-scale daylight raids, the operational concept being for these to make use of cloud cover on their routes to and from the target. One such sortie, Operation *Bullhead*, was flown on 25 November with six Wellingtons and five Lancasters tasked to attack Essen and five other targets. The 300 Squadron ORB stated '... crews were instructed to approach low level over the sea and look for opportunity targets in Holland, taking advantage of the ⁹⁄₁₀ths cloud to provide cover for the aircraft.' Of the three aircraft sent by 300 Squadron, one failed to return. Such nuisance raids became a regular feature but their effect was questionable, especially in view of fairly high loss rates.

The final months of 1942 saw a new Wellington variant enter service, one that was to give new life to what had started to become a tired and obsolete design. The Wellington X was the result of advances in developments in metallurgy that produced new light alloys of great strength; one of these, DTD646, was used for a new Wellington design, although perhaps design is too strong a word as in essence the basic Wellington III structure was used, but employing the new material.

engined types, as well as seeing service in other theatres. With some 3,084 being built, it was the most numerous of the Wellington variants and in later life became a flying classroom.

On 12 December 1942 Sqn Ldr W. R. A. Cott flew Wellington Z1418 of 544 Squadron from Benson on a night photography trial over northern France; in the event, weather conditions were poor and the mission was not a success (the first successful sortie coming on 15 December),

Wellington X X3595 of 75 Squadron; the Mark X was one of the best variants of the aircraft and entered service in November 1942. FlyPast Collection

Specification – Wellington X	
ENGINES	Two Bristol Hercules VI or XVI
DIMENSIONS	Span 86ft 2in (26.26m); length 64ft 7in (19.68m)
PERFORMANCE	Max. speed 255mph (408km/h); ceiling 22,000ft (6,667m)
ARMAMENT	6–8 × 0.303in guns, 4,000lb (1,800kg) bombs
NUMBER BUILT	3,084

This also allowed use of the higher-rated Hercules VI (1,675hp) or Hercules XVI engines and thus gave a marked improvement in overall performance. Wellington III X3374 was given Hercules VI engines to become the Mark X prototype.

This variant became the workhorse of Bomber Command for much of 1943, gradually being replaced by the four-

but it was still a significant date. The squadron had formed at Benson out of No. 1 PRU on 19 October with two Wellington IVs, Z1417 and Z1418 (plus three Spitfires and three Ansons), for experimental night photography; 8 November saw the first real trial. 'An experiment in night photography was made in total darkness, flashes being dropped from the hand-

Only seven Wellington crew members received the Conspicuous Gallantry Medal; one of those was Sgt Leonard Williamson when he brought back his aircraft after it had suffered severed damage over Duisburg. Ken Delve Collection

With a particularly bright ED-M code, LP713 of 21 OTU at Moreton-in-Marsh. R. Dobie via John Hamlin

launching chute. Tests indicate that chute launching of flashes is satisfactory.' Cameras were mounted vertically and the idea was to take line overlaps of target areas.

In late January 1943 the squadron received a visit from Dr Spencer, scientific adviser and representative of MAP on the Air Council, who expressed the view that

... night photography was of great importance and all facilities for developing it should be granted to the unit. He stated that development of more powerful flashes was in the hands of

Ordnance, he would arrange for a supply of infrared super sensitized film for the unit and that supply of K19 cameras would be investigated.

The end of that same month the unit received, on loan, 14in focal length F24 cameras, which were duly fitted to Z1418. A visit by Sir Henry Tizard, Scientific Adviser to the Air Ministry, confirmed the value of the work being done; he reported that 'Night photographs are often better than by day – and were safer to take,' although he was of the opinion that the

Mosquito would be more effective type for this work (the Wellingtons were indeed replaced by Mosquitoes in March).

Thus, at the end of 1942 the Wellington was still a very significant aircraft in terms of numerical strength within Bomber Command's operational table; indeed, it had a major boost with the formation of the Commonwealth squadrons, all of whom were to equip in due course with heavies but, for the present, became operational with Wellingtons; in the training role it was, and was to remain, pre-eminent.

(Above) The Wellington X became the backbone of Bomber Command Main Force and was a well-liked aircraft. Painted matt black underneath as an aid against being picked up in the night skies over Germany. FlyPast Collection

Z1491 of 301 Squadron failed to return from an attack on Nurnberg on 28–29 August 1942. Ken Delve Collection

Special Duties

By January 1942 the workload on 109 Squadron was such that the unit divided into three flights, operating from Tempsford, Upper Heyford and Boscombe Down. However, the squadron soon became involved with other developments and in particular the trials and development of the 'Oboe' system as a blind-bombing aid for Bomber Command. In consequence it began to give up its RCM/ELINT work, this being reflected in July when A Flight became 1474 Flight for RCM/ELINT, soon moving to Little Gransden with nine Wellington ICs, and B Flight became 1473 Flight at Upper Heyford. Both continued their special duties work with Wellingtons throughout the year, although 1473 moved to Finmere in December.

The work undertaken by the unit was both essential and dangerous. On 2 December Sgt Paulton and crew in DV819 took off at 0202 hours on a special duties flight:

Z1657 of 57 Squadron at Methwold in 1942. Ken Delve Collection

[The] operation took place across the north coast of France to an area near to Frankfurt. The aircraft was engaged on the eighteenth sortie on a particular investigation which necessitated the aircraft being intercepted by an enemy night fighter and up to this sortie all efforts to get such an interception had failed. At 0431 ... the special operator, Plt Off Jordan, had been reporting that he had received signals on his special wireless equipment which he thought were the ones requiring to be investigated. He warned the crew to expect fighter attack. A code had previously been agreed so that if the signals were picked up, the frequency would immediately be sent back to base, it being absolutely vital that this information should reach base at all costs ... Jordan warned the crew that his receiver was being saturated and to expect an attack at any moment. Almost simultaneously the aircraft was hit by a burst of cannon fire. The rear gunner gave a fighter control commentary during the attack and identified the enemy aircraft as a Ju 88. Violent corkscrew turns were used as evasive action. Jordan was hit in the arm on this first attack, and realizing now that there was no doubt at all about the signal being the correct one, he changed the coded message, a change that would tell base that the frequency given was absolutely correct and that it applied without doubt to the signal being investigated. (1474 Flight ORB)

In all the fighter made more than ten attacks and Jordan, as well as other crew members, was injured again. With the

Wellington down to 500ft the attacker broke off and Paulton was able to climb slowly to 5,000ft and head back to England. The coast was sighted at 0720 and all but one of the crew elected to stay aboard whilst the pilot ditched the aircraft. They were all picked up by boat.

Training Duties

1942 was a critical period for Bomber Command in a great many respects, not least of which was the major expansion that it underwent and the consequent huge expansion of the training empire – much of which was handled by the Wellington-equipped OTUs. Harris recognized the invaluable work that the training organization carried out:

The OTUs then [March 1942] settled down to a five-months' course involving eighty hours' flying, and maintained this standard until the end of the war; there were times when it looked as if we should have to reduce the length of the course, but in the end we got through without lowering the standard of training ... It is not generally realized how good was the work of the OTUs. They produced an endless flow of crews whose ability to cope with every conceivable sort of weather was far in advance of what any pre-war crew, civil or service, could have achieved. All this was done by instructors during what were called their 'rest periods' between

operational tours, and it was not done without casualties ... In the most dangerous flying conditions the instructors and instructional crews ran almost as much risk as the fighting crews, and they ran these risks over a much longer period than that of an operational tour. (Sir Arthur Harris, *Bomber Offensive*)

No. 22 OTU at Wellesbourne Mountford was typical of the well-established Wellington-equipped OTUs (having run its first course in June 1941), operating a satellite field (Stratford/Atherstone) and by early 1942 having a strength of forty-four aircraft. In April the unit had 414 pupils on strength and was operating five flights: A, D and E Flights as the operational flights, C as the navigation flight and B as the conversion flight. The unit was averaging over 3,000 hours a month in Wellingtons, as well as around 700 hours in its Ansons.

Constant changes were being made to the OTU establishment and courses in an effort to react to the requirements of the front-line units and many decisions were taken on a 'needs must' basis in order to overcome immediate crises rather than to develop an 'ideal' training establishment. The expansion requirements of the front-line relied on having an adequate supply of trained crews, and the number of available trained crews was also under pressure from losses (operational and training) as well as the need to send screened aircrew to the

(Above) **No. 29 Course of 22 OTU; unlike most OTU records, those for 22 OTU contain a full set of course photographs and are very well compiled.** 22 OTU records

All OTUs undertook operational missions; a board in the briefing room at 22 OTU shows 'last night's trip'. 22 OTU records

training units as instructors. In March 1942 the decision was taken to remove the second pilot from the operational bombers as this would ease the OTU bottleneck in the provision of pilots. At the same time it was decided to split the observer's role into two with the creation of a navigator and a bomb aimer. This in turn led to a requirement to increase the number of OTUs! 'A new 6 Group training syllabus became effective which required a complete re-organization of the operational flights; each flight now takes thirteen one-pilot crews. The second W/T operators were trained as bomb aimers until No. 19 Course, when thirteen bomb aimers were posted here for training.' (22 OTU ORB)

In May 1942 the two training groups were renumbered, No. 6 Group becoming No. 91 Group and No. 7 Group becoming No. 92 Group (a third, No. 93 Group, was formed in June) and by August twenty-two OTUs were either formed or forming, the target at this stage being twenty-seven such units. The same month saw the OTUs undertake their greatest opera-

tional commitment with participation in the thousand-bomber raids, providing some 30 per cent of the overall bomber force. Typical of the involvement was that by 22 OTU which committed thirty-five aircraft, fourteen operating from Wellesbourne, eleven from Stratford and ten from Elsham; four aircraft were lost on this raid.

Having completed his operational tour with 99 Squadron, John Gee was posted in late 1942 to 91 OTU at Wymeswold to become Chief Ground Instructor:

Lectures and practical demonstrations were given in a variety of subjects such as the Wellington aircraft and its systems, meteorology, theory of bombing, engine handling, dinghy drill (in the static water tank), and fighter evasion. I had a staff of three and one of them, Fg Off Wally Walters, had had pre-war experience of store and window display. He very quickly got a Wellington airframe and dressed it up in a hangar with a display of all of its equipment. It looked most impressive and in a matter of weeks we had a very efficient ground-training centre.

There was concern at the use of the training units for operational tasks and this was the subject of an ORS report at the end of the year (BC ORS report S70 dated 23 October 1942) which, in part, stated:

In order to produce the maximum weight of attack on favourable nights, the OTUs and also conversion flights have been brought in on a number of occasions to supplement the effort of the operational squadrons ... In the earlier raids in which the OTUs took part about 80 per cent of the crews were made up of screened personnel. Since the first three, however, they have usually consisted of pupils, and when screened personnel were used they were usually included in crews the majority of whom were pupils. Aircraft from the OTUs have taken part in eight raids, in one of which (Hamburg, 28–29 July) they were recalled. The other raids being:

30–31 May – Cologne
1–2 June – Essen
25–26 June – Bremen
31 Jul–1 Aug – Düsseldorf
10–11 Sep – Düsseldorf
13–14 Sep – Bremen
16–17 Sep – Essen

The big raids arouse great enthusiasm and come as a welcome break in the routine of the OTUs. The increase in keenness of the ground staff is most marked and the serviceability position is

26 OTU's LR132. The role of the OTUs increased throughout 1942 and the Wellington became the main type used by Bomber Command for crew training. Peter Green Collection

thereby much improved. The knowledge that the crews may have to go on operations before leaving the OTU makes them take their training much more seriously and also helps the instructors to relate their training more closely to operations. The majority of instructors, also, find operations a welcome change from their normal duties. There is however some reluctance to operating Wellington ICs on the part of those who have carried out their operational tour on faster and heavier aircraft.

The high losses of OTU aircraft have been partly due to the fact that the crews were mostly without operational experience. However, even if these crews had been in operational squadrons, unless they had taken part in special freshmen operations, their losses would have certainly been high, as it is known that in the operational squadrons the wastage rate of freshmen crews is appreciably higher than experienced crews. The OTU aircraft have been timed to be over the target in the middle of the attack. In view of the fact that they cannot time their movements as well as the operational crews it is desirable that this should always be done as they will then be more likely to avoid becoming stragglers and being picked off separately by the enemy defences.

The report concluded:

The OTUs have added materially to the success of those raids which have been carried out in good weather conditions. In cases where the target has not been well marked by the operational groups, they have not made any substantial contribution to the effectiveness of the raid. OTUs should, therefore, only be used when there is a firm forecast of good weather,

and it is better to cancel them at the last moment and accept the loss of effort than to employ them in any but good weather conditions. The OTUs should only be used on nights when a large force (say 500 aircraft) can be found from the operational squadrons. The output of trained crews from the OTUs will be unaffected provided that the training programme is curtailed only on nights when the OTUs are operating and that losses of OTU aircraft are promptly made good.

The September series of raids, under the code-name *Grand National,* had seen a particularly heavy OTU involvement, that against Düsseldorf on the night of 10–11 seeing 174 OTU aircraft in the total force of 476 aircraft. The plan called for four waves over the target – PFF, No. 5 Group, OTUs, No. 3 Group/PFF. Thirty aircraft were lost, including fourteen OTU Wellingtons (16 OTU being heavily hit, losing five aircraft, one of these having ditched on the outbound sortie).

The OTUs were still able to raise a note of humour, as reflected in Issue No. 1 (July 1942) of the *Wellesbourne Review:*

There is a sound of Aviodomy by night
when Wellesbourne's Wimpeys, in reluctant flight,
pass oe'r the King's Head, Ah! the natives say,
the runway tonight is B to A.

The C–D runway bears on Wellesbourne House
and you should hear the Flight Commanders grouse,
the wind is light, the runways shut, they say,
so kindly lay the flarepath B to A.

The E–F runway faces up a hill
a sight that makes most pilots feel quite ill,
and so unless a gale blows down that way
we leave the damned old runway B to A.

Maritime War

Although the Wellington had been involved in the maritime war since 1940, it was only from 1942 onwards that it really became an effective weapon in the war against the U-boats, an increased number of squadrons and the introduction of specialized equipment bringing a number of successes.

The maritime war had reached crisis point by early 1942 and, as related above, Bomber Command had been directed to add its efforts to the campaign against German capital ships. There was also a great deal of pressure for the command to release squadrons to Coastal Command for the maritime role – indeed many senior officers were of the opinion that the resources of Bomber Command could (and should) be more profitably used elsewhere. The loss of squadrons was made by Harris with ill grace; writing of the major efforts made in 1942 to expand Bomber Command, he noted:

The command struggled to raise new squadrons, complete with crews. But as far as the offensive against Germany was concerned, the greater part of this work might as well not have been done. As fast as each squadron was raised, it was transferred, not to the front-line strength of Bomber Command, but to the Middle East or other commands not concerned with the offensive against

Germany. In all, nineteen new squadrons were formed in the command during 1942, and thirteen of those were taken from us. And of the new squadrons that were left to us, three were on more or less permanent loan to Coastal Command and engaged in anti-submarine patrols. From May 1942 to the end of February 1943, additional aircraft lent to Coastal Command made 1,000 sorties while engaged in this work.

Amongst the units to 'join' Coastal Command were 311 Squadron (to 19 Group) and 304 Squadron (to 15 Group), both experienced Wellington bomber units whose Czech and Polish crews, respectively, were determined to carry the war to the Germans at every opportunity and who had already established a reputation for tenacity.

Although the German fighter patrols over the Bay of Biscay were becoming stronger and more effective, the Wellingtons proved on more than one occasion that they were able to look after themselves.

179 Squadron Wellington VIII HX379 in distinctive Coastal Command scheme and sporting the four ASV aerials that led to this variant being nicknamed 'Stickleback'. The overpainted codes of 172 Squadron can still be seen. Peter Green Collection

A pair of photographs showing a Wellington carrying out a torpedo drop. The aircraft could carry two such weapons, mounted one above the other. Ken Delve Collection

Perhaps one of the most famous incidents is that of 16 September when an aircraft of 304 Squadron was involved in a fierce fight with a number of Ju 88s. The incident is recorded in a Polish report:

While on an anti-submarine patrol over the Bay of Biscay a Wellington with Fg Off S. M. Targowski's crew flying almost at sea level was attacked by five Ju 88 fighters which came in one after the other, their cannons blazing. As a result of a comparatively short combat the Poles destroyed one and damaged another German aircraft. The remaining three Junkers decided to call it a day and flew back to France. The Wellington, although crippled by thirty-nine direct hits, returned home safely with petrol tank holed, engine, airscrew, tail-unit and fuselage damaged. None of the crew were wounded. For this gallant action, two of the crew received the *Virtuti Militari* cross and four others the Cross of Valour.

All of the Wellingtons employed by the command so far had been 'basic bomber' variants, operating primarily by day and hoping to catch U-boats in transit so that they could be attacked with bombs or depth-charges. Whilst a number of successes had been achieved, in the face of determined defence by the enemy U-boats and in the face of German fighter cover, the campaign was certainly not proving decisive. What was needed was more aircraft and a way of improving the overall strategy of the campaign.

In March 1942 No. 1417 Flight formed at Chivenor to bring the Leigh Light Wellington into service, although within weeks the unit had been redesignated as 172 Squadron under the command of Wg Cdr J. Russell (according to the squadron ORB the first three 'operationally-equipped Wellington ICs arrived, on loan from Cranwell', on 5 April). The necessity of improving effectiveness in the anti-U-boat war had given Coastal Command many a headache during 1941; it was particularly important to devise a system whereby the U-boats could be attacked when they surfaced at night to recharge batteries and change the air within the submarine. The solution was to use a system, such as radar (or ASV (Air to Surface Vessel) as it was called in this regard) that worked by night as well as day. But this was not accurate enough to permit an effective attack run, and so a system had to be developed to turn night into day for the final critical phase. As early as October 1940 Sqn Ldr Humphrey de Vere Leigh had put forward a proposal to fit a searchlight to the Wellington as a means of achieving this terminal illumination. Supported by the AOC Coastal Command, Air Chief Marshal Sir Frederick Bowhill, Sqn Ldr Leigh was tasked to develop the idea and by the end of 1940 he was working with Vickers to examine ways in which such an installation could be effected.

A trial aircraft, P9223, was fitted with ASV and a 61cm searchlight for trials – under the designation of Wellington DWI III (used for spoof purposes) – but the idea was abandoned in the summer of 1941. However, the decision was soon reversed and work commenced once more with successful trials being conducted and indeed showing great promise. The Pegasus-powered Wellington IC was chosen as the platform for the Leigh Light and aircraft were converted to have the light and ASV Mark II installed; with this fit they

The Leigh Light

The Leigh Light was a carbon arc searchlight carried on an aircraft and used in conjunction with ASV to illuminate surfaced submarines at night. The searchlight operator was situated in the nose of the aircraft from where he could control the searchlight in both elevation and azimuth. Indicators were fitted which showed the direction in which the beam would shine. The operator was thus able to train the searchlight in approximately the right direction and distance before the light was exposed. A lens giving a spread of 10 degrees in either a horizontal or vertical plane was provided which made searching for the target easier, but some expert operators prefer to use the light without the lens. The maximum effective range in ordinary weather was about 2 miles. The arc lamp was fully automatic in operation; power for the arc, which ran at 120 to 150 amperes, was obtained from seven 12v 40 ampere/hour type D accumulators and a trickle charge fitment would maintain them fully charged provided the arc was not run for more than 3½ minutes per hour. The turret-type Leigh Light was fitted to the Wellington; a 24in searchlight being mounted in a retractable under-turret with hydraulic controls. The maximum beam intensity was fifty million candles without the spreading lens and twenty million candles with the lens. Total weight of the installation was 1,100lb.

Tactical instructions. The best height to fly on patrol is between 1,500–2,500ft. When the target is picked up on ASV the height of the aircraft should be noted and the aircraft brought down to 500ft at a range slightly exceeding 1 mile to ensure that the aircraft is level when a range of 1 mile is reached. At a range of approximately ¾ mile the light is switched on. Before this the light operator should have ascertained by means of the indicator that it is aiming straight and is depressed to the correct angle – usually 6 degrees. Only a small degree of light movement should be necessary to illuminate the target. Immediately the target is lit up the aircraft should reduce height to 50 or 100ft and the normal depth charge attack made, dropping flame floats at the same time. (IGRU Report)

ed that operational success was needed before they would allocate any more resources and so the AOC decided to employ 172 Squadron before it was fully equipped, four aircraft being tasked for patrols over the Bay of Biscay on 4 June. The AHB *Narrative* noted:

The results from these first four sorties were most gratifying. Although three of the aircraft located no U-boats, the high standard of ASV operation attained during the special training with the Leigh Light was most apparent in the ease with which they located and illuminated contacts, even though these turned out to be small fishing vessels. The fourth aircraft – F/172 Squadron – contacted, homed on and successfully illuminated a large U-boat on the surface which fired a two-star recognition signal and made no attempt to dive. An accurate depth charge attack was made from 50ft altitude. While circling to examine the position of attack, another U-boat was contacted in the vicinity and illuminated. This proved to be a smaller U-boat ... having no depth charges left, F/172 carried out two machine gun attacks before having to leave the scene. The first U-boat was the Italian *Luigi Torelli* which sustained severe damage and caused her commanding officer to make for the Spanish coast at a much reduced speed. [The submarine was subsequently attacked by a Sunderland of 10 Squadron and beached at Santander.]

172 Squadron recorded the first operational day's events in the ORB:

The first operations were flown by four aircraft – HF828/C, BB513/B, BB503/D and ES986/F. Sqn Ldr J. H. Greswell in F found two U-boats and attacked one, dropping four 296lb torpex DC Mk VIII from 50ft. Three DCs exploded, one on the starboard quarter about 5yd from the hull and the other two on the port side. The second U-boat was located about 12 miles distant and was attacked from 150ft with machine gun fire, scoring hits on hull and conning tower. This notable success on the first operational effort was hailed with great enthusiasm throughout the squadron as it had proved the whole outfit to have been an outstanding success.

During June these four aircraft flew 235 operational hours, primarily in the Middle Bay area, made seven U-boat sightings and delivered attacks on three which resulted in serious damage to at least two of the submarines. The system was certainly proving itself, especially when compared with the

carried the designation GR.VIII. Other than the very obvious ASV aerials, and a few other minor equipment changes, the GR.VIII was a basic Wellington IC. It was, however, to have a significant impact on the maritime war. In the Leigh Light version, of which only fifty-eight were produced, the nose turret was removed and a Mark I nose fitted as a crew station for the light operator. Rather more GR.VIIs were given ASV and a torpedo role, 271 being so equipped.

Deliveries of aircraft were still slow and by May the squadron still only had five serviceable aircraft. The Air Ministry insist-

Specification – Wellington GR.VIII

ENGINES	Two Bristol Pegasus XVIII
DIMENSIONS	Span 86ft 2in (26.26m); length 64ft 7in (19.68m)
PERFORMANCE	Max. speed 235mph (376km/h); ceiling 19,000ft (5,758m)
ARMAMENT	4 × 0.303in guns, depth charges, torpedoes
NUMBER BUILT	394

statistics for the Whitley night operations (using ASV and flares) with no sightings in 195 operational hours. On 24 June Admiral Dönitz issued an order that U-boats were to transit the Bay of Biscay submerged – day and night. However, the first successful Wellington operation took place on the night of 5 July when Plt Off Howell (an American) and crew in Wellington H of 172 Squadron caught the U-502; the depth-charges were well placed and the U-boat sank immediately:

Four DCs were released from 50ft across its bows from starboard to port as it was in the act of crash-diving, the decks and conning tower still visible. The rear gunner opened fire as the Wellington passed over and as the spray from the exploding DCs subsided, he saw a swirling mass of water.

This was the first confirmed kill by a Leigh Light-equipped aircraft and the first by a Wellington. The squadron claimed another damaged U-boat in July – U-159 on 12 July (to Plt Off Howell again) – whilst, on 27 July, 311 Squadron recorded its first success when Sqn Ldr Stransky damaged U-106 in a daylight attack. This squadron made the only confirmed 'kill' by 19 Group in August when, on the 10th, Fg Off Nyult sank U-578. As with all maritime operations, the routine was very much one of many hours of inactivity, followed by a few minutes of intense action – often against false targets – with few actual U-boat sightings or attacks.

The situation was considered very serious by the Germans – hence the order that U-boats were not to transit the Bay by night. But with the increase in day fighter

cover, they transitted the Bay on the surface by day – a move that was countered by increased Coastal Command patrols and the employment of long-range fighters. The AHB *Narrative* said in summary that:

From these events it can be said that the advent of Leigh Light Wellingtons, although never exceeding four or five operational aircraft in June and July, marked the commencement of an effective offensive in the Bay of Biscay which seriously worried the U-boat Command, harassed the crews in an area hitherto comparatively safe and by the increase in passage time, greatly curtailed the number of days a U-boat could spend in an operational area ... The complete surprise and helplessness of the few U-boats attacked in June and July 1942 by this novel weapon encourages speculation as to the possible results if two or even one whole

148 Squadron crew pose with DV561 at LG224 in November 1942. G. Caldecott

A posed publicity shot of torpedoes and their specially-modified Wellington at Malta. The Wellingtons were a vital part of the anti-shipping war being fought from Malta. Ken Delve Collection

squadron had been employed instead of the penny packet actually available.

In his dispatch on Coastal Command operations, Air Chief Marshal Sir Philip Joubert stated his conviction that 'Our belief that the airborne searchlight was the solution to the problem of night operations seemed justified and I asked that steps be taken to produce the Leigh Light on a scale sufficient for all large aircraft on anti-U-boat operations.'

The U-boats had a somewhat easier time from August as this was the tunny-fishing period and they were able to hide amongst the mass of small fishing boats that confused the aircraft radar. At the same time, the Germans were developing a detector to allow them to pick up the ASV signals and so give U-boat commanders warning of the presence of enemy aircraft; this 'Metox' system was being fitted by September and had a detection range of 30 miles – far in excess of that at which a Wellington ASV operator could detect the submarine. The solution for the hunters was to employ radar of a different frequency and this was duly done, after some delay, with the introduction of the centimetric ASV III.

The success of the system led to its being employed in other areas where U-boat tar-gets were likely to be found; therefore in August a detachment had moved to Wick, in the extreme north-east of Scotland, to operate against the northern U-boat transit lanes. On 1 September this detached flight of 172 Squadron became 179 Squadron. After a few hectic weeks at Wick, with some successes, the unit moved to Gibraltar, arriving at its new base in the latter part of November. U-boats frequently transited the Straits of Gibraltar to bases in southern France and Italy and prior to the arrival of the Leigh Light Wellingtons they had been able to do so with some degree of immunity at night.

The Bomber Command *Quarterly Review* (No. 4, Jan–Mar 1943) summarized an attack by a Wellington of 304 Squadron:

At 1140 hours on 2 September Wellington A/304 came across an Italian submarine travelling at 8kt, in the Bay. An attack was made up track, and four out of the six depth-charges fell alongside the submarine, which was completely obliterated by the spray. On the run up, the aircraft machine gunned the U-boat and several of the crew collapsed on the deck. The submarine did not reply, except by firing two five-star red cartridges. Immediately after the explosions an oil patch 400ft across appeared, and the submarine soon lost way and came to a standstill. The aircraft circled again and made two bomb attacks, releasing one 250lb AS bomb on each occasion but missed by 10 and 20yd respectively. The Wellington circled again and made five machine gun attacks, expending 2,500 rounds. As a result ten men in bathing costumes dived off the submarine. The submarine now had a heavy list to port and was well down at the bows; part of the starboard forward hydrophone PLANE showed. The attack evidently inflicted severe internal damage on the submarine and temporarily crippled it. Subsequent information shows that this submarine was the *Guiliana*, which arrived in the Spanish port of Santander in a damaged condition the next day.

Three further Wellington squadrons joined the maritime war in the UK before the end of the year: 547 Squadron formed in October, becoming operational at Chivenor in December; and 544 Squadron formed at Benson in October to become a Coastal Command PR unit with a mixture of types, A Flight being equipped with Wellingtons for night photography. 612 Squadron re-equipped at Wick in November, receiving GR.VIIIs with Leigh Lights. None of these units was truly operationally until 1943.

September brought an upsurge in anti-submarine patrol activity as Coastal Command began to implement its plans for the protection of Allied convoys that would be involved with Operation *Torch*, the landings in North Africa.

Middle East

The primary task of much of the Allied air power in the Western Desert was the destruction of Axis supply lines, especially the weakest link – sea communication with southern Europe. For much of 1942 the Wellingtons continued to operate against shipping, both at sea and in harbour, with bombs and torpedoes. Having reached a high point at the end of 1941, the Allied advance had faltered and given the Axis forces time to re-organize; Rommel received a limited amount of supplies and reinforcement and with those he launched a counter-stroke in early 1942, sweeping the Allies back to the borders of Egypt and a defensive line at El Alamein. Without the well-applied use of air power during this critical period, it is likely that the retreat would have become a rout.

14 March saw Eric Barfoot flying a 70 Squadron Wellington as part of a squadron-strength attack on the Italian airfield at Calato Lindos, Rhodes:

The journey was uneventful, but as we approached Rhodes at about 10,000ft we could see that a terrific anti-aircraft barrage was being put up over the harbour. We thanked our lucky stars that another squadron had the harbour as a target and skirting the town by a few miles, we made several bombing runs on a poorly defended Italian aerodrome. On our final bombing run I was startled to see two rows of tracers skimming over our starboard wing; our rear-gunner opened up and, on the end of the tracers, a Fiat CR.42 sailed by out to starboard with not many more knots on his clock than we had. The front gunner bade him farewell with a long burst. Bombs gone we made our detour, watching *Flak* and bomb bursts in the town. We landed at LG 104 after 5½ hours. The harbour had not been bombed, it had been shelled by Navy destroyers and the Wellington attack on the airfield had been a diversion.

Benghazi was the most frequent of the strategic targets; so frequent that 70 Squadron crews referred to this as their 'Mail Run' and even created a squadron song (to the tune of *Clementine*). The song did vary from time to time; this particular variant was that sung during the Kabrit period:

Down the Flights each bloody morning
Sitting waiting for a clue
Same old notice on the Flight Board
Same old target, guess where to.
– chorus –
Seventy Squadron, Seventy Squadron,
Though we say it a with a sigh,
We must do this bloody Mail Run every night
Until we die.

Take off for the Western Desert
Fuka, 60 or 09,

Same old Wimpey, same old target,
Same old aircrew, same old time.

Forty Wimpeys on the target,
Two were ditched down in the drink,
Then three others pranged on landing,
Bloody hell, it makes you think.

Fighter coming into starboard,
Bloody Hell we'll have to shift,
Find the bloody gunner sighting,
On the fighter for a drift.

Stooging round the Western Desert,
With the gravy running low,
Wish to hell I could see Fuka,
In the shit storm down below.

And old Tennant from his photos,
Said we seldom reached BG,
Sees no bombholes in the roof tops,
Only craters in the sea.

Try to get your thirty ops in,
Without your Wimpey being hit,
If you do you'll go to Blighty,
If you don't you're in the ...!

Oh to be in Piccadilly,
Selling matches by the score,
It might be a little chilly,
There'd be no Mail Run any more.

As the Allies withdrew in the face of Rommel's 1942 offensive, the situation approached crisis level and air power became even more important; the Wellington squadrons of 205 Group were withdrawn to the Canal Zone and continued their maximum effort operations:

Double sorties by tired aircrews, flying aircraft that were equally tired and kept serviceable only by the superhuman exertions of ground crews working without rest. Once Rommel had been checked in the first week of July, the immediate task was to prevent supplies reaching the enemy. Tobruk was the main supply port and from July onwards it became the target for all the aircraft that 205 Group could put into the air ... The enemy had built up one of the most vicious concentrations of heavy and medium AA defences ... one particularly dangerous and effective battery of heavy guns was christened 'Eric' by the crews. In their minds they pictured 'Eric' as a fat, bespectacled, but very cunning Hun, who waited, clock in hand, ready to give the order for his battery to fire when the night bombers arrived. A coloured cartoon of 'Eric' hung on the wall of the briefing room and many

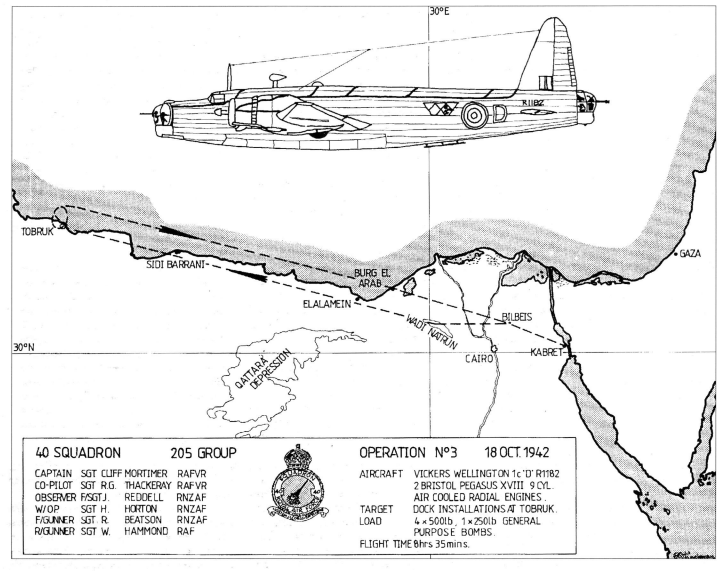

A typical 40 Squadron mission, flown by Reg Thackery, as part of 205 Group's strategic campaign.
Reg Thackery

jokes were made about this fictitious character. While over the target, however, crews treated 'Eric' with due respect. To meet the strong defences of Tobruk, the Maw Plan – initiated by the Officer Commanding No. 108 Squadron – was introduced, by which the greatest possible number of bombers was brought over the target at the same moment. This plan of a Blitz time saved casualties and proved effective in attacks on other well-defended targets. (RAF Middle East Review No. 4)

The pace remained hectic. Reg Thackery joined 40 Squadron at Kabrit as a second pilot:

In August 1942 we were all posted to No. 2 Middle East Training School for conversion to night bombing on the Wellington IC. Training commenced at RAF Kabrit but was soon transferred to RAF Aqir near Tel Aviv; some sixty hours later we were back at Kabrit to join 40 Squadron. By the time I reached the squadron a regular pattern of long-range ops to Tobruk had been established under Wg Cdr Ridgway. My first trip as a second pilot was, inevitably, to Tobruk and the skipper, a New Zealander, Flt Lt Morton, was on his second tour. He was a keen type and by Christmas 1942 had become the squadron commander. This first trip lasted eight hours and I had not

previously been in the air for more than five hours and so had recourse to the caffeine tablets provided and managed to keep awake to handle the aircraft on the long flight to and from the target. The skipper, of course, did the take-off and landing and the time over the target. Our target was the dock area at Tobruk but there was a great deal of cloud and eventually Morton ordered an attack on a heavy gun position north of the harbour. During the bombing run we lost height from 13,000 to 6,000ft to avoid the *Flak* but saw the bursts, smelt the cordite and felt the bumps. The bomb load of 250lb and 500lb bombs were released by our observer at 9,000ft. The flight back was uneventful and we landed back at Kabrit in daylight having been airborne since 2240. I slept for about twenty-four hours after that initiation and it was a week before I was again on the order of battle – to Tobruk again.

Torpedo Bombing

The most significant development for the Wellington squadrons in 1942 was the employment of the air-dropped torpedo; this was largely due to the trials work undertaken by 38 Squadron. The trials had begun the previous December in response to the need for increased striking power against Axis shipping, the torpedo having proved itself to be an effective weapon in the hands of the Beaufort anti-shipping squadrons. The advantage with the Wellington would be its greater range and its ability to carry two torpedoes. Standard aircraft required a number of modifications, such as removal of the nose turret and changes in the bomb bay to allow two of the standard Mk 12 torpedoes to be carried.

The first practice drop was made by 38 Squadron's Commanding Officer, Wg Cdr John Chaplin, on 20 December, and having proved the basic soundness of the concept, an intensive training period took place in the first few months of 1942 to refine the technique. The first operational sorties took place, but without success; further tactical changes were made with the aircraft being given long-range fuel tanks and, by operating from some of the forward airfields, attacks being made on harbours in Greece. The first success came on 27 March when three aircraft attacked shipping in Patras harbour, with Plt Off Swingler claiming a 15,000-ton MV.

March also saw the operational debut of another Wellington unit in the Middle East; 221 Squadron had arrived at LG39 in January (although a detachment remained at Luqa for some time) equipped with Wellington VIIIs carrying ASV. The success of this equipment in the UK had led to the decision to employ it in the Mediterranean theatre and the tactical concept developed was for an ASV-equipped Wellington to locate enemy shipping at night and then drop flares to illuminate the target for the torpedo-carrying Wellingtons to attack.

Although its main base was at Shallufa, 38 Squadron, having acquired the torpedo-bomber role late the previous year, was soon sending detachments to forward airfields for anti-shipping work. Typical of

this was that recorded in the ORB for 23 January:

> Five aircraft required to attack convoy endeavouring to reach Tripoli, and to destroy the escorting battleships. Aircraft to operate from El Adem – four aircraft from B Flight and one from A Flight left Shallufa for El Adem. In addition two other A Flight aircraft left for El Adem to operate from there and delivered torpedo attacks on the convoy.

Also typically, this mission was cancelled the next day, although the aircraft remained on standby at El Adem for a few more days.

In the meantime, more aircraft were being sent to Heliopolis to be modified for torpedo dropping and crews were practising night torpedo attacks against HMS *Sagitta* in Suez Bay. The torpedo had proved itself a very effective weapon and the long range of the Wellington, plus its ability to carry two torpedoes, would make it a valuable addition to the anti-shipping strike force (although on certain occasions when an overload tank was fitted the aircraft would carry only one torpedo). As more aircraft became available, the squadron sent a detachment, of only two aircraft, to Malta – the first such leaving for Malta on 27 February.

Following a conference attended by the squadron commander, 38 Squadron was instructed to maintain a detachment of torpedo aircraft at LG05 for the duration of the moon period. They were soon in action, a typical engagement being that of 22 May when an ASV Wellington of 221 Squadron worked with DV542 (Sgt Youens) and AD597 (Sgt Flanagan) of 38 Squadron:

> At 0130 hours Sgt Youens received a revised position for convoy from ASV aircraft. He set course for estimated position, repeatedly checking by bearings on ASV aircraft. At 0215 hours Sgt Youens sighted the convoy consisting of two destroyers and two MVs, one large of about 8–10,000 tons and the other 2–3,000 tons. The convoy was in echelon 1,200yd apart with the destroyers on the flanks. He attacked the large MV, approaching to the stern of the starboard destroyer. The destroyer opened fire with 12–14 Bofors-type guns, hitting the aircraft and causing damage. As the aircraft came round to the north-east of the convoy, Sgt Youens saw smoke screen beginning centering on the target ship. He could not see whether there was smoke coming from the stack or whether it was the result of a hit. The ASV aircraft reported that clouds

of smoke were pouring from the ship and the next day a reconaissance aircraft reported a large MV beached some 30 miles north of Benghazi with a gaping hole in the side. It is therefore claimed that Sgt Youens hit the ship. The aircraft was damaged considerably, hits being registered on flaps, main surface and aileron of starboard wing, starboard side of fuselage, port engine cowling and port engine wheel covers. The aircraft succeeded in reaching LG05. Sgt Flanagan did not sight the convoy until 0320 hours and it was effectively screened by smoke so that no favourable opportunity for attack was presented. (38 Squadron ORB)

Torpedo strikes were also being made by the Malta detachment:

> Five aircraft torpedo strike from Malta led by Flt Lt Robinson; all aircraft were homed on to the Italian fleet successfully. The ASV aircraft dropped flares in an excellent position but great difficulty was experienced in trying to attack owing to a very thick smoke screen. Fg Off Foulis succeeded in penetrating the smoke screen and managed to get in two attacks. He did not see any results due to the smoke screen but the ASV aircraft saw a red glow and it is thought that at least one of the torpedoes found its mark. The rest of the aircraft did not attack and brought their torpedoes back.

A similar attack was made the following night by five aircraft but, again, only one was able to drop both torpedoes.

July was a typical month for the squadron with 144 operational sorties (1,132 hours), dropping 78½ tons of bombs, eighty-six mines and sixteen torpedoes. At this stage the squadron was still carrying out its own training regime for 'torpedo captains', although this ceased in October when No. 5 METS began to run a comprehensive training scheme.

In mid-September Sqn Ldr Robinson was carrying out low-level bombing trials in Suez Bay:

> The object was to ascertain whether a 1,000lb bomb when dropped from a height of 100ft or less would bounce on the water for a certain distance or whether it would plunge straight in as soon as it touched. Two bombs were dropped, one from 70ft in a shallow dive and one from 70ft straight and level. Both disappeared beneath the surface immediately.

The anti-shipping force in the Mediterranean was increased in November when 69 Squadron at Luqa, Malta, received a number of experienced torpedo captains from 38 Squadron.

Indeed there were a number of changes in the latter part of the year, recorded in colloquial style by 38 Squadron's ORB for 27 November. 'As arranged at the conference yesterday, three 'Goofingtons' were received from 221 Squadron and conversion of these to 'Snoopingtons' was started immediately; three of our 'Fishingtons' were transferred to 5 METS.'

Special Operations

Meanwhile, the RCM/ELINT unit, 162 Squadron, continued to operate its specially equipped Wellington ICs from Shallufa and detached locations, having responsibility for the entire Mediterranean area. The unit had formed on 4 January as the Signals Squadron at Kabrit under Wg Cdr H. S. Rusher, the nucleus of six aircraft having been provided by 109 Squadron. Having been designated as 162 Squadron, the unit moved to Shallufa and was soon undertaking trials with captured German tank radios, an Army unit arriving with this equipment on 12 January in order to test the effectiveness of the jammers. Two aircraft were fitted out for these tests; the tests involved a T1360T transmitter and the intention was to establish the height and range at which jammers were effective at varying distances between ground stations.

In the meantime, the first operational sorties had been flown on 8 January when Plt Off Fenton (with Lt Baker of the Signals Branch as the special operator) flew Wellington 'X' from LG09 on an SSR (Special Signals Reconnaissance) of Crete and the Greek Islands:

Left Shallufa at 1415, arrived LG09 at 1510. Operation consisted of signals investigation of Crete and the Greek Islands area. Although visibility was bad and accurate pinpoints difficult to obtain, Lt Baker gathered useful information. As dawn was breaking on return to the coast, the aircraft returned direct to Shallufa, landing at 0840 having taken off at 2230. (162 Squadron ORB)

The gathering side was by far the most important side to the squadron's activities, but in October a number of aircraft were equipped with 'Jostle' equipment to jam German ground communications, especially the tactical nets on tanks and AFVs as part of the overall support plan for the Allied Alamein offensive.

On 30 June three aircraft moved to Shallufa from Bilbeis (the squadron having moved here in April) for operations over the battlefield; one failed to return from this sortie, having been involved in a mid-air collision.

Eric Barfoot completed his tour of operations with 70 Squadron in July and was posted to the Ferry Flight at Fayid. 'We were given a Wellington IC, Z8734, as a taxi. We became a collection and delivery mob scouring the Middle East and Western Desert, rescuing old and new, serviceable and damaged kites. We collected several – and I left my silver cigarette case in one of them!' After a short spell with this unit he moved to Kabrit to join No. 4 Middle East Training School (METS) with its variety of equipment, including Wellingtons. The school was also involved with training elements of the Long Range Desert Group (LRDG) in parachute jumping, as well as undertaking the occasional operational parachute drop. After one such, Eric, his colleague Harry and an LAC engine fitter were flown by Hudson to Gambut No. 3 to pick up Wellington DV677 which had force-landed there after an LRDG mission:

The airfield was deserted and the Hudson flew off, leaving us to inspect the 'Wimp'. The port motor was OK on run-up, but one magneto on the starboard motor was totally unserviceable, and the other unreliable. There was no way to make contact with base and take-off was out of the question. We explored the landing ground, finding lots of German and Italian garbage; on one dump the LAC found some scrap German dry batteries, the centre pole of which was a solid stick of carbon. We needed magneto brushes and so sat down to whittle and file these sticks of carbon to a diameter of about ⅛in, and approximately ½in in length. Finally, after three days, Harry made one and the fitter, our saviour, made three. Brushes fitted I warily tried the engines as Harry and the airman took turns in cranking. Pessimism disappeared as the engine burst into life and elation took over as the mag drops were within bounds. The flight home went without a snag.

Another unit to arrive in theatre during 1942 was 458 Squadron RAAF; this unit had formed in the UK in August 1941 and flown operations with Bomber Command from October 1941 to January 1942, at which time it was ordered to move to the Middle East. However, the piecemeal arrival of aircraft and crews meant that these were 'acquired' by other units and the groundcrew, having arrived in late

May, acted as a Maintenance Unit for other Wellington units. However, in September the unit came together once more and, equipped with Wellington VIIIs, joined the maritime war, the first mission being flown on 1 November.

DWI Wellingtons of 1 GRU were still active throughout the year and still operating detachments to various areas as required from their home base at Ismailia. Typical of these was a two-aircraft detachment in late November,

... for operations from Mersa Matruh and Tobruk as soon as these ports fell into our hands. The following day [3 November] experiments were carried out at Ismailia to list the efficiency of DWI aircraft on German mine units by a technical officer from the C-in-C staff, Mediterranean Station. As an afterthought a subsidiary experiment was carried out on a British mine unit. In well-informed quarters the ability of DWI aircraft to deal with enemy mines was never doubted, and the result of the experiment merely confirmed previous tests. Great surprise and satisfaction was caused, however, when the British mine unit was also easily fired. This immediately placed greater importance in the employment of DWI aircraft at Western Desert ports where it was known that large numbers of British mines were laid. The two Wellingtons, P2518 and L4227, left Ismailia on 9 November for Gianaclis. The following day, in company with an air-sea rescue Wellington carrying water and rations, they took off for LG 104, landing at 0730 hours. P2518 was airborne at 0940 hours and proceeded to Mersa Matruh in order to sweep the channel and harbour for Red Mines. L4227 was unable to sweep due to loss of oil from a leaking pipe.

There was then some confusion as to the Navy requirements for further DWI work in this area and Tobruk, although Philip Dawson as OC of the GRU was keen to undertake the task, stating in his report that 'the primary function of the DWI aircraft is to carry out a searching sweep for finely set magnetic mines in order to reduce the danger to minesweeping vessels.' He had his way and a third aircraft was summoned from Ismailia:

Aircraft P2518 was airborne at 1330 hours (14 November from Gambut Main) and set course for Tobruk where sweeping was commenced at 1345 hours. No naval sweepers had arrived at the harbour, and it was noticed that town was practically deserted. On the twelfth run of the sweep a mine was exploded in the channel at the north entrance to the harbour. Altogether thirty-eight runs were made over the harbour and outer channel before the aircraft returned to Gambut, landing at 1635 hours.

The following day two aircraft made sweeps over the harbour and a second mine was exploded. The Navy were pleased with the results and requested that Derna be swept; this was duly done, though the crew of P2518 received a shock when they were attacked by a Ju 88 which had just bombed Derna:

After this attack the crew were greatly relived to see the enemy fly out to sea. That they were extremely lucky in not being shot down will be appreciated when it is realized that the aircraft have no armament or armour plating. Even one engine put out of action would have caused the aircraft to crash as no height can be maintained on one engine. This would most likely have been equally as disastrous as being shot down as a DWI aircraft which had to ditch off Port Said in 1941 with engine failure due to its laden condition went straight under leaving no survivors.

Benghazi was the last of the ports to be swept by this detachment and on 1 December the Wellingtons returned to Ismailia.

The night of 23–24 October saw the opening of the final battle of El Alamein and the bomber Wellingtons flew double sorties against Axis positions and supply routes. Allied air power moved forward with the advance and even strategic squadrons like the Wellingtons became mobile, attacking retreating Axis troops and also keeping up the pressure on supply lines, including ports in Italy.

The year ended on a high point for the Allies in North Africa with the successful landings under Operation *Torch* commencing on 8 November, the intention being to seize the Vichy French territory and then attack the German forces from east and west and so squeeze them out of North Africa. The Wellington units played a full and active part in all of the associated air operations. In November the squadrons of 238 Wing (40 and 104) moved to Luqa to make it easier to attack ports such as Tunis, Bizerta, Sfax and Tripoli that were being used to supply the Axis forces in Tunisia. Nearness to targets meant that the squadrons could fly double sorties, although on 19 December an attack on Luqa by Ju 88s caught the Wellington force between sorties and nine aircraft were destroyed.

As more airfields were captured, so various air assets were moved forward and additional squadrons deployed from the UK, including the Wellington-equipped 142 and 150 Squadrons, both of whom had been operating as part of Main Force, Bomber Command since late 1940. Both units moved to Blida, Algeria in December 1942 and formed 330 Wing. When the aircraft deployed from the UK they brought a number of groundcrew with them so that they could become operational as soon as possible; the first missions in their new theatre were flown on 28–29 December with an attack on the docks at Bizerta.

Far East

The outbreak of war with Japan on 8 December 1941 was not unexpected, but it provided yet another drain on the already strained military resources of the British Empire. In January 1942 two UK-based Wellington squadrons, 99 Squadron at Waterbeach and 215 Squadron at Newmarket, were instructed to send groundcrew by sea to India and to prepare to move to that theatre of operations. Aircraft were ferried out in February and

Parachutists lining up to board a 215 Squadron Wellington at Chaklala, October 1942.
Andy Thomas Collection

March, many falling prey to Middle East acquisition *en route*! It was a slow, frustrating period for both units and it was summer before they were in a position to start flying once again; 215 Squadron had moved to Pandaveswar on 17 April, an airfield with a single runway and almost no facilities. The groundcrew had received instruction on the Wellington IC from a 40 Squadron detachment (groundcrew only) at Asansol. The first operation took place on 24 April but the poor weather conditions led to many instances of aircraft being bombed-up but then the mission being cancelled. Between 9 May–22 June the squadron undertook many supply-dropping sorties, food and medical supplies being dropped to the retreating armies in Burma. The airfield at Pandaveswar became unusable in the summer monsoon and detachments operated from Dum Dum and Alipore, supply dropping remaining the primary task. Meanwhile, 99 Squadron had been sending crews to operate with 215 Squadron whilst they themselves were still in the process of working up. In late August they moved to Pandaveswar but by that time 215 Squadron had moved to St Thomas' Mount and in September began flying maritime missions off the east coast of India, the first such being flown by Sqn Ldr Skinner in DV574 on 1 September.

> Operationally it was a month of dull monotony, no enemy sightings were made, although all aircraft carried either depth charges or bombs none were expended – except on the 25th when a DC fell off an aircraft during take-off but fortunately without damage to the aircraft or its occupants.' (215 Squadron ORB.) In October the squadron moved to Chaklala for training 'devoted to container dropping and in giving air experience to paratroopers.'

Aircraft were modified for the new roles and by December the squadron was also flying night paratroop drops.

No. 99 Squadron had also been on the move, ending up at Digri by late October in preparation for a renewed bombing offensive; the first operation took place on 18 November when eight aircraft deployed to the ALG at Fenni to attack the airfield at Meiktila:

> Despite considerable lack of facilities at Fenni, all aircraft took off on time and a highly successful attack developed at Meiktila, weather conditions being excellent with bright moonlight.

Many bursts were seen on the target and all aircraft returned safely to Digri, the aircraft piloted by Fg Off Brown being intercepted for a short while by an enemy fighter. (99 Squadron ORB)

Airfields remained the priority targets for the rest of the year, but the squadron expressed a few concerns:

> The chief concern from a technical viewpoint to be drawn from the 1½ months' operations in India was that it would not be possible to maintain in India the same high operational serviceability that prevailed in England. This was due firstly to the very tight supply position in India and, secondly to the variety of technical difficulties encountered in the new climate. The net result of these two factors was that a higher serviceability than eight or nine aircraft was rarely possible with the sixteen I.E. [Initial Establishment] aircraft allowed by the establishment. Also, by the end of the month there were no less than thirty-one complete crews on the strength of the squadron, and in consequence the problems of employing all these aircrew became acute. Strong representations were made to have a considerable number of these crews posted away, and whilst some were sent away during the month, fresh arrivals kept the aircrew strength practically the same figure. (99 Squadron ORB)

CHAPTER FOUR

1943: Goodbye to Bomber Command

The Wellington Xs of Bomber Command were gradually replaced during 1943 by the four-engined heavies and by the end of the year had all but vanished from front-line service. FlyPast Collection

Bomber Command

In the latter part of 1942 a number of squadrons had formed with Wellingtons; one such had been 466 Squadron RAAF which was formed at Driffield with Wellington IIIs on 15 October as part of No. 4 Group. In late November the first of the squadron's operational Mark Xs arrived, the first, HE368, arriving on 25 November. It caused

> ... a great deal of interest among squadron personnel since no-one was quite certain as to the difference between the two types of aircraft. After being on view for a short while the aircraft was wheeled into the hangar for the necessary modifications to be effected with the

object of getting it flown and tried out as soon as possible.

By 6 December the squadron had eighteen such aircraft on strength and was undertaking intensive training in order to become operational early in 1943. Having moved to Leconfield on 27 December, 466 Squadron was declared operational on 1 January but the jubilation was crushed a few days later,

> ... when a signal was received from Command ordering that the Wellington X was to be used for local day flying only until further notice. As a result of eight failures of the ball races in the rear turret it was decided by No. 4 Group that turret changes should be carried out on eight more aircraft which were under suspicion.

The signal arrived on 6 January and on the 11th the squadron was placed non-operational pending the results of an investigation by the Ministry of Aircraft Production into the turret failures.

Two days later the squadron flew its first operation when six aircraft were tasked for a minelaying sortie; all had to fly an air test which included a thorough test on the turrets. All six took off at 1600 for the Terschelling Island area but HE152 lost the dinghy compartment cover (and dinghy) on take-off and so had to return to base. The remaining aircraft set course in formation and arrived in the target area just before dark, descending to 100ft to lay their mines. All returned safely. Such minelaying missions became the norm for January, during which period the squadron flew forty-seven sorties but lost four aircraft. (Indeed, 466 Squadron was to become something of a specialist mine-laying unit and in August 'a record number of mines – 236 – were laid, establishing the squadron as the leading mining squadron in Bomber Command.')

The year opened slowly with small-scale raids on Essen and on 14 January Harris was given a new directive to concentrate on U-boat bases in France: St Nazaire, Lorient, Brest and La Pallice. Lorient was duly attacked by 122 bombers (including thirty-three Wellingtons) on 14–15 January, this night seeing the debut of No. 6 Group in the strategic bombing offensive. Two major raids on Berlin had no Wellington participation but then, on 26–27 January, 139 Wellingtons were part of a 157-aircraft force that attacked Lorient again. This continued to be a significant target into late February and the Wellingtons always comprised the major element of the strike force.

On the night of 5–6 March Harris unleashed what became known as the Battle of the Ruhr – a concerted effort to destroy this vital industrial centre in what Bomber Command saw as a potentially war-winning offensive. Essen was the first target and 442 bombers (including 131 Wellingtons, of which four were lost) caused heavy damage to the Krupps works and surrounding areas. Although many other cities were also attacked in subsequent weeks, the Wellington force took part in only a small proportion of these, the next being 158 Wellingtons (as part of a 457-aircraft force), again to Essen on 12–13 March. However, by April they were present on most of the major attacks – Kiel, Duisburg, Frankfurt, Stuttgart, Mannheim and Dortmund.

By May 1943 the Wellington units still accounted for a significant part of Bomber Command's strength, despite an ever-increasing number of four-engined bombers entering service. Typical of the targets under attack was Dortmund and in the Bomber Command Review for April–June 1943 the attacks on this target are summarized as:

Dortmund is one of the chief centres of the German heavy industry. It is also the great transport centre at the east end of the Ruhr, corresponding to Duisburg in the west. In addition to handling railway traffic to and from the Ruhr industries, it deals with a vast quantity of through traffic to central, north and east Germany, and is the terminus of the Dortmund–Ems canal. Traffic on this canal has recently gained in importance from the considerable transfer of German sea-traffic from Rotterdam to Emden. The virtual elimination of this industrial centre in two attacks at a total cost of sixty-nine aircraft missing is in some ways the most remarkable achievement of Bomber Command, up to date. The havoc caused was great. Not only was the centre of the town largely burnt out, but direct damage to factories and transportation was

Wellington ORBAT, April 1943

Bomber Command		No. 93 Gp	
No. 1 Gp		Bramcote/Finningley	18 OTU
Binbrook	12 Sqn	Hixon	30 OTU
Kirmington	166 Sqn	Lichfield	27 OTU
Hemswell	199, 300, 301, 305 Sqns	Wymeswold	28 OTU
Holme	101 Sqn	**Coastal Command**	
Breighton	466 Sqn	No. 16 Gp	
		Benson	544 Sqn
No. 3 Gp		No. 17 Gp	
Mildenhall	149 Sqn	Cranwell	3 OTU
Newmarket	75 Sqn	Limavedy	7 OTU
Gransden Lodge	192 Sqn	Turnberry	1 TTU
No. 4 Gp		No. 18 Gp	
Driffield	196 Sqn	Tain	547 Sqn
Leconfield	466 Sqn	No. 19 Gp	
Tholthorpe	429 Sqn	Chivenor	172, 179, 547 Sqns
Burn	431 Sqn	Talbenny	304, 311 Sqns
No 5 Gp		RAF Gibraltar	
Scampton	57 Sqn	Gibraltar	179 Sqn
No. 6 Gp		**Mediterranean Air Command**	
Croft	420, 427 Sqns	Blida	142, 150 Sqns
Dishforth	424, 425, 426, 428 Sqns	Gibraltar	179 Sqn
No. 8 Gp		AHQ Malta	
Warboys	156 Sqn	Luqa	69, 221, 458 Sqns
No. 91 Gp		Middle East Command	
Harwell	15 OTU	Bir el Gardabia	37, 40, 70, 104 Sqns
Lossiemouth	20 OTU	Berka	38 Sqn
Moreton-in-Marsh	21 OTU	Bilbeis	162 Sqn
Pershore	23 OTU	Ismailia	1 GRU
Wellesbourne Mountford	22 OTU	Shallufa	det of 221 Sqn
No. 93 Gp		221 Gp Calcutta	
Chipping Warden	12 OTU	Chaklala	215 Sqn
Cottesmore	14 OTU	Digri	99 Sqn
North Luffenham	29 OTU	Tanjore	36 Sqn
Upper Heyford	16 OTU		
Wing	26 OTU		
Westcott	11 OTU		

166 Squadron operated Wellington IIIs for a few months in the early part of 1943 from Kirmington.
Peter Green Collection

(Below) **X3763 of 425 Squadron failed to return from an attack on Stuttgart in April 1943.**
Ken Delve Collection

widespread. In particular, the damage to Hoesch AG, one of the largest steel-producing undertakings in Germany, was so severe as to make production impossible for a considerable time.

The two raids in this period can be summarized thus (*see* box below).

Of the 596 aircraft on the first raid, 110 were Wellingtons and six of these were lost. This was the first major attack on Dortmund, bombing was accurate and heavy damage was caused. On the second raid 151 Wellingtons were involved and

again six were lost. The latter raid also brought a Conspicuous Gallantry Medal (CGM) to Sgt Stuart Sloan, a bomb-aimer with 431 Squadron. In confusion over the target area, the pilot baled out and Sgt Sloan, along with the navigator, Sgt Parslow (who was awarded the DFM) and wireless operator, Fg Off Bailey (who was awarded the DFC) flew the aircraft back and landed it at Cranwell. Sloan was granted an immediate CGM, a field commission, and was sent to train as a pilot.

The awards are listed in Air Ministry Bulletin 10527 under RAF Awards No 589:

CGM – Sgt Stuart N. Sloan
DFC – Fg Off John B. G. Bailey
DFM – Sgt George C. W. Parslow

One night in May 1943 Fg Off Bailey and Sgts Sloan and Parslow were members of the crew of an aircraft detailed to attack Dortmund. Shortly after its bombs had been released, the aircraft was badly damaged by AA fire whilst held by the searchlights. Evasive action was taken by putting the aircraft into a steep dive but this proved ineffective and the bomber was subjected to heavy fire whilst still illuminated. The situation became critical but Sgt Sloan, displaying superb skill and determination, eventually flew clear of the defences and headed for this country. A hatch was open and could not be closed, the rear turret door was also open and wind of great force blew through the length of the aircraft. All the lights

Date	A/C sent	A/C attacked	Bombs		Losses
			HE	incendiary	
4–5 May	596	534	842	738	31
23–24 May	826	764	1,167	2,248	38

This side view of LP700 shows that despite having beam guns in some variants, the Wellington was simply not heavily enough armed for the night war of 1943; this, plus a poorer performance and lower bomb load than most of the newer types meant that its operational days in Bomber Command were numbered.
FlyPast Collection

Wellington Xs dotted around an airfield in August 1943. FlyPast Collection

in the navigator's cabin were extinguished but in the face of extreme difficulty, Sgt Parslow plotted a course. On the return flight, he and Fg Off Bailey assisted Sgt Sloan in every way within their power and eventually this gallant airman flew the badly damaged bomber to an airfield and effected a good landing. In appalling circumstances, these members of aircrew displayed courage, determination and fortitude of the highest order.

The CGM had been instituted by George VI in November 1942 'for acts of conspicuous gallantry whilst flying in active operations against the enemy' and of 110 awarded during World War Two, seven were awarded to Wellington aircrew:

13–14 March 1943	Flt Sgt G. Ashplant	166 Sqn
12 March	Flt Sgt G. F. Keen	427 Sqn
8–9 April	Sgt L. F. Williamson	428 Sqn
14–15 April	Sgt E. F. Hicks	466 Sqn
12–13 April	Sgt J. P. McGarry Sgt T. P. Petrie	70 Sqn 70 Sqn
12–24 May	Sgt S. N. Sloan	431 Sqn

The Wellington strength table for 1943 shows the rapid run-down in strength from the middle of the year (*see* box, below).

The high loss rates of April to June were primarily from attacks on German towns and cities. This was the period of the Battle of the Ruhr (March to July) with Bomber Command making a concerted effort to cause critical damage to the German industrial heartland. The overall loss rate was running at between 3½–5 per cent and it was evident by now that the Wellingtons were starting to take an increasing number of losses (along with the Halifax) mainly due to their inferior performance. Whilst some squadrons suffered little loss over the period, others were hard hit – 429 Squadron, for example, losing ten aircraft in the period 11–25 June.

Whilst the Wellingtons continued to play their part in the Main Force offensive they were also very active on the minelaying campaign, which also caused some losses. In the period April–June 1943 Bomber Command flew 1,485 'Gardening' sorties during which 4,191 mines were laid ranging from the Baltic to the coasts of Spain. The Bomber Command *Quarterly Review* stated that the primary purposes of this campaign were:

Date	A/C	Crews	A/C+Crews	Loss Rate (night ops)
Feb	147	183	137	2.7 per cent
Mar	197	220	184	3.2 per cent
Apr	164	193	158	5.0 per cent
May	123	157	121	5.1 per cent
Jun	126	133	117	5.2 per cent
Jul	97	93	89	3.4 per cent
Aug	70	74	68	3.6 per cent
Sep	42	44	38	1.0 per cent
Oct	25	30	25	0.8 per cent
Nov	16	17	15	0.7 per cent
Dec	11	11	11	0.5 per cent

1. To cause serious embarrassment and dislocation to the enemy's vital seaborne traffic, especially in regard to raw materials for the Ruhr and military supplies either for the Russian Front or for the Norwegian theatre of occupation;

2. To assist the Battle of the Atlantic by interrupting the passages of U-boats leaving or entering the French west coast bases, and by rendering the Baltic U-boat training areas unsafe;

3. To interfere with the arrivals and departures of blockade runners, armed merchant raiders, iron ore ships and sundry traffic using the Gironde River or other Atlantic ports;

4. To force the enemy to maintain numbers of experienced personnel and much valuable material for the purpose of sweeping his widely spread harbours and channels.

Two consecutive nights in particular are indeed noteworthy in the history of minelaying by RAF aircraft. On the 27–28 April, 160 aircraft laid 458 mines in areas along the French Coast and Frisian Islands. On 28–29 April, 226 aircraft laid 593 mines in the Heligoland Bight, off the Norwegian coast, in the Kattegat and Baltic approaches, and off Baltic ports from Kiel to the Gulf of Danzig. Thus, in less than forty-eight hours, 386 aircraft had laid 1,051 mines from the Spanish frontier to the Gulf of Danzig.

The Wellington contribution had been thirty-one aircraft the first night, for no loss, and forty-seven the second night,

from which six failed to return; as mentioned before, losses from these 'less hazardous' missions were often high.

The Battle of the Ruhr continued throughout the early part of the summer, incorporating a new directive of 3 June that instigated the Combined Bombing Offensive with the Americans, as Operation *Pointblank*. This had no immediate effect on the targets being attacked as many of Harris's preferred cities were included on the list. Bomber Command carried the war to Germany's cities throughout the year, new tactics, techniques and equipment being introduced in an effort to counter the growing strength of the German defences and to obtain greater accuracy and weight of attack. However, throughout the latter half of the year Wellington strength continued to decrease and by September was of little overall significance within Bomber Command.

Throughout this history we have made little mention of the wide range of 'other' units that included Wellingtons amongst their establishment (a partial list of these is included in the appendices). However, one such unit was the Bombing Development Unit (BDU) which formed in February 1943 and included two Wellingtons amongst its various aircraft 'to carry out trials and experiments with any new bombing or navigation equipment produced for the command'. Units such as the Central Gunnery School operated a number of Welling-

tons as did various other training organizations – often with no reference to the presence of such aircraft within their official establishments. The type also made a useful transport aircraft and one of the units to use Wellingtons in a support role was 24 Squadron on transport and liaison duties. Wellingtons were frequently used for the Hendon to Belfast 'run', and on other routes that were serviced by this transport unit.

Special Duties

On 4 January, 1474 Flight became 192 Squadron, the Wellington Is and IIIs being phased out the following month and replaced by Mark Xs (although the unit also used Mosquito IVs and, from the summer, Halifax Vs). The unit remained at Gransden Lodge until April when it moved to Feltwell (and eventually, in November, to Foulsham), performing an Electronic Intelligence (ELINT) role. The unit was also involved with the development of new equipment for the RCM force. By the summer it was using other airfields as ALGs, Chivenor, Davidstow Moor and Predannack being used for operations in connection with the Bay of Biscay campaign.

The other specialist unit, 1473 Flight, likewise made a number of moves during the year, ending up at Little Snoring in September as part of the RAF's new RCM organization, No. 100 Group. It moved to

Fighter affiliation between CGS Wellington IA N2887 and a Mustang. Peter Green Collection

Vickers Warwick

Whilst not a direct part of this story, it is appropriate to give some mention to the Vickers Warwick as the lineage of this aircraft is firmly linked to that of the Wellington, or perhaps it would be more accurate to say, alongside that of the Wellington as the designs were progressed at the same time, the Warwick being intended as a more powerful heavy bomber. To take the argument even further it could be said that the Wellington was a scaled-down Warwick!

The design of the Warwick, to Specification B.1/35, was taking place at the same time as that of the Wellington – it was by no means a 'follow-on' to the Wellington – and both types had, for obvious reasons, many common design features. Numerous changes were made during the design stage, not least in the variety of engines which were specified, and the first flight, of K8178, took place on 13 August 1939 with Vulture engines. Development was, however, slow and it was not until January 1941 that orders were placed with Weybridge, the intention still being that the type would enter service as a bomber. The two initial production variants were to be the Warwick I, with Double Wasp engines, and Warwick II, with the Centaurus. It was, however, all too late and the type would not have been an effective bomber by the time it reached squadron service. The design did show promise

(Above) **Warwick BV403 carrying a Mark II airborne lifeboat.** FlyPast Collection

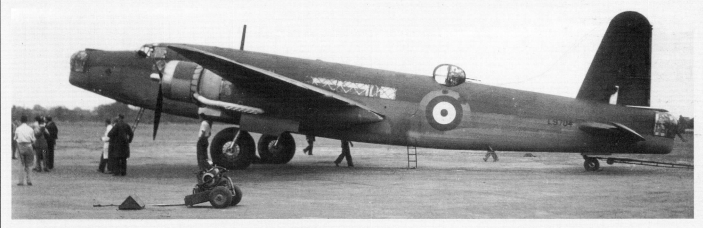

Warwick L9704. FlyPast Collection

(Left) **Looking very much like a Wellington, Warwick I HF944 in its airborne lifeboat role and wearing D-Day stripes.** FlyPast Collection

and it was decided that it could perform a useful role as a transport and troop-carrying aircraft and it was in these roles, initially as the C.1, that the Warwick began its career, serving with the British Overseas Airways Corporation as well as a number of military users. However, it is, perhaps, in its maritime guise that the aircraft is best remembered and especially that of Air/Sea Rescue.

An order was placed in 1943 for ASR variants equipped with Lindholme Gear or airborne lifeboats. The first unit to be equipped was 280 Squadron at Langham in August 1943. Further ASR variants entered service, as did a number of GR versions, and the Warwick served with a number of units.

Wellington IA N2990 in transport configuration with 24 Squadron, but with dummy gun turrets to fool enemy fighters. FlyPast Collection

Foulsham in December and was there joined by 192 Squadron (who in January 1944 absorbed the flight).

Maritime War

The early part of 1943 brought two new Wellington variants into service, both for the maritime role; the GR.XI first joined 407 Squadron in January and the GR.XIII joined 612 Squadron in March.

The Wellington XI was developed from the Mark X, HF720 being the first of 180 production aircraft (105 by Weybridge and 75 by Blackpool). The aircraft was equipped with the tried and tested ASV II, and thus carried the distinctive four aerials along its spine (which earned all such Wellingtons the nickname 'Stickle-backs'), although this equipment was not fitted to every Wellington XI.

Specification – Wellington XI	
ENGINES	Two Bristol Hercules VI or XVI
DIMENSIONS	Span 86ft 2in (26.11m); length 64ft 7in (19.57m)
PERFORMANCE	Max. speed 255mph (408km/h); ceiling 22,000ft (6,667m)
ARMAMENT	4,500lb (2,000kg) bombs
NUMBER BUILT	180

The Wellington XIII was also a development of the Mark X, but was given two 1,735hp Hercules XVII engines, thus making it amongst the most powerful of all the Wellington variants. The first production aircraft was HZ551 and a total production run of 883 followed (the last operational examples did not leave RAF service, with 294 Squadron, until April 1946). Like other GR variants, this one was equipped with the distinctive ASV II; it was primarily intended for torpedo operations. The GR.XII was another maritime variant of the Mark X, entering service in December 1942 and, carrying ASV III, was intended for anti-submarine operations; only fifty-eight were built.

The number of Wellington units involved in the battle against the Axis U-boats increased during 1943; two in particular had successful years – 172 Squadron with 19 Group and 179 Squadron operating from Gibraltar. No. 172 Squadron had formed at Chivenor in April 1942 from 1417 (Leigh Light) Flight, which itself had only been in existence since March (see previous chapter). The first victory of the year went to Fg Off G. D. Lundon in the early hours of 19 February when he came across U-268 on the surface and, catching it unawares, sank it with four depth-charges. By spring 1943 the Wellington VIIIs had gone and, until August, the squadron operated Mark XIIs, these remaining in service until October but having been joined by Wellington XIVs in August.

The increased German U-boat activity in the Bay of Biscay and the British determination to gain the upper hand in the U-boat war led to a number of both tactical and technical developments. Amongst the latter was the fitting of ASV III to the squadron's aircraft from March to counter German use of the Metox detector. Success soon followed. The first contact and attack using ASV III was made by Wellington /B of 172 Squadron on 3 March; the commander of U-333 reported that he '...received no warning on his Metox set and that his boat was slightly damaged in the attack – the Wellington was shot down'. The aircraft, MP505, flown by Flt Sgt J. Tweddle, was, in fact, undamaged, and, in turn, thought that it had inflicted mortal damage on the U-boat. (Although the RAF narrative records the U-boat as U-333, it appears to have been U-525.)

However, in general, the number of sightings had fallen drastically in recent months, in part due to a change of tactics by the Germans but primarily due to the warnings they received from Metox of the presence of an ASV aircraft. It was hoped that the introduction of the 10cm ASV III would redress the balance and, as a trial, Coastal Command instituted Operation Enclose. Eight squadrons (including the Wellington-equipped 172, 304 and 311) of No. 19 Group were allocated to this operation for the period 20–28 March, covering a 140-mile band running north–south across the Bay, the idea being to 'maintain a constant stream of aircraft sweeping south and returning on the reciprocal track'. The operation was considered to have been a success, twenty-six sightings being made and two U-boats being claimed: U-332 damaged on 21 March and U-665 being sunk the following day, both falling to 172 Squadron.

547 Squadron Wellington VIII. Andy Thomas Collection

The official caption reads: 'An RAF mechanic, working on a Coastal Command base in the Azores, pauses for a moment to admire the sturdy oxen used by local labour on the airfield.' FlyPast Collection

This 'ribbon' tactic became standard and *Enclose 2* was flown from 5–13 April, an additional Wellington unit, 407 Squadron, taking part. This experienced Coastal Command unit had moved from Scotland to Chivenor in March and received Wellington XIs and XIIs (plus XIVs from July onwards) to join the intensive 19 Group campaign over the Bay. *Enclose 2* brought a number of sightings and two successes, although only one of these fell to the Wellingtons, Plt Off Whiteley of 192 Squadron putting paid to U-376 on 10 April.

Having formed with Leigh Light Wellingtons at Docking in January, 407 Squadron began operations in March, moving to Chivenor the following month to strengthen the Bay of Biscay patrols. April brought 179 Squadron back to the UK, to

Predannack, to strengthen Coastal Command's anti-submarine force and this experienced unit was soon heavily engaged. The ribbon patrol line was changed to reflect intelligence analysis that the U-boats were using different routes and a new patrol was instituted under Operation *Derange*.

April also saw 547 Squadron become operational in its torpedo-bomber role, the squadron having formed the previous October at Holmsley South (moving to Chivenor in December and then Tain in January 1943). The original intention was to 'counter blockade runners into and out of the Bay of Biscay; to work in this area at long range equipped with ASV to operate in conjunction with shadowing aircraft'.

172 Squadron continued to show their expertise and recorded two more scores, damaging U-566 on 26 April, U-437 on 29

April and U-415 on 1 May. The RAF's anti-U-boat campaign was paying dividends and causing enormous disruption to U-boat operations; on 28 April the U-boat commander, Admiral Dönitz, ordered a change of tactics with the U-boats to submerge at night and only surface during the day for the minimum time. The number of day attacks began to increase and with little option left, a number of submarine commanders fitted extra armament on their boats and elected to stay on the surface and fight it out with their attackers – on 6 May this became official policy and two U-boats were equipped as *Flak* boats. This, added to the policy of group sailings by the U-boats, led to the climax of this phase of the Battle of the Bay in July and August.

Wellingtons claimed four U-boats during this period, three being sunk by 172

Wellington GR.XIII, still with the distinctive aerials of the early versions of ASV; the type entered service
with 612 Squadron in March 1943. FlyPast Collection

Unusual view of a Coastal Command Wellington XIII, probably JA144. FlyPast Collection

Squadron and one being damaged by 547 Squadron. This latter unit's first success in its new role (although, as yet, on day operations only as Leigh Lights had not been fitted) came on 2 August when Plt Off J. Hermiston attacked U-218. Although the depth-charge attack was unsuccessful, the machine-gun attacks caused a number of casualties as well as minor damage.

On the same day, 'At 0932, Wellington C/407 Squadron had re-located U-106 and immediately delivered a low-level

replaced the *Musketry* and *Seaslug* areas with a new series of zones: *Percussion* A to E, Area C being the main one for the Wellington Leigh Light squadrons. It covered the area 45–42 degrees north and 11–9 degrees west, although it was subsequently decided that the Wellingtons did not have sufficient range to satisfactorily cover the southern part of this box, and so their operations were restricted to the northern part, the southern area being covered by Leigh Light Catalinas. It was

Specification – Wellington XIV	
ENGINES	Two Bristol Hercules XVII
DIMENSIONS	Span 86ft 2in (26.26m); length 64ft 7in (19.68m)
PERFORMANCE	Max. speed 250mph (400km/h); ceiling 16,500ft (5,000m)
ARMAMENT	6 × 0.303in guns, 4,000lb (1,800kg) bombs
NUMBER BUILT	841

GR.XII JA144; the Wellington XII entered service with 172 Squadron in December 1942 but only fifty-eight were built. Ken Delve Collection

attack in *Flak* rendered inaccurate by the excellent smothering fire from the front guns. The depth charges were well placed and seriously damaged U-106 which had to turn back for home, signalling for assistance.' (AHB *Narrative*, The RAF in the Maritime War.) The submarine had been attacked by Sunderlands before found by the Wellington and was hit again by Sunderlands, finally being abandoned by her crew.

As part of the continual re-appraisal of the operational areas, Coastal Command

obvious, and had been for some time, that the Leigh Light Wellingtons were of prime importance to cover the nearer areas and so, in August, the AOC requested that 304 and 547 Squadrons should re-equip from night torpedo-bomber to Leigh Light.

August also brought another Wellington variant into operational service, the GR.XIV. This variant carried ASV III in a chin turret, thus losing the standard nose turret, although a dummy nose was painted on some aircraft, as well as the now fairly standard Leigh Light. Powered by two

1,735hp Hercules, the variant was an effective maritime weapon and 841 were built at the various Vickers plants.

The experts of 172 Squadron had no more luck during 1943, but UK-based Wellingtons did score twice more, Plt Off E. O'Donnell of 407 Squadron sinking U-669 on 7 September and W/O I. Gunn of 612 Squadron sinking U-96 on 10 November.

The *Percussion* series of areas was extended to include *Percussion* E to be covered by the aircraft operating out of Gibraltar (a Coastal Command station); this is an

A mud-spattered Wellington XI, MP521, photographed in January 1943; this variant entered service that month with 407 Squadron, some 180 being built. FlyPast Collection

appropriate point at which to look at the Wellington operations from the Rock. 179 Squadron had formed in September 1942 by expanding a detached flight from 172 Squadron at Skitten to squadron status. The unit had moved to Gibraltar with its Wellington VIIIs in mid-November 1942 (*see* previous chapter) and was a critical asset in the battle against U-boats passing through the Straits. The first Wellington XIVs arrived in August – just in time for a renewed burst of activity.

In September Dönitz had ordered seven U-boats to run the Straits of Gibraltar in the no-moon period to reinforce the Mediterranean squadron after the collapse of Italy. The first of these U-boats attempted the passage towards the end of the month; in the 48-hour period from 0247 on 24 September, U-667 was attacked six times by 179 Squadron (for the loss of one aircraft) and severely damaged, being forced to retire. U-223 received numerous scares, though no actual attacks, and reported that the passage

was impossible (a reflection of the effect of the RAF's campaign on the submariners' morale). Dönitz ordered the remaining U-boats not to try.

As the nature of the maritime war changed, so Coastal Command had to alter its pattern of patrols; one aspect of this was the creation of 247 (Azores) Group which came into being in late 1943 following negotiations between the British and Portuguese governments. Wellington detachments were amongst those sent to the Azores to conduct anti-submarine patrols; for example, 179 Squadron sent a detachment from Gibraltar to Lagens (this eventually returned to Chivenor in mid-April 1944). The detachment scored two successes in November: on the 19th, Fg Off McRae located and sank U-211, whilst on the 28th Sqn Ldr Knott in HF168 attacked and sank U-542.

U-boats were not the only threat to concern Coastal Command, and at a conference on 20 August the Air Ministry agreed that action needed to be taken to

counter the threat from German E-boats. As part of a new tactical plan it was decided to use ASV-equipped Wellingtons for reconnaissance, to work in conjunction with Fleet Air Arm Albacores as the attack element. This was subsequently modified to give 415 Squadron a flight of Wellington XIIIs with ASV III along with an Albacore flight. By late October the Wellington element was almost complete and tactical concepts were studied that resulted in the inception of Operation *Deadly*, the first mission taking place on 3 November. A tactical conference on 6 October had decided that four patrol areas should be established east of the main convoy route and that the Wellingtons should fly whenever conditions favoured E-boat operations.

The long hours of darkness during the winter months favour the employment of E-boats against our east coast trade routes. The intention is to locate enemy light surface forces and vector our light surface forces on to them.

The distinctive chin-mount for the centimetric ASV III as seen on Wellington XII MP512 in January 1943.
FlyPast Collection

Superb shot of rocket-carrying Wellington XIV MP714. FlyPast Collection

(Opposite) **Wellington XIV with underwing rocket projectiles. The rockets had proved an effective anti-shipping weapon on other types such as the Beaufighter.** FlyPast Collection

415 Squadron are to maintain three serviceable aircraft at Bircham Newton with effect from 27 October 1943. They are to be prepared to fly any two of the patrols detailed in Appendix C whenever the weather conditions favour the employment of E-boats against our eastern coast trade routes at night ... The aircraft is to continue to shadow the enemy force, remaining as nearly as possible over them and switching on Rooster until our own light coastal forces and enemy forces are seen together on the screen, when the aircraft is to drop a flare and continue to illuminate the enemy. (No. 16 Group Operation Order 6/1943, Operation *Deadly*)

The tactical concept had been changed from using an air striking force to that of using light naval forces; however, No. 16 Group issued another instruction, for Operation *Gilbey*, in January 1944 as an extension of the tactical concept for 'Night torpedo attack using flares dropped by special aircraft' – the special aircraft being Wellingtons and the strike aircraft, torpedo Beaufighters.

Training Role

Expansion of the bomber force continued throughout 1943 as an increasing number of squadrons were formed or re-equipped with, in most cases, the four-engined heavies such as the Halifax and Lancaster. It was, however, the Wellington that bore the brunt of the work at the Operational Training Units throughout the country; the number of OTUs peaked in December 1943 with 22½ units (with a strength of

almost 1,300 aircraft) receiving input of crews for training. As Sir Arthur Harris said in his *Despatch on War Operations*,

... it was quickly found that only aircrew with operational experience could successfully train crews from the OTU stage onwards; but owing to the constant expansion of the front line, and the rate of casualties at the height of the war, which did not allow for a large number of tour-expired aircrew becoming available as instructors, there was always a lag in the number of pilot instructors. For a considerable period there was also a deficiency in the number of navigators and air bombers ... in consequence of this, until well into 1944, training units had to struggle along with their strength of instructors well below establishment. Moreover, instructors, having once started to instruct, were kept in the training units very much longer than was originally intended, owing to the difficulty of finding the capacity to train new instructors when in the course of time they became available. The work done by some of the long-term instructors was tremendous.

The same could also be said of the Wellington itself; at a time when front-line bombers were in short supply, the trusted old Wimpey proved to be a rugged, reliable and essential workhorse in the vital training role, a role in which its part has all too often been overlooked.

At the beginning of the year the situation appeared stable and the training course well established; indeed, there was a surplus of most trades except pilots, although the decision to reduce the pool of spare pilots per operational squadron from

six to one (plus the commanding officer) eased this. However, by April Bomber Command was over one hundred crew short, due to an increase in loss rates plus a change of policy that required an increase of two crews per squadron. To overcome this problem it was decided to increase the OTU intakes from sixteen to eighteen crews every two weeks. This matching of input to output was a continual problem for the training units; the 'training tap' could not be turned on and off at short notice. The output requirement was set at 383 crews in March with a planned increase to 622 by December. To meet this increase it was decided to increase the number of medium bomber OTUs to twenty-four by September, partly achieved by increasing the size of some of the existing units and creating new units; for example, in March, 18 (Polish) OTU was increased to full size to become a standard OTU with a Polish flight. By June 1943 there were 19½ OTUs, all but four (Whitleys) being equipped with Wellingtons. A full-size OTU had a notional strength of fifty-four aircraft and was capable of producing thirty-two crews a month in the summer and twenty-two in the winter.

There were supposed to be forty-seven electricians at 16 OTU, there were actually sixteen to look after sixty-four Wimpeys. The Wellington was beloved of everybody, aircrew and ground-crew and I knew every one of my sixty-four. It may sound crazy but to me they were children who needed the loving care we lavished on them. They weren't bits of metal, wood and fabric, they

Wellington X HE508 of 84 OTU. Peter Green Collection

Fine line-up of 30 OTU aircraft being prepared for a
Nickel **sortie, 11 September 1943.** Ken Delve Collection

(Below) **Z1732 of 12 OTU.** Ken Delve Collection

were living creatures whose needs were real and demanding. (Gerard Duncan)

John Long was posted to 21 OTU at Moreton, but did most of his flying from the satellite at Enstone:

On arrival we were directed to one of the hangars where the completely undirected process of 'crewing up' took place. Pilots, navigators, wireless operators, bomb aimers and gunners all milled around, making their categories and names known to each other as the random selection process went on. Having crewed up, through the rest of July and on into September we became a 'unit'. We were learning not only how to operate our war machine but also about each other ... we practised war-load take-offs,

fighter affiliation, navigation and dropped real sticks of bombs. I spent 13½ hours (6½ at night) at the controls of the Wellington, learning enough to get us home if our pilot, Tommy, got hit on operations. I always flew in the 'second dickey' seat and, to all intents, that's what I was ... as well as back-up navigator, gunner and wireless operator because, when push came to shove, I could have stepped into their shoes too!

Preparing aircraft for a Nickel sortie; these leaflet-dropping sorties were used almost as a 'final test' on the OTUs. Ken Delve Collection

Gerard Duncan was an aircraft electrician on Wellingtons at 16 OTU, Upper Heyford, and he recalls that life could be quite hairy for the groundcrew, especially if invited to go along on a test flight, as happened 'one fine day in October 1943':

The test pilot instructed me on my duties during flight, instructions such as noting the readings on the various instruments as required by himself. Before the pilot ran up the engines he checked movable items in the cockpit such as the escape hatch above his head, which he found to be not performing as it should, so he called to one of the riggers who came up the outside of the fuselage to make an adjustment which satisfied the test pilot, although it was still sticking. He signalled the flight sergeant to run up the engines, one at a time, on the mobile starting battery. Whilst all this was going on I was having difficulty with the entrance hatch – it would not stay shut so I was obliged to stand with one foot on it to keep it shut. Once airborne the pilot gave me a list of the instruments that would need to be checked – this was like a foreign country as most of them meant nothing to an aircraft electrician whose usual job was engine magnetos, bomb gear, batteries and aircraft lighting! The single engine tests were carried out and the pilot was setting up for a full power check on both engines when there was an almighty crack from the port side of the cockpit, the canopy flew open, the pilot shot out of the opening and the exit slammed shut trapping one poor aircraft electrician in a now pilotless Wimpey. The canopy blew shut and the exit hatch blew open such that I could squeeze through the opening. I remembered to pull the ripcord and so floated

down in some discomfort as I had not put on the harness in the correct fashion.

After a summer when expansion was the watchword, in November, Bomber Command requested a slowing down of OTU output as too many crews were clogging up the system further down. This was in part due to a reorganization of the HCUs and also to a reduction in the loss rates. Thus, each OTU had seven courses: five in training, one on leave and one awaiting posting. Typically, 22 OTU had 420 pupils in October (eighty-seven pilots, sixty-eight navigators, sixty-six WOP/AGs and 159 air gunners), with Courses 50 to 54 in training and an aircraft strength of forty-seven Wellington IIIs and eleven Wellingtons Xs.

Middle East

The major air effort in the first half of 1943 was in support of the Allied operations in Tunisia, with all of the Wellington units being involved. The Wellington IIIs of 150 Squadron were primarily tasked against ports and airfields, the latter often in conjunction with protecting Allied convoys; the ORB recorded for 17 February,

... a maximum effort was requested for convoy protection, our job is to ground the German aircraft at Elmas and Decimmomannu. Three waves of aircraft are to go against each target and aircraft are to stay in the area for 1½ hours. It is hoped to keep the enemy on the ground all night.

In the event, however, the mission was scrubbed at 1830; nevertheless, the overload fuel tanks were left fitted to the aircraft as it was anticipated that the same tasking would occur over the next few days. The same happened over the next two days: the Wellingtons were on standby but poor weather conditions prevented the sorties taking place, but the same bad weather also prevented the Germans from operating and so protected the convoy. Typical targets at this time were the docks at Trapani and Ferryville and the airfields at Elmas, Vallacidro and Medenine. There were also a number of special operations, such as that of early January when Plt Off Roberts of 150 Squadron was tasked with dropping supplies to encircled French troops.

However, great effort was also expended in rather more direct support of the ground forces; this was especially true from late February with the start of the Eighth Army offensive. The 70 Squadron ORB records two typical missions: On the night of 25–26 February,

... the target was Gabes West LG, a *Stuka* base, but instead of spreading the attack over a period as done on previous nights, the two wings concentrated on a blitz with aircraft of 37 Squadron providing [flare] illumination for each of the targets. One of them was to fire Verey cartridges to indicate that there were good targets on the LG, otherwise the town would bear the full weight of the attack ... [and, on 9 March,] ... most effort was devoted to helping the army break through the Mareth Line by

January 1943 and HE115 of 40 Squadron at El Adem after a forced landing due to fuel starvation.
Reg Thackery via John Hamlin

The strategic port of Benghazi shows the effect of Allied bombing; the stern of an ammunition ship rests on the Cathedral Mole. Ken Delve Collection

attacking troop and MT concentrations. Albacores were used as illuminators on these sorties.

The Germans fed in major reinforcements but these, after some initial success, had little effect and by April the German air corridor had been all but destroyed. After the collapse of the Mareth Line, 205 Group concentrated at Kairouan; the final attack in this campaign was made on the night of 11–12 May by twelve Wellingtons of 40 Squadron on the Hammamet–Menzel –Timimi road.

To Italy

The Axis forces in Tunisia finally surrendered on 12 May 1943. A few days before this, No. 330 Wing was formed, under Gp Capt J Powell, within 205 Group, and comprised 142 and 150 squadrons at

Malta to rejoin the rest of the squadron at Protville towards the end of May, to become part of 332 Wing within the Coastal Air Force.

good results were obtained. Our aircraft went down to 100ft to machine gun seaplanes lined up on the tarmac. Lido di Roma seemed to be defended by a single machine gun. (150 Squadron ORB)

It was now both possible and desirable to increase the bomber strength for this next phase and as part of the air build-up a further four Wellington squadrons arrived in theatre. Three of these, 420, 424 and 425 Squadrons, all Canadian units, went to form 331 (RCAF) Wing at Kairouan/Zina,

Foggia, with aircraft of 40 Squadron at the main base for 205 Group's strategic bomber force after the move to Italy. Peter Green Collection

The Wellington force operating from Malta had been strengthened in January when 221 Squadron moved to Luqa from Shallufa and re-equipped with Wellington XIs and XIIs as part of 248 Wing under AHQ Malta. Likewise, a detachment of 458 Squadron became operational out of Malta during January with its Wellington VIIIs, some of which were equipped for torpedo bombing – the detachment left

Fontaine Chaude, Algeria. Amongst the memorable missions flown by 150 Squadron was one to Rome on 16 May when twelve aircraft were despatched to drop leaflets and also to attack the seaplane base at Lido di Roma:

... all crews clearly identified Rome in the brilliant moonlight before dropping their leaflets. Lido di Roma was also found successfully and

becoming operational in June. Their first mission took place on 26 June when 420 and 425 Squadrons attacked the airfield at Sciatica. The following day saw 424 Squadron's first operation, the plan being for twelve aircraft to attack San Giovani; only eight were actually bombed up in time because of problems with facilities at the airfield and of these one dropped a bomb on take-off (which went un-noticed!) and one had a puncture on take-off, causing the aircraft to crash, breaking the starboard wing.

Meanwhile, part of the Allied build-up called for the seizure of the fortified islands of Lampedusa and Pantelleria, both of which were subjected to heavy air attack, in which many of the Wellington squadrons played a full part, flying bombing missions nightly between 25 May and the surrender of the islands in mid-June. Following one raid on Lampedusa, the 150 Squadron diarist was quick to comment that 'that the raid was successful may be deducted from the fact that the island surrendered to our forces the very next day.'

Throughout June and into July the Allied air forces attacked targets in Sicily and mainland Italy:

On 25–26 June [we] were given a new and interesting target on the east coast of Italy, namely the oil refinery at Bari. Twelve aircraft took off but over the target area was considerable haze and extreme darkness persisted making identification difficult. Only three crews claim to have positively identified the target and the majority bombed fires which they considered to have been in the target area. However, subsequent photographs showed that the target had been missed.

Such industrial targets were a rarity and the major effort remained that against lines of communication, airfields and tactical support of ground operations. The above extract from the 150 Squadron ORB does, however, highlight the continued problems of accurate bombing on nights when the weather was poor – the bomber squadrons in this theatre were not (yet) as well provided with blind flying aids or tactics such as pathfinder forces as their colleagues in Main Force Bomber Command.

In addition the Wellingtons also conducted a vigorous anti-shipping campaign. It was as part of this effort that the fourth new unit, 36 Squadron (which in due course became part of 338 Wing), became involved, initially flying ASW missions with its Wellington VIIIs. In a slightly surprising move, the unit had come from India – where lack of Japanese submarine activity had made their services somewhat

redundant – and moved in to Blida in early June (the groundcrew eventually arriving late in July).

The assault forces hit the beaches of Sicily on 10 July under massive air and naval support. This event was recorded in all of the squadron ORBs; the 40 Squadron books says,

... on the night of 9–10 July the invasion of Sicily began and to 40 Squadron was allotted an important part in assisting First Airborne Division which was to advance from Augusta towards Syracuse where they would take up positions near the town and await our attack. The confidence of the military authorities in the accuracy of Wellington bombing was such that a bomb line only 500yd from our target was accepted.

The ORB then says that a signal was received from the CO of the Division, Major General Hopkinson. 'I would be most grateful if you would let your aircrews know how much their efforts on that night were appreciated by the Army, and I would like to add my personal thanks to you for all the trouble you took to make it a success.'

LN385 of 150 Squadron at Foggia in August 1943. Andy Thomas Collection

No. 205 Group had 123 Wellingtons airborne that night supporting the landings.

It was not only bombs that were being dropped on the Axis forces in Sicily; there was also an intensive leaflet campaign. (Indeed, the Wellingtons were dropping an ever-increasing number of leaflets on various places in Italy as Allied intelligence indicated that it would take little to drive Italy out of the war.) A message was sent to 40 Squadron by the colonel commanding the Psychological Warfare Branch:

[The] first interrogations of prisoners from Sicily shows that everybody has seen the leaflets and has welcomed them. In Palermo and Messina the leaflets you dropped calling for peace demonstrations were followed by such demos. Practically all the leaflets distributed in the Italian campaign were carried by the Wellingtons. I have so stated in my official report and congratulations for your co-operation in a task which we know adds something to the risk of your missions.

The campaign in Sicily went well and with tactical air support progress was rapid, and by early August the Axis forces were facing their own Dunkirk; this was recorded in the ORBs of a number of the Wellington units as they began a new phase of operations. The 40 Squadron diarist wrote on 5 August:

The campaign in Sicily having reached a stage at which evacuation attempts by the enemy might be expected, tonight's target was the beaches above Messina where the presence of small boats for this purpose was suspected. Fourteen aircraft operated, ranging up and down the 10-mile stretch of beach in search of suitable targets. One crew descended to 1,000ft to machine gun the beaches.

The night was not without loss, however, and two of 40 Squadron's Wellingtons failed to return. Sicily finally fell on 17 August and Major General J. H. Doolittle, commander of NWASAF (North West African Strategic Air Force) sent a signal to 205 Group for the Wellington squadrons:

I wish to further congratulate you and the entire Wellington force, for since 1 July until the fall of Sicily on 17 August the Wellington force has flown a total of 3,020 sorties, an average of sixty-two sorties a night, have dropped in that time 5,300 tons of bombs on enemy lines of communication and have dropped 20,739,000 *Nickels*. The

Wellingtons have sustained a total loss of fifty-one aircraft, a percentage of 1.7 per cent. This excellent record is going to be difficult for any organization in our Allied Air Force to duplicate.

The Allied advance took its next major step in September with the first ground forces landing on mainland Italy, and the air plan included key roles for the strategic bombers. Attacks on the lines of communication were considered to be the strategic key and Operation *Strangle* was designed to deny the enemy freedom of movement and thus the ability to move his forces to threatened areas or re-supply those already engaged. A significant element in the movement of troops and supplies was the railway and much effort was expended on trying to shut down the rail network in Italy by attacking key node points, especially marshalling yards and, later, bridges. The former were, in theory at least, good targets for strategic bombers such as the Wellingtons. August 1943 saw a particularly concentrated effort against key yards. On 1 August American bombers attacked Naples marshalling yard, attempting to close all the entry/exit points; that night some fifty bombers of 205 Group were tasked to shower the area with incendiaries and delayed action bombs. Unfortunately, poor weather meant poor results. The following extract from the 70 Squadron ORB details a typical attack:

For the second time in three nights the group effort of fifty aircraft was turned to the Bagnoli Marshalling Yards, Naples. Eight aircraft were detailed and crews briefed out but only seven took off, 'S' being unserviceable with magneto trouble, and the reserve 'O' taking the place of 'U' who stuck whilst taxiing and had port engine overheat. Of the seven which took off, all claimed to have arrived in the target area, five on bombing and two illuminators. Illumination was well concentrated over target, although some flares illuminated Pozzvoli area further west. Bombing seems to have been well concentrated too, despite considerable searchlight and *Flak* opposition, upwards of twenty searchlights being reported from the Naples area. *Flak* consisted of accurate heavy from target area, tracer from Pozzvoli. Weather good, no cloud. Bombing 2354 to 0001 from 8–11,000ft, 12 × MC 500lb with ¼sec delay, 13x500lb GP with ¼sec delay and 20x500lb GP with long delay.

September saw yet another Wellington unit in theatre with the formation, at

Berca, of 294 Squadron by giving squadron status to the Air Sea Rescue Flight which had performed invaluable work; the primary task was ASR in the eastern Mediterranean and the squadron was rarely together at one place, detachments being operated from a number of airfields from Palestine to Libya.

Enemy air opposition continued to be light but over certain targets the *Flak* defences were still significant and not all of the bombing missions were without loss, albeit on most occasions loss rates were never on the same scale as those suffered by Main Force over Germany. One exception to this was a raid against Turin in late November in which seventeen Wellingtons from the total force of seventy-six were lost – a horrendous loss rate when compared against all previous missions. Report N7 (dated 12 December 1943) from the ORS examined 'Losses on the Turin raid of November 24/25' The report began:

ORS (MAAF) was requested by 205 Group to attempt to determine the causes of the heavy losses incurred on the night of 24–25 November during the course of a raid against the ball-bearing factory at Turin. Losses were:

Unit	A/C Despatched	FTR	Remarks
231 Wing			
37 Sqn	14	4	2 crews later returned
70 Sqn	13	3	1 crewman survived
236 Wing			
40 Sqn	14	3	
104 Sqn	11	2	
330 Wing			
142 Sqn	14	5	1 crew later returned
150 Sqn	10	0	

While a number of factors must have contributed to the losses, there can be no doubt that the major factor involved was the difference between the weather found and that predicted. North of Corsica aircraft were flying continuously in cloud and had little or no opportunity of measuring their drift, as a result many were blown eastwards. Icing, cloud and turbulence prevented many crews from navigating correctly north of Corsica. It is probable that several aircraft became lost completely and being unable to discover their position were eventually forced into the sea ... There are good grounds to believe that many aircraft made landfall in the neighbourhood of Spezia and continued northwards to the same latitudes as Portofino without realizing that they were over land. In this event low flying aircraft would cross the coastline early and eventually crash on the high ground (4,000ft) in the neighbourhood of Spezia; for example, one pilot was surprised on breaking cloud to find himself in a narrow valley near Spezia and was only able to turn with difficulty.

The report concluded that it was unlikely that any of the losses had been directly due to enemy action and made recommendations concerning provision of meteorological forecasts and additional navigational training for some crews.

John Long joined 150 Squadron in November:

Our next operation was on 1 December – to drop 200,000 leaflets on the German and Italian troops in front-line positions. The leaflets carried the message, in German and Italian, that it was only a matter of time before Hitler would be brought to his knees, and for the Italians to pack it in! As we made our landfall at Gaeta, we started our run across Italy to the opposite shore at Pescara. We could see the artillery duels going on below. It fell to me and Doug Phipps to go down the back to the flare chute where the groundcrew had stacked the leaflets and wait for Tommy to tell us when to push out Italian ones and when to push out German ones. Phipps wasn't having any of this 'under the door delivery' stuff and kept shovelling them down the flare chute regardless of language! On 4 December word came that we were moving to Italy. Once again we packed up our parrots and monkeys, struck camp and loaded X for X-Ray with everything but the kitchen sink, and duly left for Cerignola. The aircraft was unevenly loaded because of its assorted but unusual load of extraneous equipment. We hit some peculiar air currents over Sicily and the kite became difficult to control, and we nearly came to grief. The weather turned very dirty over Sicily and it was an anxious time, flying blind around Etna but we finally made our new base in three hours.

By December the group had concentrated on airfields around Foggia:

We had our share of maintenance problems whilst at Foggia Main, mainly, I hasten to add, due to the environment rather than the Wellington itself. The big problem was with

tyres and I had a nice introduction when, having skidded off the wet clay runway at Cerignola, we landed at Foggia and the port tyre burst – fortunately at the end of the landing run. Having loaded up with tools, boxes, tents, beds, Jerry cans and whatever (concentrating the weight around the main spar) from floor to ceiling, I'm sure we did things to the C. of G. not envisaged by Barnes Wallis!

The tyre problem arose from the fact that the aerodrome had been bombed and shelled by us in its capture and the Germans had reciprocated when they were driven out. This led to a liberal sprinkling of shrapnel and splinters which sank below the surface during the winter; as the top soil was eroded this debris, firmly stuck in, appeared causing havoc with tyres. Thanks to the vigilance of the riggers, the electro-magnet which was built for sweeping the dirt runway and taxi-ways, plus the numerous checks carried out between missions, there were surprisingly few take-off incidents.

However, a small number of Wellingtons had also been playing a vital role in the electronic war; a detachment of 192 Squadron operated in theatre in the first half of 1943, mapping radars at various points around the shores of the Mediterranean. This work was recorded in a series of reports issued by the Operational Research Section of the MAAF; typical of these was report E.1 concerning *Freya* coverage in south-east Italy. In part it stated:

This investigation flight was carried out on 8 August by 192 Squadron detached flight in order to study *Freya* coverage on the south-east and south coasts of Italy from Vieste to Cape Santa Maria di Leuca and then to Cape Spartivento; (Wellington HE232/F, pilot Sqn Ldr Fernbank and special operator Fg Off Wilhelmson). The aircraft took off from Blida at 2105 and landed at Malta at 0545 having flown at heights of 500–2,000ft ... Two points of interest emerge. One is the use by the enemy of frequencies as high as 142.6 mcs (this has since been confirmed by American investigation flights); the other is the reception of *Freya* signals such a long way inland in mountainous country. This would suggest the use of very high sites in the Naples–Licosia area, possibly some little distance inland.

Such missions were of vital importance to Allied intelligence in putting together a clear picture of the capabilities of the enemy air defence systems. 192 Squadron was not, however, the only Wellington unit involved in this work as 162 Squadron was still operating a small number of aircraft on similar

duties. In January the unit had a detachment of two aircraft in Malta, a typical mission being that of 1 January when 'one Wellington operated from Malta on RDF investigation, course Malta–Cape Scalanbri/Santa Crace–Scilla–Capri–Naples–Siapani–Malta. The aircraft also bombed a concentration of searchlights at Trapani.' (162 Squadron ORB.)

Such sorties out of Malta were frequent events while the main Wellington part of the squadron operated from such places as Gambut and Benina, although aircraft were always in short supply. This situation worsened during the year, leading the diarist to comment,

... very little to report ... spares problems make it difficult to maintain high standards of serviceability. The total of 351 hours was possible owing to the fact that the squadron was allocated one Wellington X, this aircraft alone completing over 100 hours in August. Results have shown that if the squadron were re-equipped with Mk III Wellingtons, much better results could be obtained. (162 Squadron ORB)

Wellington strength had been reduced in October when the Canadian squadrons of 331 Wing returned to the UK. In November, No. 205 Group HQ moved to Ariana, near Tunis and its squadrons settled at nearby airfields. However, the offensive in Italy progressed rapidly and by the end of the year most units had moved to Italy, initially to Cerignola for a few days but eventually settling on the airfields around Foggia.

Far East

The two Wellington units continued the same routine in the early months of 1943, 215 Squadron with its supply and paratroop work and 99 Squadron with bombing operations against Japanese airfields, Heho being the most frequent target. However, by spring the situation had changed and it was planned to bring the units together as No. 170 Wing to become a strategic bombing force. In March, 215 Squadron moved to Jessore and sent crews to Digri for operational training with 99 Squadron; the first sortie mounted from Jessore was led by Wg Cdr Webster on 16 April when eight aircraft attacked enemy-held villages on Akyab island. April saw 99 Squadron moved to Chaklala and also the arrival of the first Wellington III (DV678) and X (HE641) from the Karachi ferry pool – 215

Squadron was also re-equipping with Wellington Xs. There was still some debate as to the future role of the squadron and a decision was delayed as to the fitting of parachute-dropping modifications to the new aircraft. By May it had been decided that the aircraft should not be modified and in that same month the squadron

(ACSEA) was formed under Air Chief Marshal Sir Richard Peirse as a combined Anglo-American air arm and with a more extensive geographical area under command, although this had no immediate effect on the bomber units. It remained a year of mixed fortunes with aircraft serviceability causing problems and periods when

creeping line-ahead search for a U-boat or life-boat'. Nothing was found and on the way back the aircraft became lost and had to force-land, fortunately with no serious injuries. The squadron flew searches for the lost aircraft and three days later Wg Cdr Green found them, dropped supplies and then landed nearby to pick up the crew.

Kairouan, 1943, and Wellington IV DF704. Andy Thomas Collection

moved the Jessore and began a period of intensive training with the new variants:

> Load tests with the new types gave an easy take-off with loads up to 4,000lb, and with the max load, heights of 11,000ft with full petrol were reached. Instruction was also begun for all air gunners on the new four-gun Fraser-Nash turret, but a serious difficulty here was the fact that many aircraft had been delivered from the UK with a faulty type of ball bearing in the turret and arrangements had to be made to fly from England supplies of the correct bearings. (99 Squadron ORB)

In June the squadrons began flying daily reconnaissance sorties of the Bay of Bengal and Arakan coast, although bombing missions were also being flown as and when weather conditions allowed. In August 1943 Air Command South East Asia

sickness amongst air and grounds crews also curtailed operations.

The bomber force was not the only Wellington unit in theatre as by late 1943 there were three Wellington-equipped squadrons engaged in maritime operations – 8 and 621 Squadrons at Khormaksar and 244 Squadron at Sharjah. The primary role of all these units was convoy escort and anti-submarine patrol of the Indian Ocean and adjacent coastal waters. No. 621 Squadron had formed on 9 September at Port Reitz under Wg Cdr P. Green with sixteen Wellington XIIIs as part of 246 Wing within AHQ East Africa. Three days later they were instructed to send a detachment of eight aircraft to Mogadishu, the first of these deploying on 18 September. Plt Off J. Glover flew the first operation from Mogadishu in HZ802 on 24 September, 'a

1 October brought a signal from 246 Wing that the operational detachment at Mogadishu was in future to carry six Torpex depth charges. By the middle of the month the whole squadron had moved to Mogadishu from Nairobi, but was soon running detachments at such places as Scuiscuiban and Bander Kassim. They also undertook 'colonial policing' at the request of local army commanders, flying reconnaissance missions looking for 'armed native raiding parties'.

> It was felt that Aden would be the scene of the more intensive operations and, following a special conference in November to examine the GR position in the whole Indian Ocean, a complete Wellington squadron was transferred from East Africa to bases covering the approaches to the Gulf of Aden. (RAF *Mediterranean Review* No. 7)

CHAPTER FIVE

1944–45: Final Operations

Special Duties

In the fifth year of its war, the Wellington was still playing a significant part in the Allied air effort at home and overseas. Although Bomber Command had a number of Wellington squadrons still operational within Main Force, these were all in the process of being re-equipped or re-roled, No. 1 Group removing the type from operational service in March. Thus, by spring 1944 the only unit within Bomber Command was 192 Squadron at Foulsham in the bomber support role as part of No. 100 Group, the squadron including a flight of, on average, six Wellingtons (these remained operational until January 1945). The Wellingtons continued to play a vital role throughout 1944; typical missions were those on 1 October when 'six SDFs to locate signals believed to be associated

with enemy radar-controlled missiles were undertaken on this date and all were carried out successfully. Four Wellingtons [and two P-38 Lightnings] patrolled an area about 30 miles off the Dutch coast between Walcheren and Texel' (192 Squadron ORB). The last Wellington operation was flown on 7 January 1945 when Fg Off Stephens and crew took HZ415 on an 'SD over the North Sea to investigate enemy beam signals connected with the launching of flying bombs and believed to emanate from marker buoys. Bad weather curtailed the flight.'

From May 1944 another specialist unit was in action, 69 Squadron having reformed at Northolt to operate Wellington XIIIs on night photo reconnaissance over Europe, becoming part of 34 (PR) Wing within 2nd Tactical Air Force (TAF). The squadron eventually became the first

Wellington unit to be based in northern Europe, moving to A12/Balleroy in September 1944. The aircraft used photo flashes for its night photo task but also carried flares for illuminating 'areas of interest' in order to locate targets worth photographing. Having moved to Melsbroek in late September, the squadron flew missions covering German lines of communication – the only safe time for the Germans to move was at night when the cover of darkness grounded the overwhelming Allied tactical air power. They were still present at that airfield on 1 January when the *Luftwaffe* launched Operation *Bodenplatte*, a last-ditch attempt to cripple Allied air power by destroying it on the ground. Although the overall plan was a disastrous failure, it did account for a number of Allied aircraft, including eleven of 69 Squadron's Wellingtons.

Wg Cdr Shaw, OC 69 Squadron, and other squadron members pose in front of Ritchie's Wonder at Melsbroek, Belgium, in October **1944.** Ken Delve Collection

Wellington ORBAT, July 1944

91 Gp			19 Gp		
Honeybourne	24 OTU		Chivenor	172, 304, 407 Sqns	
Lossiemouth	20 OTU		Docking	524 Sqn	
Moreton-in-Marsh	21 OTU		Predannack	179 Sqn	
Wellesbourne Mountford	22 OTU		St Eval	547 Sqn	
92 Gp			247 Gp, Azores		
Bruntington	29 OTU		Azores	det of 172 Sqn	
Bruntingthorpe	19 OTU				
Chipping Warden	12 OTU		MACAF		
Desborough	84 OTU		Bone	458 Sqn	
Husbands Bosworth	85 OTU				
Market Harborough	14 OTU		205 Gp, Foggia		
Silverstone	17 OTU		Amendola	142, 150 Sqns	
Upper Heyford	16 OTU		Foggia	40, 104 Sqns	
Wing	26 OTU		Tortorella	37, 70 Sqns	
Westcott	11 OTU				
			242 Gp, Taranto		
93 Gp			Grottaglie	221 Sqn	
Finningley	18, 30, 86 OTUs				
Lichfield	27 OTU		AHQ Eastern Mediterranean		
Ossington	82 OTU		Berka	38 Sqn	
Peplow	83 OTU		Edcu	162 Sqn	
Wymeswold	28 OTU		Gambut	det of 38 Sqn	
100 Gp			HQ Aden		
Foulsham	192 Sqn		Khormaksar	8, 621 Sqns	
			Masirah	244 Sqn	
2 TAF, 34 Wing					
Northolt	69 Sqn		West Africa Command		
			Dakar	344 Sqn	
16 Gp					
Bircham Newton	415 Sqn		225 Gp, Bangalore		
			Santa Cruz	203 Sqn	
17 Gp					
Silloth	6 OTU		231 Gp, Calcutta		
Haverfordwest	4 RFU		Jessore	99 Sqn	
Killadeas	12 OFIS				

The sole operational Wellington element within Bomber Command was now 192 Squadron with 100 Group and this unit continued its ELINT work throughout 1944. With the advent of other types into the role, the Wellingtons, now concentrated into A Flight, spent most of their time patrolling over the North Sea. When the Germans launched their V-2 attacks on the UK the RAF responded with its 'Big Ben' patrols, trying to catch the ballistic missiles at launch, and as part of this strategy the Wellingtons of 192 Squadron flew virtually round-the-clock patrols.

The last of the Wellington Xs left the squadron's operational register by early January 1945, bringing to an end another chapter in the Wellington story.

Maritime War

By 1944 the primary operational role for home-based units was in association with the maritime war, especially within No. 19 Group, five of whose ten ASW units were equipped with Wellingtons, three of these having Leigh Light aircraft.

The squadrons soon notched up their first attacks for 1944, Wellington MP756 of 612 Squadron attacking and damaging U-373 on 3 January. 'On *Percussion* patrol a radar contact was made and after homing in a surfaced U-boat was seen in the Leigh Light, depth-charges being dropped from 75ft, 80ft ahead of the swirl left by the crash-diving sub.' The U-boat was picked

The only Wellington unit to operate with Second Tactical Air Force, 69 Squadron, flew night reconnaissance missions. Ken Delve Collection

The Luftwaffe **attack on Allied airfields on 1 January 1945, Operation** Bodenplatte, **scored few successes, but it did manage to destroy a significant number of 69 Squadron's aircraft.**
Ken Delve Collection

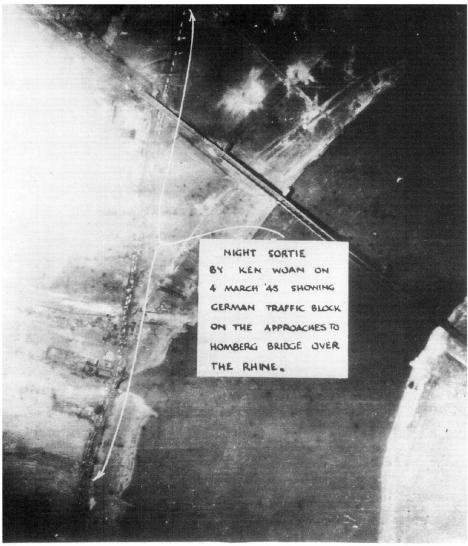

NIGHT SORTIE BY KEN WOAN ON 4 MARCH '45 SHOWING GERMAN TRAFFIC BLOCK ON THE APPROACHES TO HOMBERG BRIDGE OVER THE RHINE.

Night reconnaissance photo taken by 69 Squadron in March 1945. Ken Delve Collection

(Above) **Wellington X LP805 of the Malta Communications Flight.** Andy Thomas Collection

172 Sqn. Wellington using ASV VI to locate, track and attack a German U-boat using only the radar return from the Schnorkel. Jan 11 1945.

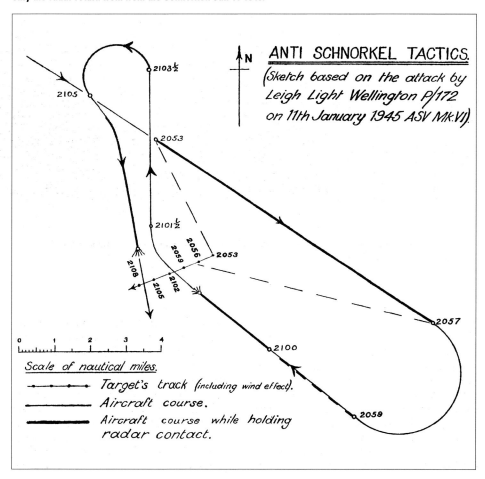

up again a few minutes later, but as the Wellington had no depth charges left it called a Halifax of 224 Squadron to the scene and this aircraft made a depth charge attack. The following night Wellington HF185 of 304 Squadron attacked and damaged U-629. The only other attack that month was on the 30th when Flt Sgt Richards in MP183 of 172 Squadron sank U-364 whilst on a *Percussion* patrol over the Bay of Biscay. Return fire from the U-boat, however, brought down the Wellington with the loss of its crew.

The introduction of the *Schnorkel* – which allowed U-boats to run their diesel engines, and so recharge their batteries, whilst submerged – had given the U-boats a significant tactical advantage and it was increasingly difficult for Coastal Command's aircraft to locate their enemy, especially at night. The Coastal Command *Quarterly Review* for early 1945 included an account of a Wellington attack:

On 11 January, Wellington P/172 was patrolling on a course of 124 degrees when at 2053 hours the radar operator picked up a contact at a range of 3½ miles bearing green 30 degrees. The captain checked target speed and when at 2057 hours contact bore 160 degrees range seven miles, turned starboard onto course 308 degrees. During this turn contact was lost but was regained intermittently at seven miles down to 3½ miles when it became steady. Height had now been lost to 200ft and contact remained dead ahead with no change of course. The captain continued homing to one mile when the Leigh Light was switched on. Nothing was seen owing to haze, and the aircraft climbed on course 360 degrees to 700ft for approximately two minutes and then turned to port on to a course of 140 degrees. Contact was regained at five miles bearing green 25 degrees and the aircraft altered course 30 degrees to starboard. Height was reduced to 150ft at three miles and when range was one mile Leigh Light was switched on illuminating a *Schnorkel*, course 220 degrees at 5kt. Sighting was made first by the second pilot and then immediately afterwards by the captain and navigator. The Wellington released six depth charges set to shallow depth, spaced at 60ft. The *Schnorkel* was visible at the time of the attack. The depth charges entered the water slightly ahead of the *Schnorkel* and the rear gunner saw at least four explosions. Two hundred rounds of tracer were fired into the depth charge plumes. The aircraft turned back to search the surface between the flame floats and two Mark II marine markers were dropped, but nothing was seen on account of smoke and haze.

given to the problems that the naval force would encounter, including the threat from U-boats and E-boats. As part of the pre-D-Day work-up, Sholto Douglas, as C-in-C Coastal Command, decided to

... temporarily curtail the operations of the searchlight squadrons in order that they make full use of the comparative lull in U-boat activity to complete a period of intensive training before the summer. This decision entailed an appreciable reduction in the operational effort of the Leigh Light squadrons but I decided to accept it in order to ensure the highest possible standard of skill in the night operational procedure. (Sir Sholto Douglas, *Despatches on Coastal Command Operations*)

April saw the formation of 524 Squadron at Davidstow Moor, the unit being equipped with ten Wellington XIIIs for the 'location and flare illumination of E-

In the event, Operation *Deadly* was suspended in late April as Coastal Command forces began their re-organization in preparation for D-Day.

Thus as the Allied landings grew nearer, Coastal Command had seven Wellington-equipped units ready for action: 172, 304, 407 and 612 at Chivenor, 179 at Predannack, 415 at Bircham Newton and 524 at Davidstow Moor. June 1944 was a particularly busy month for the anti-submarine units as intensive operations were flown in conjunction with the Allied amphibious assault at Normandy, the landings themselves taking place on 6 June. Although few U-boats were actually sunk, a number were damaged and the high level of air operations certainly restricted the activity of the German submarine force. 172 Squadron was amongst the most experienced of anti-U-boat units; typical of the missions flown by the

March 1945 and 458 Squadron pose for the camera at Gibraltar; the unit had been operating its Wellington XIVs from the Rock since January. K Ripley

The report stressed the importance of this attack. 'The captain and crew are to be congratulated on an excellent performance. It is encouraging to note that a *Schnorkel* can be held on ASV, while a speed check is made and that the aircraft can return to the spot having failed to carry out an attack at the first attempt.'

With the Allies finalizing their plans for the invasion of France, much attention was

boats so that attacks could be delivered by other aircraft or naval surface forces'. This was a further development of the moves already taken in late 1943 under Operations *Deadly* and *Gilbey*.

In April the Wellington squadrons involved in such tasks were also authorized to carry eight 100lb anti-submarine bombs, for which a Mk XIV bombsight had been fitted to the aircraft, so that they could, if required, make their own attacks.

squadron was that of 13 June when Plt Off L. Harris and crew in Wellington XIV MP789 sighted and attacked a U-boat:

At 2338 hours 4750N 0537W had radar contact at eight miles. Homed, experienced heavy *Flak* at one mile, switched on Leigh Light and illuminated a fully surfaced U-boat at ½ mile. Front gunner opened fire and then six depth charges were dropped straddling the stern of the U-boat. Continuous *Flak* was experienced during run in and rear gunner replied. Twice it was believed that the U-boat had submerged but it suddenly opened fire again and so 'Y' took evasive action. A 2359 hours a faint yellow glare was seen in position of flame floats which was followed by a very heavy explosion and a long streak of fire on the surface. A large column of black smoke rose to 1,000ft.

The submarine was U-270, a Type VIIC, and the attack had caused damage that was serious enough for her to be taken out of operational service.

Flt Lt Hill, 179 Squadron, on 7 June, U-989 to Sqn Ldr Farrell of 407 Squadron the same day, U-270 to Plt Off Harris of 172 Squadron on 13 June, and U-971 to Fg Off Foster of 407 Squadron on 20 June. John Saul served with 612 Squadron:

Joined OTU at Silloth on 30 November 1943 and upon completing our training were posted to 612 Squadron at Chivenor in March 1944. Whilst at Chivenor we took part in Operation *Cork*, when the English Channel was virtually sealed off against U-boats and surface craft

squadron had now been equipped with the new Mark 6a radar and this enabled the crew to detect a *Schnorkel* and allowed for blind bombing using the radar. It had a 360-degree timebase and gave very accurate map-like picture on the radar screen. In the event of a hostile blip, the operator fixed the blip, this allowed the aerial to follow the return no matter what the aircraft's attitude was. The captain then homed on to the hostile, and at three miles three lights came on – green, amber, red. The bomb-bay doors were opened and the navigator primed the bombs. At two miles the green

A camouflaged XIII, JA105. FlyPast Collection

Wellingtons of 19 Group claimed one sunk – U441 by Flt Lt Antoniewicz and crew in Wellington HF331 of 304 Squadron on 18 June – and four damaged (U-415 to

from attacking the D-Day landings. On 6 September the squadron was posted to Limavady to combat the *Schnorkel* menace that was at that time taking a toll of shipping. The

light went out, at one mile the amber light went out. When the red light went out the bombs were released and hopefully were accurately aimed at the target.

(Above) **April 1944 and GR.XIV MP818 of 36 Squadron; this aircraft was one of those transferred to the French Air Force in September 1946.** FlyPast Collection

407 Squadron GR.XIV at Chivenor, December 1944.
Andy Thomas Collection

A 179 Squadron GR.XIV wearing D-Day stripes at Predannack. R C B Ashworth

(Below)
MF639, a Wellington XIII of 415 Squadron, at Bircham Newton in May 1944.
Andy Thomas Collection

With detachments at Gibraltar and Lagens, 179 Squadron was spread thin but there was little option as Coastal Command's ASW aircraft were overstretched. Countless hours of night patrols were rarely rewarded with sightings, and 1945 opened badly when, on 8 January, Fg Off Davidson, taking advantage of bright moonlight, attacked the surfaced U-343. Lined up at 80ft the Wellington dropped its depth charges but return fire from the submarine set the port wing of the aircraft on fire. The aircraft went out of control

and crashed into the sea, the pilot being the only survivor. Many U-boats were now heavily armed – some indeed had been turned into *Flak* boats – and making such attacks was highly dangerous.

Meanwhile, the Azores detachment continued its routine of convoy escort and anti-submarine patrols, and although sightings were rare, 172 Squadron claimed two victims: Plt Off Armstrong (HF168) sinking U-231 on 13 January and Fg Off Finnessey (HF183) putting an end to U-575 on 13 March.

Wellington strength was reduced in October when the Canadian squadrons of 331 Wing returned to the UK. In November, No. 205 Group HQ moved to Ariana, near Tunis, and its squadrons settled at nearby airfields. However, progress of the offensive in Italy was rapid and by the end of the year most units had moved to Italy.

In October the C-in-C requested that two Leigh Light squadrons be transferred from the Mediterranean in order to reinforce Coastal Command in covering the south-west approaches as 'unmistakable signs were obvious of a policy of close investment of the British Isles' (Sholto Douglas); two squadrons were duly returned and were equipped with Wellington XIVs.

At the tail-end of the year another squadron was formed to join the anti-submarine war. 14 Squadron already had a distinguished wartime career as a bomber squadron, most lately flying Marauders in

sions began, though the squadron did not fly its first operation until early 1945.

The Wellington was fairly straightforward compared to the high-performance Marauder, but pilots had to get used to accurate instrument flying over long night periods. They also had to learn to descend at night, on bearings given by the radar operator, down to a height of 250ft. To

to such low level and then at a distance of half a mile to target to switch on the Leigh Light. Crews had to learn low-level straddle bombing techniques in daylight as well as in darkness. (Dr Vincent Orange *et al*)

The final Wellington U-boat kill was made on 2 April 1945 by W/O R. Marczak and crew of 304 Squadron, who put paid to U-

The Rock of Gibraltar provides a dramatic back-drop to these GR.XIVs of 458 Squadron in January 1945.
Peter Green Collection

Italy; however, it had disbanded in September and began to reform at Chivenor in October. The first Wellington XIVs were received the following month and conver-

avoid ditching in the sea a radio altimeter activated at 400ft with three lights, amber, green and red to indicate critical heights. On a bumpy night it was wearing and tense work going down

321. The end of the war brought a rapid end to the Wellington units of Coastal Command, six disbanding in June; and the final one, 621 Squadron at Langham, on 7 July.

524 Squadron moved to Langham in late 1944 to undertake anti-E-boat operations off the Dutch coast. Andy Thomas Collection

(Below) **The lines of the original Wellington are still very much in evidence in this late-war shot of MP714.** FlyPast Collection

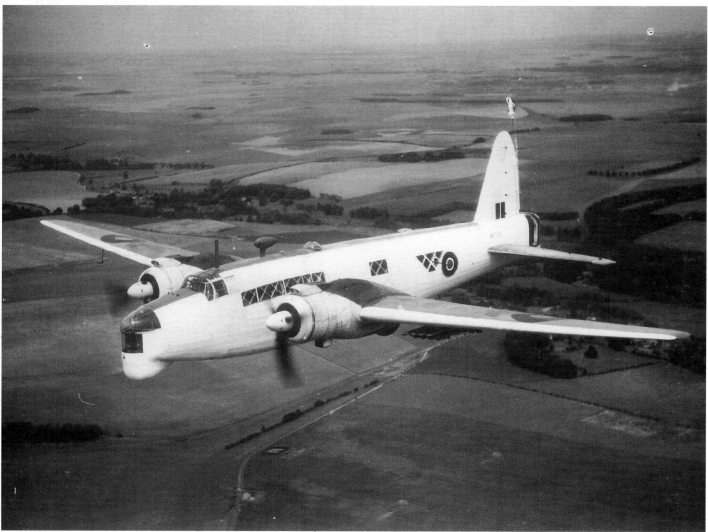

One of the longest-serving Wellington units, 304 Squadron, was flying maritime operations up to 1946, having received its first Wellingtons in November 1940; this is Wellington XI HZ258 in 1944.
Andy Thomas Collection

Training

The Aircrew Training Bulletin No. 19 for August 1944 including an article entitled 'Bomber Command Training' and this gives a good insight into a standard Wellington OTU:

The name Bomber Command suggests – and rightly – heavy attacks on the enemy. However, a very large part of its energies are devoted to training the heavy bomber crew, which normally consists of: pilot, navigator, air bomber, wireless operator, flight engineer and two air gunners. The training organization through which all crews must pass before they become operational is divided into five separate stages:

1. Operational Training Unit – ten weeks, forty day and forty night flying hours.
2. Air Crew School – two weeks, no flying.
3. Conversion Unit – four weeks, twenty hours day and twenty hours night.
4. Lancaster Finishing School – two week, five hours day and five hours night.
5. Squadron conversion – one week, five hours day and five hours night.

OTU

The air crew meet for the first time at the OTU and during the first two weeks of ground course are given certain discretion in sorting themselves out into complete crews (with the exception of the flight engineer who does not arrive until later). The flying course starts with conversion to the Wellington aircraft, gradually progresses through various stages and ends up with a leaflet raid in a Wellington over enemy-occupied territory. The syllabus includes the following exercises:

1. Synthetic training. Link trainer, AM Bombing Teacher, radar, clay pigeon shooting, turret training.
2. Gunnery. Combat manoeuvres, air-to-sea firing, air-to-air firing, fighter affiliation exercises by day and by night.
3. Bombing. High-level bombing by day and by night, bombing on cross-countries, infra-red bombing, demonstration of pathfinder technique and target indicators.
4. Navigation. DR navigation, cross-countries, radar training.
5. Operational Training. Night exercises with the night fighter, searchlight and anti-aircraft organization in this country. Leaflet raid over enemy territory.
6. Drills. Dinghy, parachute, fire, oxygen, crash drills.
7. Operational Procedures. Darky, searchlight homing, SOS.

There are, of course, many other subjects which have not been mentioned – for instance engine handling, the air-sea rescue service, and standard beam approach, in each of which considerable training is required.

The fact that the OTU (Wellington) part of the training of an aircrew member takes up

Bundles of leaflets arrive at the aircraft for another Nickel sortie, and *(left)* **are attached to the bomb beams, May 1944.** Ken Delve Collection

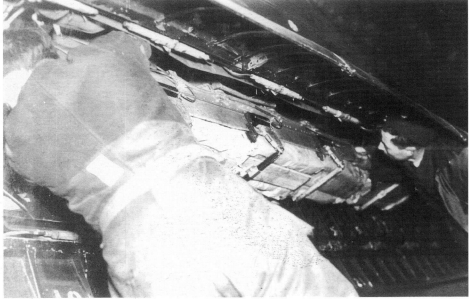

such a large proportion of the overall training time and flying hours is indicator enough of the importance of the Wellington in the Bomber Command training machine.

As a typical OTU operating in 1944, 22 OTU at Wellesbourne Mountford had an almost even mix of Wellington IIIs and Xs amongst its eighty aircraft, as well a number of Martinet Is for target towing. The course sizes had grown once more in the early part of 1944 and comprised twenty-eight to thirty crews, a total of 654 pupils under training (January 1944), the majority of the aircrew being Canadian. Bomber Command revised its requirements in April after wastage rates had proved higher than anticipated and discussions were held on how to increase the

OTU and HCU throughput. The Wellingtons of No. 22 OTU flew, in a typical summer month, almost 5,000 hours (just under 2,000 of which were by night) and operational sorties, invariably *Nickels*, were a routine part of the course. Typical of this was May when student crews operated on four nights:

5 May – six aircraft to Fontainbleau, Melun, Etampes;
9 May – five aircraft to Laval, Le Mans;
10 May – six aircraft to Angers, La Fleche, Rennes;
22 May – five aircraft to Paris, Creil, Compiegne.

The *Nickel* sorties were then halted for a while but a signal from 91 Group on 29 June stated '... that *Nickel* ops are to recommence. 91 Group has been limited to thirty-two per month and it is proposed to divide these as follows: No. 21 OTU –

ten per month, No. 22 OTU – twelve, No. 24 OTU – ten.'

June 1944 saw the bomber OTUs at just about their maximum strength, and although all were established for Wellington Xs it will be seen from the following table that virtually all of them were operating a mix of IIIs and Xs. Of the OTUs listed below, on 22 June 1944, 14, 15, 82 and 83 were ½ size whilst 20 and 22 were 1½ size, all the rest were standard (*see* box below).

No. 91 Group	Base	Mk X	Mk III
20 OTU	Lossiemouth	36	26
21 OTU	Moreton-in-Marsh	39	9
22 OTU	Wellesbourne Mountford	26	31
24 OTU	Honiley	36	6
No. 93 Group			
11 OTU	Westcott		37
12 OTU	Chipping Warden	21	19
14 OTU	Market Harborough	36	
15 OTU	Upper Heyford	7	20
17 OTU	Silverstone	22	11
26 OTU	Wing	22	18
19 OTU	Bruntingthorpe	17	30
84 OTU	Desborough	31	
No. 93 Group			
18 OTU	Finningley	30	10
27 OTU	Lichfield	19	17
28 OTU	Wymeswold	38	4
30 OTU	Hixon	23	12
82 OTU	Ossington	23	12
83 OTU	Peplow	23	2
86 OTU	Gamston	22	

Wellington T.XVIII NC928 with a Mosquito nose for radar training of night-fighter crews.
FlyPast Collection

27 OTU Wellington X, out of Lichfield in 1944. The OTUs remained busy for most of 1944, but then came a dramatic and rapid run-down. Alan Walker

By July the situation had changed once again and the War Cabinet was looking at ways to cut back the strength of the training units, primarily because an overall manpower shortage would not permit the planned expansion of the bomber force (at one stage the plan had been for a heavy bomber force of 4,000 aircraft); it was decided, therefore, to restrict the expansion of the bomber force and thus to reduce the number of OTUs to fifteen by the end of 1944 and to six by March 1945.

Accident rates at OTUs remained, in general, quite high, although 22 OTU received a signal from Air Vice-Marshal J. A. Gray, AOC 91 Group on 11 November, 'Congratulations on October's 3,600 flying hours without accident, and this after four months of over 1,000 hours per accident.' Sadly, November had its share of tragedy with two fatal accidents on the 20th, LN460 exploding in mid-air and MF509 crashing in Wales, both with the loss of their crews.

By the end of 1944 a number of OTUs had been disbanded, five actually disappearing from the ORBATs – but four new ones had been created: 10 OTU at Abingdon, which received forty-nine Wellingtons Is, 16 OTU at Upper Heyford, 29 OTU at Bruntingthorpe and 85 OTU at Husbands Bosworth.

A number of other training units operated Wellingtons during this period. No. 1692 BSTU (Bomber Support Training Unit) at Great Massingham had a UE

Wellington XII of 76 OTU in Cyprus 1944. Andy Thomas Collection

The plan was to have only a handful of OTUs in operation by mid-1945; this is AI-Q of 20 OTU at Lossiemouth. Peter Green Collection

(Below) 77 OTU's MP757 in March 1945; this Wellington XIII served with a number of training units, eventually crashing on take-off from El Adem on 5 October 1945. Andy Thomas Collection

of two Wellingtons although for most of the time none were actually available! It was a similar picture with the Bomber Command Instructors School (BCIS) at Finningley which, in December 1944, had an establishment that included twenty-two Wellingtons but had only four such aircraft on strength.

The training routine continued into 1945 but with a progressive run-down. The original plan to have only six OTUs in use by March 1945 had long been abandoned and as the war ended in May there were still fifteen Wellington-equipped OTUs operating within 91 Group and 92 Group.

Italian Operations

Wellington squadrons remained an important part of the bomber strength of strategic air forces in the Mediterranean/Italian theatre; the capture and repair of the major series of airfields around Foggia enabled even more squadrons to move to

Winter 1944 at Foggia Main, home to the Wellington strategic bombing force of 205 Group. R Allonby

19–20	Monfalcone
22–23	Padua West marshalling yard
23–24	Padua North marshalling yard
24–25	Sofia marshalling yard
26–27	Vincenza marshalling yard
28–29	Milan–Lambrate marshalling yard
29–30	Sofia marshalling yard Fano/Cesano rail bridges

Maurice Lihou, a pilot with 37 Squadron, has published an excellent account of 205 Group operations (*It's Dicey Flying Wimpeys in Italian Skies*) in which he recounts the 28–29 March attack on Milan:

... they arrived over the target which was clearly visible below, the earlier cloud having dispersed. They arrived late in the target area as did the aircraft sent to illuminate it. The target was therefore well illuminated for them and they attacked with one stick of nine 500lb high explosive bombs. Bursts were seen towards the west end of the yards, where it was later reported that a direct hit had been made on the roundhouses, starting a fire. Bombing was well concentrated in the area and four large explosions were seen in the centre of the yards. Subsequent reconnaissance proved that the raid was very successful.

After they had attacked it with the usual excitement of fires, flares, *Flak* and tracer, they had just finished the thirteen-second straight and level run to take the photograph when the cockpit suddenly lit up! They were bathed in a brilliant white light ...Good God, we were in a searchlight! For one horrible moment he panicked ... pulling himself together, he called 'hang on' and he flung the aircraft into a dive; first left and then right. He opened the throttles and pulling back on the stick began to climb trying to get out of it, but it was too slow. Putting the nose down he started to dive again. Quickly he pulled out of the dive and once again started to climb with full power. The engines were screaming. He weaved left to right, right to left. It seemed incredibly slow but he couldn't go any faster. Still the searchlight held them; he stall turned. Down he went again, zigzagging as the aircraft sped downwards. Flak shells with their orange spurts of flame were bursting all round them. The smell of cordite made him feel sick. Slowly he pulled the stick right back – nose up

Italy from their previous bases in North Africa.

40 Squadron, under the command of Wg Cdr J. D. Kirwan DFC, moved to Foggia Main in December 1943 with its Wellington Xs, although a few Wellington IIIs remained operational for the first few months of 1944. The first operation from the new location was flown on 7 January 1944 to attack the Reggiane aircraft factory at Reggio Emelia; the squadron ORB recorded that,

... thirteen aircraft took part in the attack, although one returned early with an unserviceability; three were tasked to drop flares and the others to drop bombs in what proved to be a good attack. A photograph taken the next day by a B-17 showed good results, all of which was achieved by the Wellingtons of this wing. So successful was this combined night and day attack that a booklet is being prepared by MASAF giving the whole story and copies of this are to be sent to General Spaatz and to the Air Ministry. In the opinion of experts the factory is now useless.

All of the squadron's aircraft returned safely but Flt Sgt Fielder, the wireless operator in Wellington HF386, baled out over Bologna 'under the misapprehension that the aircraft was out of control when it dived steeply to avoid *Flak*.'

Aircraft production facilities remained high on the target list for the first half of the year along with railway facilities; indeed this latter category, as part of Operation *Strangle*, was the most important individual target category. Targets included marshalling yards, bridges and even stretches of rail line. Road and rail targets were also attacked in February in support of Sixth Corps in the Anzio bridgehead; for example, on 12 February the squadron flew double sorties (that is, two in the day) to attack the road from Campoleone to Cecchina, a sector occupied by the Hermann Göring Armoured Division. This type of mission continued into March. The Allies gathered an air armada of 2,903 aircraft (including eighty-six Wellingtons) to support Operation *Shingle*, the Anzio landings. Support for the Anzio bridgehead was also given by 70 Squadron, whose ORB records that 'gradually as the weather improves our air umbrella increases and the position of our troops on the beachhead becomes better, although still fairly serious'. March, indeed, saw 205 Group on a particularly intensive spell of attacks on marshalling yards, with almost nightly operations from 11 March onwards:

March	11–12	Genoa marshalling yard
	15–16	Sofia marshalling yard
	16–17	Sofia marshalling yard
	18–19	Plovdiv marshalling yard

and they started to climb again. He could feel the strain on the aircraft as he pulled out of the dive; how that aircraft never broke up was a miracle ... just at that moment they flew out of the entangling beam.

The sturdy old Wimpey often surprised its crews with its ability to take such harsh handling; a Bomber Command pilot once said, 'there was a warning on the main spar that the aircraft must not be dived at more than 280mph; we had just pulled out at 360mph and were still flying!'

performed marvels and kept serviceability at nearly 90 per cent.

From Foggia the Wellingtons could not only attack other areas in Italy, but could also strike into Austria and across the Adriatic into the Balkans. Typical of these was that to the Manfred Weiss armament plant at Budapest on 3 April in which thirteen Wellingtons of 40 Squadron participated:

The first attack by the RAF on Budapest was the closest thing that we had to coming to a disaster. Our bomb load was incendiaries. By the

the aircraft. We struggled to a straight and level attitude, discovered that the port engine was damaged and set course for home. We limped over the mountains of Yugoslavia and dropped down over the Adriatic to avoid possible fighter attack. We were the last kite back. The aircraft had taken twelve direct hits in the fuselage and wings. A piece of *Flak* had pierced the engine and embedded itself into one of the blades of the supercharger impeller. Although Tommy finally had to feather it, the engine gave us just enough power to get over the Dalmatian coast mountain range.

O-Orange of B Flight at Foggia, 1944. R Allonby

A number of low-level attacks were made in an attempt to hit bridges that had proved immune to high-level bombing; one such mission was flown on the night of 29–30 March when two aircraft attacked the rail bridge at Fano whilst three other aircraft dropped flares to illuminate the target area. The two bombers, Wg Cdr Kirwan in LN769/G and W/O Bradshaw in LN759/L, took off at 1900 hours and each scored near misses with their 4,000lb bombs. In March the squadron had flown 121 sorties, dropped 180 tons of bombs and lost one aircraft. The groundcrew had

time we were due to bomb, things had really warmed up. Light and heavy *Flak* was all around us and fires were burning on the ground. It was not difficult to pick out where the action was! I had no sooner called out 'bombs gone' then 'crunch, crunch, thump, thunk' ... and Wellington LP118 went into a steep dive. We had been clobbered by heavy *Flak* and having bombed from 11,000ft were down to 4,000ft before Tommy's voice came over the intercom 'don't worry chaps, I've got her'. I was helplessly glued to the bomb aimer's cushion because there was no way to struggle upright from the head-down position forced on me by the diving attitude of

Once again a number of aircraft were tasked to drop flares:

This gave excellent illumination and eleven bombers attacked, seeing numerous bursts in the target area. There was moderate inaccurate heavy *Flak*, moderate to intense light *Flak* and about twelve searchlights; several crews saw probable night fighters. Flt Sgt Redden (JA511/Y) and crew were on their bombing run when the starboard engine cut out, probably hit by a stray burst of *Flak*. In spite of this the bomb run was completed and a hit scored on a large building in the centre of the target area, followed by a large fire. On the return the aircraft was forced to ditch off Termoli. This was successfully accomplished and all crew rescued, though the captain sustained a broken shoulder, elbow and forearm. The crew were rescued by a Walrus.

A number of daylight sorties were flown, usually on 'special operations' such as that of 8 April when eleven Wellingtons attacked German troops at Hiksic, Yugoslavia, at the request of Tito's partisans. The ability to call on such air power was greatly appreciated by the partisan units, who by mid-1944 were often fighting more as regular troops than as guerrillas. All such daylight missions were given fighter escort – in this instance, Spitfires.

The Wellington units were kept very busy and performed a wide range of tasks including bombing, supply dropping, minelaying and leaflet dropping. Minelaying had proved to a very effective operation in the North Sea and Mediterranean and as part of the Allied plan to cripple German supply routes it was decided that the Danube, a vital strategic transport route, and one on which traffic had increased by 200 per cent since the destruction of the rail network, should be mined. The task fell to 205 Group and the first missions were flown in April; nineteen Wellingtons and three Liberators undertaking the first operation on 8–9 April, forty mines being laid near Belgrade. Maurice Lihou was one of the 37 Squadron pilots on the 12 April operation:

Loaded with two 1,000lb cucumbers they set off. One good thing about this trip was that the met. had forecast good weather in order for the crews to find the 'cucumber beds' in the moonlight and be able to fly at 200ft between the banks of the river. On the other hand it meant that it was going to almost like a daylight attack in the bright moonlight and they would be clearly visible to the enemy defences.

The squadron were to sow their cucumbers in a patch of the river between Nova Sad and Belgrade ... In the brilliant moonlight they found the vegetable patch. Flying low along the Danube with the river banks rising on either side of them, they could clearly see motor traffic with dimmed headlights moving along ... They laid their deadly traps and went in search of barges to shoot up. It wasn't long before the first barges came into sight sitting low in the river, chugging along and leaving a tell-tale wake of white foam behind them ... The burst of machine gun fire filled the aircraft and they flew over the barges.

For 40 Squadron the minelaying of the Danube proved particularly costly on 1 July. Eight aircraft were tasked to drop mines between Pancevo and Smederevo (east of Belgrade) and all were met with heavy, accurate cross-fire from both banks of the Danube; two aircraft were lost (LN744/N and LP497/A) whilst three others were damaged and one rear gunner killed. This night saw the heaviest effort with No. 205 Group sending fifty-seven Wellingtons (and seventeen Liberators) who dropped 192 mines for the loss of four aircraft. The Wellingtons did not take part in the minelaying in August but did fly a few more missions in September and early October, the last one being 4–5 October.

Minelaying in the Danube was fun! We flew to Belgrade and identified the stretch of river, south of the city, that had been allocated to us. We were loaded with two 1,000lb mines which were equipped with parachutes which opened quickly to lower the mines gently into the water, to avoid detonation on impact. To successfully plant the mines we had to get down to 50ft. This precision flying and on-the-spot delivery was just what appealed to our illustrious skipper. Down we went, me in my usual prone position ready to press the bomb tit when Tommy gave the word. Lower and lower we went, with no illumination other than reflections from the river, which I could see flashing by below. Jerry could have thrown stones at us, much less AA. (John Long)

The importance of the Wellingtons in the offensive strength of Allied air power was demonstrated in a number of studies undertaken by the ORS. One of these (N13 dated 13 June 1944) was tasked to examine the 'Sustainable effort of the six Wellington squadrons of 205 Group':

It was required to determine the scale of effort that could be maintained by the six Wellington squadrons of 205 Group; it became apparent

that at the present, the sustainable effort of these squadrons would be limited by the rate of replacement and of repair of aircraft rather than by wing or squadron maintenance output. In the period March to May 1944 the squadrons flew 17,704 operational and 2,035 non-operational hours, losing seventy aircraft to all causes. The busiest month was May with 1,350 sorties and thirty-two aircraft lost. Wing and squadron personnel are extremely short of even the most elementary equipment. Their facilities for working are rudimentary and it is difficult to maintain effort during the heat of the day. There is also a shortage of spares at wing and squadron level. The establishment of the six squadrons is 120 Wellingtons; in May the strength was 114 aircraft of which, on average, eighty-one were declared serviceable. The scheduled rate of replacement from the UK is forty-two Wellingtons monthly, of which thirty are allocated to 205 Group and twelve for the OTUs. As at 25 May, 172 aircraft were held at MUs, ninety-seven of those awaiting repair having estimates of over fifteen days; a further thirty-one were held by the two Repair and Salvage Units. The holdings of these two organizations need to be reduced.

The main RAF bomber element in Italy was 205 Group with its HQ at Foggia. In July 1944, 205 Group's Wellington strength comprised:

231 Wing (Tortorella) – 37 Sqn, 70 Sqn.
236 Wing (Foggia) – 40 Sqn, 104 Sqn.
330 Wing (Amendola) – 142 Sqn, 150 Sqn.

Report N24 issued by the Operational Research Section of NAAF/MAAF summarized the 'Effort and casualties by aircraft of 205 Group March–September 1944'. At this time the group comprised six Wellington squadrons (as detailed above), plus, for part of the period, three Liberator squadrons and one Halifax squadron. The statistics given for the Wellington units are detailed in the box below.

	Night Bombing	Leaflet	Day/Special	Total sorties	Total hours
Mar	756	3		759	3,987
Apr	1,028	5	8	1,041	5,233
May	1,331	15	16	1,362	6,634
Jun	1,103	19		1,122	5,426
Aug	860	8		868	4,529
Sep	1,016	9		1,025	4,847
Totals	7,026	87	24	7,137	30,706

Tortorella, Italy, 1944 and 37 Squadron aircraft on the way to another sortie. Note the unusual finish on the rear aircraft. Peter Green Collection

A lonely-looking 104 Squadron aircraft in Italy October 1944. Philip Dawson

Kalamaki, Greece in March 1945 with GR.XIIIs of 221 Squadron. The squadron deployed here in October 1944 to carry on its maritime work, but also for supply-dropping as communications in Greece were chaotic. Andy Thomas Collection

The sad end of many fine aeroplanes, a Middle East (?) graveyard of countless Wellingtons.
Peter Green Collection

The report further stated that:

8.5 per cent of sorties were non-effective through technical problems or weather (a figure of 10.4 per cent for the Liberators and 11.4 per cent for the Halifax). During the major part of the period the targets attacked outside of Italy were strategic in character, whereas those in Italy were mainly tactical, being attacked in support of army operations. Casualties on targets outside Italy were far heavier per hundred sorties than on targets inside Italy. This is mainly due to the considerably stronger defences of such targets as Budapest, Bucharest, Ploesti and Munich, and possibly to some extent the long duration of each flight. Losses on targets outside of Italy averaged 3.4 per cent whereas those in Italy were 1.1 per cent.

In August and September the Wellingtons of 205 Group were active every night with formations of, on average, fifty aircraft, but with occasions when more than eighty were airborne from all four wings.

The No. 205 Group Wellingtons were not the only ones operating from Italy; in September the Wellington VIIIs of 458 Squadron moved to Foggia from Alghero as submarine and shipping targets were few and far between further south. Ken Ripley was with the squadron when it moved to Italy:

We were stationed at Foggia on anti-submarine patrols over the Adriatic but then I was sent

with the 'A' Flight detachment to Cecina (near Pisa) ostensibly to undertake anti-sub patrols off southern France prior to the Allied invasion of that area. The ground party moved by road in a convoy via Naples and Rome. Two days after arrival at Cecina the operation was cancelled and we had to make the horrendous road journey back to Foggia.

In Yugoslavia the partisans, led by Tito, were very active and giving the Germans enormous problems; from time to time the Wellington squadrons were called upon to fly support missions for the partisans. The first such mission for 40 Squadron was flown on 29 October when sixteen aircraft each carried six supply containers to a drop site north-east of Kotor; despite the fact that a number of aircraft had to drop using Gee co-ordinates, having been unable to find the visual markers, most of the containers were recovered by those for whom they were intended. Partisan supply became the main role in November, by which time 40 Squadron had almost doubled in size, having received crew and aircraft from 330 Wing (142 and 150 Squadrons) which disbanded in October. In November some 664 containers were delivered.

In the autumn, German forces began to abandon Greece, helped on their way by Allied air power, including the Wellington units. However, in December the Greek

communist organization, ELAS, endeavoured to take control of the country and civil war erupted. On 13 December,

... fourteen aircraft were stripped of bomb sights and other equipment to act as transports owing to the urgency of the situation in Greece where ELAS is operating against our forces. The aircraft flew to Grottaglie and loaded with men and equipment to move to Hassani, Athens. The fourteen aircraft that took part moved 122 men and their equipment.

The special duties ELINT aircraft of 162 Squadron, operating from Idku since April 1944, had few missions to fly, the majority of the work being calibration; throughout the summer their workload decreased to such an extent that the unit was disbanded on 25 September, its calibration duties being taken over by 26 AACU. The end of the year also brought a reduction in the strength of 205 Group when, in mid-October, 330 Wing left the command (142 and 150 Squadrons disbanding), although many of their aircraft were distributed to the squadrons of the remaining wings. The Monthly Statistical Summary for the Wellington component of the North West African Strategic Air Force (NWASAF), to which 205 Group belonged, showed an average daily availability of 130–150 aircraft during the period October–Novem-

A somewhat broken ME933 of 77/78 OTU at Ein Shemer on 2 November 1944.
Peter Green Collection

ber – not particularly good from a notional strength of over 300 aircraft; the table below was extracted from the MAAF Summary document.

Famine Relief

One of the more unusual tasks for the Wellington in 1944 was its involvement with supply flights as famine relief to tribesmen in the Hadhramaut region of Arabia, an area under the control of the authorities in Aden. A Famine Relief Flight was formed in April and by 7 May had a strength of six Wellington Xs, fresh from the UK, having been modified by 168 MU for supply dropping. Operating from Riyan, but also using a number of other improvized landing grounds, the aircraft flew numerous sorties up to the end of June, at which point they were withdrawn due to a mix of serviceability problems and the belief that the worst of the famine was over.

The flight was a mixed RAF and Army formation, the aircrew being taken from the Middle East Training School at Ramat David, and ground personnel coming from 168 MU. A specially made landing strip was prepared at Qatn and a test flight on 28 April proved its suitability. The next day three Wellingtons flew two sorties each and delivered 216 bags of grain. On 18 May the aircraft started supply dropping in four areas: Tarim, Ghuraf, Einat and Seiyun, each aircraft carrying three tons of grain to drop, and so only one further landing was made at Qatn. By the end of May the flight had flown 163 sorties and delivered 5,505 bags of grain plus 8¼ tons of milk. The aircraft, however, were feeling the strain of operating in these conditions and in June two suffered engine failures, one resulting in a crash, whilst a third aircraft crashed whilst landing at Riyan. This venture by the Wellington into humanitarian aid had been a great success.

Far East

The formation of South East Asia Air Command (SEAAC) on 16 November 1943 (under Air Chief Marshal Sir Richard Peirse) had brought a change in the operational boundaries of a number of RAF organizations and in due course incorporated units flying from Aden covering the Indian Ocean, the Gulf of Oman and the eastern seaboard of Africa. Two units in this area re-equipped with maritime Wellingtons for maritime reconnaissance and anti-shipping duties. At Khormaksar, 8 Squadron received its first Wellington XIIIs in December, flying its first operational sortie on 2 January and being up to full strength of sixteen aircraft by the end of January. Meanwhile, at Sharjah, 244 Squadron received its first Mark XIIIs in February, the entire squadron moving to Masirah the following month.

By late February the squadron, now under the operational control of AHQ Aden, had seven Wellingtons on strength but was facing serious problems with both inadequate facilities at Masirah and the poor state of some of the aircraft; the engineering report in the February ORB stated that,

> ... several had to be put unserviceable on arrival. All except one were found to need considerable servicing of elevator trimmer tab controls and two trimmer tab boxes were found to be unserviceable ... no information has been received on

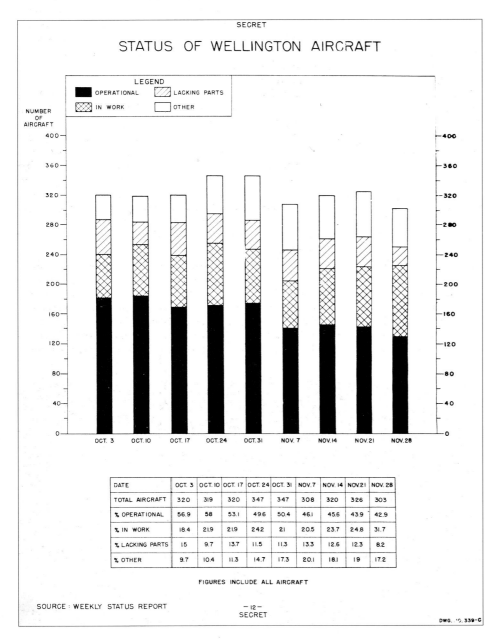

STATUS OF WELLINGTON AIRCRAFT

LEGEND
■ OPERATIONAL ▨ LACKING PARTS
▨ IN WORK □ OTHER

NUMBER OF AIRCRAFT

DATE	OCT. 3	OCT. 10	OCT. 17	OCT. 24	OCT. 31	NOV.7	NOV. 14	NOV.21	NOV. 28
TOTAL AIRCRAFT	320	319	320	347	347	308	320	326	303
% OPERATIONAL	56.9	58	53.1	49.6	50.4	46.1	45.6	43.9	42.9
% IN WORK	18.4	21.9	21.9	24.2	21	20.5	23.7	24.8	31.7
% LACKING PARTS	15	9.7	13.7	11.5	11.3	13.3	12.6	12.3	8.2
% OTHER	9.7	10.4	11.3	14.7	17.3	20.1	18.1	19	17.2

FIGURES INCLUDE ALL AIRCRAFT

SOURCE : WEEKLY STATUS REPORT

– 12 –
SECRET

DWG. No. 339-C

Status of Wellington aircraft in Middle East.
Middle East Statistical Summary

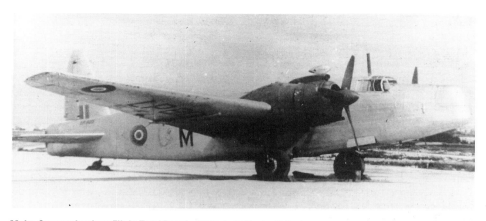

Malta Communications Flight T.10 LP805 in 1946. Andy Thomas Collection

The stick was accurately placed and it was estimated that two fell within lethal range. Three minutes later as the aircraft climbed to observe results, the submarine began to surface, listing to port. It opened fire, which was returned by the rear gunner. The aircraft continued to shadow and before leaving the area had the satisfaction of seeing another Wellington of the same squadron carry out an attack. The submarine was hunted for the rest of the day. In all twenty further sorties were flown and six further attacks made by 8 and 621 Squadrons ... it fought back all day and fired at every aircraft that came within range. On the morning of the 3rd a Wellington reported seeing it stationary south of Ras Hafun and on fire and it was finally reported as scuttled; a Royal Navy party went ashore to round up survivors. [It had taken twenty-two sorties, forty-five depth charges and 7,800 rounds of 0.303 ammunition!] (RAF *Middle East Review* No. 7)

the modification necessary to enable a stick of six depth charges to be dropped. A local mod has been devised to be carried out if the authorized one has not arrived in time. (244 Squadron ORB)

The first operational sortie was flown from Masirah on 24 March, Flt Lt G. Burton taking HZ897 for a 6½-hour patrol as close escort to a convoy. By this time the squadron was running detachments at other bases, partly to ease the problems at Masirah and partly for operational convenience, four aircraft, for example, having moved to Khormaksar on 10 March.

A second unit equipped with Wellington XIIIs moved into Khormaksar in late 1943, 621 Squadron arriving in December from Kenya. This latter unit operated detachments from a number of landing grounds, such as Scuscuiban, Riyan, Socotra, Bandar Kassim and Mogadishu. A fourth anti-shipping unit had arrived within the operational theatre towards the end of 1943,

203 Squadron giving up its Baltimores in the Western Desert and re-forming with Wellington XIIIs at Santa Cruz.

As with maritime squadrons in other areas, the routine was one of long, weary patrols over the vast ocean areas with few sightings of enemy vessels. However, one early success was scored by 621 Squadron when, on 2 May, Flt Lt R. Mitchell attacked and damaged U-852 in the Gulf of Aden. The six depth charges had caused serious but not fatal damage and the Wellington summoned other aircraft to the area. Over the next two days aircraft from 8 and 621 Squadrons made further attacks and when the warship HMS *Falmouth* arrived on the scene the submarine commander scuttled his boat.

As the aircraft manoeuvred to attack, the submarine began to crash dive. At 800yd the front gunner opened fire, his tracer consequently hitting the base of the conning-tower, and at 50ft the attack was made with six depth charges.

No. 244 Squadron was still having little luck; by May all detachments had been recalled and the squadron was busy re-organizing, but 'Efforts hampered by persistent and discouraging unserviceabilities which show no signs of improving. The inexplicable tendency of our engines to empty their oil tanks through the breathers in half a minute is the most frequent and most alarming.' The engineering officer added,

... serious trouble has been experienced with the Hercules engines, which have been the cause of three forced landings and has occurred on nine aircraft inspections on ground runs. It appears to be due to a failure of the oil scavenge system. The failure causes loss of all engine oil in the tank. No oil is returned from the engine to the

Specification – Wellington XIII	
ENGINES	Two Bristol Hercules XVII
DIMENSIONS	Span 86ft 2in (26.26m); length 64ft 7in (19.68m)
PERFORMANCE	Max. speed 250mph (400km/h); ceiling 16,000ft (4,848m)
ARMAMENT	6 × 0.303in guns, torpedoes
FIRST FLIGHT	March 1943
NUMBER BUILT	843

Wellington XIII of 8 Squadron at Salalah, February 1944. Andy Thomas Collection

tank and the engine, on becoming full of oil, pushes it out through the engine breather. In the majority of instances the scavenge filter is found clogged with large granules of carbon – samples of the oil have been sent to Aboukir for test and analysis. [It did indeed turn out to be a problem with the oil.]

including airfields and, more especially, lines of communication and supply targets, typical of these being the marshalling yards at Prome and Mandalay, plus the junctions and stations at Pyinmana and Maymo. On 20 January 215 squadron dropped the first 4,000lb bomb (on

intercepted whilst attacking the Victoria Lakes supply dump at Rangoon on 8–9 April:

... five enemy aircraft similar to Navy Os flying in loose formation over the target area at 12,670ft. The formation split up and two enemy

36 Squadron GR.XIV at Reghaia in August 1944. Andy Thomas Collection

Three of the four squadrons continued their Wellington operations into 1945; 203 Squadron, however, re-equipped with Liberators in November.

The maritime squadrons remained busy into the autumn period; in June, for example, 621 Squadron flew seventy-two operational sorties (518 hours), although most of these were convoy escorts. However, by November the situation had changed and most squadrons were flying less than a hundred operational hours a month. Nevertheless, all three Wellington GR units remained in place up to the end of the war, 621 Squadron even re-equipping with Mark XIVs in January 1945.

The two bomber squadrons remained active for the first half of 1944, targets

Sagaing), having received a suitably modified aircraft only a few days before.

April was a time of great operational effort by air and ground crews, and other personnel of the squadron. The push westwards by Japanese troops towards Imphal was largely responsible for the increased activity and twenty-three operations, by varying numbers of aircraft, were undertaken. Many sorties were flown in bad weather conditions, and aircrews displayed much resource and resolution in dealing with problems, relatively few operations were abandoned on account of adverse weather. (215 Squadron ORB)

Japanese fighters did make the odd appearance; Flt Sgt Lee and crew in LN486 were

aircraft came in on the starboard quarter in a diving attack but without firing. Our aircraft opened fire from 300yd firing a short burst of about four seconds, enemy aircraft did not return fire. Our aircraft then immediately turned starboard, straightened out and enemy aircraft both came in to attack again, this time from dead astern. Our rear gunner again opened fire at 300yd and tracer was seen to enter one enemy aircraft which dropped quickly away and was not seen again. (99 Squadron ORB)

The intensive operations in support of the Imphal area continued into May but by the latter part of the month, and into June, many aircraft from both squadrons were involved with ferrying bombs and operations with Troop Carrier Command. The

Khormaksar, Aden, May 1945 and 621 Squadron's NC829. Andy Thomas Collection

Wellington ORBAT, July 1945	
91 Gp	
Abingdon	10 OTU
Honeybourne	24 OTU
Lossiemouth	20 OTU
Moreton-in-Marsh	21 OTU
Silverstone	17 OTU
Wellesbourne Mountford	22 OTU
Westcott	11 OTU
2 TAF, 34 Wing	
B78/Eindhoven	69 Sqn
16 Gp	
Langham	612 Sqn
17 Gp	
Silloth	6 OTU
19 Gp	
St Eval	304 Sqn
4 Gp	
Bramcote	105 OTU
47 Gp	
Stoney Cross	242 Sqn
MACAF	
Gibraltar	458 Sqn
Foggia	38 Sqn
205 Gp, Foggia	
Foggia	40, 104 Sqns
Tortorella	37, 70 Sqns
AHQ Eastern Mediteranean	
Aqir	dets of 221, 294 Sqns
Benina	dets of 221, 294 Sqns
Edcu	294 Sqn
El Adem	dets of 221, 294 Sqns
Aden	
Khormaksar	621 Sqn (plus dets at Socotra and Scuisciban)
West Africa Command	
Douala	344 Sqn (plus det at Port Etienne)

last Wellington operation was flown on 15 August by a 99 Squadron formation, eight aircraft attacking the supply dumps at Pinlebu; both units converted to Liberators and the Wellingtons were ferried to 352 MU at Allahabad for disposal.

Postwar

The last production Wellington was a Mark X, RP590, delivered to the RAF on 25 October 1945. It served with No. 1 PRFU (Pilots Refresher Flying Unit) and the Flying Refresher School, and was struck-off-charge on 3 April 1950.

Very few Wellington operational units survived into the postwar era, and most of those that did had disappeared by late 1945–early 1946; indeed, for most, the immediate post-war period was an almighty anti-climax; for personnel based overseas the main concern was that of trying to get back to the UK as soon as possible. There was still work to be done, however, and as the shape and size of the postwar RAF had not yet been determined it was important to keep squadrons operationally effective. Many Wellington units took on transport roles during this period as there was a shortage of such aircraft. The last operational user was 38 Squadron,

RP550 of 201 AFS; note the 'Accident prevention concerns you' notice beneath the fin.
Ken Delve Collection

Trials Use

Wellington III BK461 was used by Dunlop for tests on their Compacta tyre *(right)* **at Honiley in 1945; one of many trials uses of the Wellington that we have not had time to cover in this history.**
Harry Holmes

One of a number of Wellingtons used as engine test beds, W5389 is seen here with an experimental Whittle W2B engine in the tail and with four-bladed propellers on its Merlin 62s.
Peter Green Collection

Fleeting mention has been made from time to time in this history of 'other' usage of the Wellington, including that of trials by industry and RAF agencies. A very wide range of military users operated the Wellington in various guises in the 1940s, many of these having one or two aircraft, or even as single 'hack' aircraft; others, such as the Air Transport Auxiliary (ATA) not only ferried Wellingtons around the UK, but also used a few as communications aircraft. Records of many of these uses are poor and the only evidence in many cases is a log book entry, personal memory or a photograph. The RAF's trials and tests organizations, such as the A&AEE and RAE were major 'users'. The aircraft was, of course, used by the airframe and engine manufacturers as a test bed, but it was also used for somewhat wider trials; for example, it was a popular engine test bed, the Wellington X performing this role with a number of engine manufacturers. Bris-

tols used RP484 for feathering tests and LN718 for the Hercules 100, whilst LN715 was used by Rolls-Royce for testing the Dart turboprop. Early Whittle jets were tested, mounted in the tail section, of Wellingtons W5389, W5518 and Z5870.

Weapons were also tested on the aircraft from squadron level, often with local modifications, to manufacturer level; Vickers, for example, fitted a 40mm gun turret to the upper fuselage of L4250 and Z8416 carried a Vickers S gun. Some trials were not a success: X3286 was modified as a glider tug for Horsa gliders but proved unsuitable for this role. The aircraft also appeared in a number of transport conversions, often as one-off versions for specific purposes or geographical areas. The British Overseas Aircraft Corporation used at least four Wellingtons, on loan from the RAF, during the middle part of the war for passenger/freight on routes to the Mediterranean and India.

which bade farewell to its Wellington XIVs in December 1946. The type did, however, survive somewhat longer in the training and support roles.

Alan Walker, having flown as an Air Cadet passenger in Wellingtons of 10 OTU, Stanton Harcourt in 1944, later joined the RAF as a pilot and flew Wellingtons Xs at 201 AFS (Advanced Flying School) at Swinderby in the summer of 1948:

Having trained on Tiger Moths and Harvards it was somewhat daunting to be confronted with this large black twin-engined monster. The Wellington Xs at Swinderby in 1948 were OTU dual B.Mk Xs and were still in their wartime matt black/camouflage finish, overpainted with FTC yellow bands and codes. Though some have eulogized over the Wellington I cannot say that I entirely share their enthusiasm. Though undoubtedly strong, it was very flexible, and it was a little disconcerting to be taxiing out behind another Wellington which appeared to wobble like jelly! After take-off the wing tips would come

Wellington NA928, a T.10 with Hercules 16 engines in June 1949. The T.10 was a useful crew training aircraft and served with a number of units. FlyPast Collection

Thorney Island, 1950, and T.10 RP389 of 201 AFS. Peter Green Collection

A Wellington fuselage being used as a crew trainer at 201 AFS Swinderby, 1948. Peter Green Collection

(Below)
A Wellington X of 201 AFS out of Swinderby in January 1949; the yellow spinners denote that it is from B Squadron. Alan Walker

into view above the engine nacelles. The tips of the huge three-bladed wooden Rotol propellers passed within a few inches of the pilot's cockpit windows, and a red warning bar was fitted across each of the sliding windows. When cruising at high boost/low revs for economy one could count each yellow blade tip of the port propeller as it passed one's nose, each one on a very slightly different path. In spite of its powerful engines, the Mark X's performance with one engine stopped and the prop feathered was pretty marginal.

The fuel system management was almost Byzantine in its complexity, with manually-operated cowling gills also to be watched. The flap system was diabolical, with a complex mechanism of pulleys and cables supposed to adjust the trim automatically as flaps were lowered. This usually meant having to push hard forward on the control column to maintain airspeed on the landing approach. In all I flew forty-six hours as a pilot on the Wellington X and I have considerable admiration for those who actually went to war in these strange contraptions!

The postwar period also brought the only foreign air force use of the Wellington (the RAAF, RCAF, Polish and other wartime users had all come under the RAF 'umbrel-la' of squadrons). In April 1946 eight aircraft were delivered to Greece (ME890, 907, 940, MF190, 466, 643 and NC148 and 433). The French *Aéronavale*, though, was the biggest user, acquiring thirty-nine aircraft, and possibly more, for use on maritime reconnaissance and torpedo attack tasks.

The Wellington served on with various training units in the UK during the late 1940s and early 1950s, performing pilot and other aircrew training tasks, but eventually the RAF retired its last Wellington, T.10 LP806, from No. 1 ANS in March 1953 – the Wimpey era had ended.

A number of Fleet Air Arm units operated Wellingtons, albeit most for a short time only; here, a burnt-out HZ470 at Hal Far with 765 Squadron in March 1946. Ray Sturtivant via John Hamlin

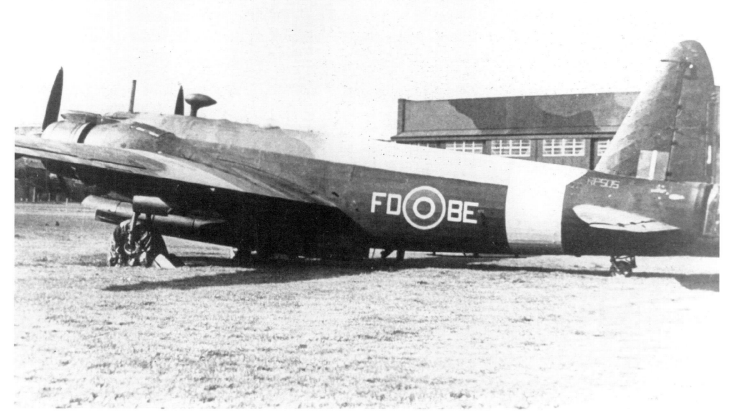

Finningley 1946 and RP505 of 202 AFS. Ken Delve Collection

January 1949 and T.10 RP569; this aircraft served with the CGS. FlyPast Collection

RP550 wearing the 9X code of 20 MU. Ken Delve Collection

(Top) **Wellington XIV HF237 out of Ein Shemer.**
Ken Delve Collection

(Above) **One of only two overseas users postwar;
a GR.XIV in French service during 1950.**
Peter Green Collection

(Right) **RP468 in its guise as G-ALUH, which it wore
for a series of radar trials off the coast of Norway.**
E. J. Ridings via Peter Green Collection

All-silver T.10 FF-ON of 2 Air Navigation School landing at Thorney Island in 1950.
Peter Green Collection

Impressive car and a very clean VIP Wellington in the Middle East. Peter Green Collection

CHAPTER SIX

Wellington Survivors

Very few Wellingtons survive, even as substantial fragments; indeed, the only complete example is that held by the RAF Museum. Considering that the type survived into the 1950s as a navigation trainer it is tragic that this is the only survivor.

Aviation archaeology groups often recover fragments of Wellingtons and many aviation collections in the UK include such material; likewise, in Holland the various recovery groups have come across a number of Wellington wrecks and crash sites over the years.

The Brooklands Museum project is magnificent (*see* below) and no doubt other Wellingtons survive in 'reasonable condition' in lakes in the UK or even in Europe. The Halifaxes that have come out of Norwegian lakes (W1048 at the RAF Museum and NA337 in Canada) show the preservative qualities of the pure lake waters of Norway. With the current high interest in recovering and restoring historic aircraft it is quite likely that the number of 'surviving' Wellingtons will increase in the next few years. The chances of seeing one fly again is unfortunately not high, as such projects invariably require a substantial portion of original airframe as a starting point (as well as impressive amounts of funding).

The only significant survivors are:

I   L7775 (substantial remains),
          Wellington Aviation Art,
          Moreton-in-the-Marsh

IA   N2980, Brooklands Museum

T.10   MF628, RAF Museum, Hendon

Wellington T.10 MF628, RAF Museum

This is the only 'true' surviving Wellington. It was built in 1944 at Squire's Gate and entered RAF service on 11 May 1944. It later went to 1 ANS at Hullavington,

The tail section and wings of L7775 were recovered from a mountain; the tail section now resides at the Wellington Aviation Museum, Moreton-in-Marsh. Ken Delve Collection

The sole surviving intact Wellington, T.10 MF628 (but now converted to look like a B.X) at the RAF Museum, Hendon. FlyPast Collection

eventually being sold back to Vickers in January 1955. Fortunately they preserved it and presented it to the RAF in 1964. It was subsequently transferred to the RAF Museum on 26 October 1971.

Wellington IA N2980, Brooklands Museum

The following article first appeared in the February 1997 issue of *FlyPast* magazine and is reproduced here by kind authority of the author, Robert Rudhall, and *FlyPast* magazine.

Wellington Re-born

ON SEPTEMBER 21, 1985, a 'monster' rose from the watery depths of Loch Ness in Scotland. This was not the 'monster' that many have been searching for and a

few have claimed to have seen over the years, but this was a monster of a restoration project, a World War Two Vickers Wellington bomber!

Wellington IA N2980 was taken on charge by 149 Squadron at RAF Mildenhall on 29 November 1939, and served with them until late May 1940. During its time with 149 the Wellington took part in raids on Heligoland Bight, Wilhelmshaven, Hanover, Sylt, Aachen and Namur, among others. Transferred to 37 Sqn on 30 May 1940, it took part in seven operational sorties until being taken on charge by 20 Operational Training Unit at RAF Lossiemouth on 6 October 1940.

On New Year's Eve, 1940, this particular Wellington met its Waterloo, when, after taking-off from Lossiemouth on a routine training sortie, the starboard engine failed. Flying through heavy snow showers, it was obvious to the pilot, Sqn Ldr David Marwood-Elton, that a return

to base was out of the question and there was no choice but to put the aircraft down as fast as he could. The order to bail out was given and six trainee crew members took to their parachutes, leaving Marwood-Elton and his co-pilot, Pilot Officer Slatter, to make the best of it! Flying through a gap in the clouds the pilot saw an expanse of water, which turned out to be Loch Ness, and decided to put the crippled Wellington down in the water. Carrying out a text-book ditching the pilot and co-pilot took to the dinghy as the Wellington slipped beneath the surface of the cold waters. It took just ninety seconds for the Wellington to sink to the bottom of the Loch!

The story of the quest to bring this bomber back to dry land after some forty-five years hidden below the surface of the Loch has been well documented over the years and nowhere better than in Robin Holme's 1991 book, *One Of Our Aircraft* (copies of which are still available from the Brooklands Museum shop).

The task of restoring Wellington N2980 has been taking place ever since the bomber arrived back at its birthplace on 27 September 1985. Considering the time the aircraft spent in its watery grave it was in a remarkable condition when it was raised. Bearing this in mind, what might be a 'remarkable condition' when raising an aircraft to the surface, is still 'a 'pretty awful' condition when it comes to restoring the aircraft to a presentable condition!

The job of putting the *Wimpey* back into one piece has been an absolute nightmare of logistics and hard work for the many people who have toiled long hours over many years in a hangar at Brooklands. Now after nearly 96,000 man hours of work the Wellington project is coming towards its conclusion. Having said that, there is still a fair bit to do on the aircraft's internals and what the members of the team call the 'fiddly bits'

When Wellington IA N2980 *R for Robert* came out of the lake it was in two major parts, the forward fuselage and wings, and the rear fuselage and tailplane. Much of the structure between these assemblies had come away over the years in the Loch. The rebuild team at Brooklands were faced with two options. 1: Leave the aircraft as it was, in two parts, and display it on the floor of the hangar looking as it was when it came out of the water, or 2: Attempt to restore the bomber and fabricate new-build structure so that the aircraft could stand on its undercarriage and to all intents and purposes be 'complete'. The latter was obviously the harder of the two options and after much deliberation it was this one which was chosen.

To replace the missing parts of the aircraft was going to be a big job and some 'outside' help would be needed. Bob Casbard, who led the restoration team for 5½ years told *FlyPast*:

Our main objective is to restore the Wellington so that it has sufficient structural strength which would enable it to stand on its own undercarriage and if necessary be moved locally within the hangar. After surveying the airframe, we rapidly discovered that in order to complete the bomber we needed a source of aluminium to make the 'new-build' geodetic structure. My predecessor on the team contacted Alcan, the British-based aluminium company, to ask if they could help with the supply of some light alloy sections for the work needed on the aircraft.

September 1985 and Wellington R-Robert emerges from Loch Ness. *FlyPast Collection*

The Wellington is made up of tubular longerons and geodetic members. The latter are made up of 2¾in channel sections. On top of this there are extruded sections for the wishbones and butterfly sections, which are the means of joining the geodetic sections together and joining the geodetic sections to the tubular longerons. It's a complex structure!

After our initial approach to Alcan, they came back to us with the offer of making the actual dies needed to manufacture the aforementioned parts. This was an incredibly generous gesture and a godsend to the restoration team. We had to finance the making of the dies, but for an investment of £850 Alcan supplied us with between 8,000 and 9,000ft (2,743m) of material, which to put it mildly was fantastic!

It's been a definite case of *déjà vu* at Brooklands, as the new-build parts for the

Wellington have been made using the same techniques used on the original prototype Wellington built in the Vickers factory at Weybridge during the mid-1930s. Each part of the geodetic structure has had to be stabilized and held in place with packing blocks and then cut and hand bent to the shape needed on the aircraft. This is a long and laborious process, but it's been the only way to achieve the team's aims.

Since the Wellington arrived back at Brooklands there has been a total of around 250 people who have worked on the aircraft over the past eleven years. Different team shifts are run on different days, in order to stop people getting in each other's way, and the most the team has 'fielded' on one day is between fifteen and twenty. With this number of volunteers all trying to 'do their bit' the Wellington can become pretty crowded at times. Therefore the importance of organizing the various teams has been critical to the project's success.

Quite a number of smaller parts of the aircraft have been restored off-site by certain members of the restoration crew. John Lattimore, current project co-ordinator explained:

Some of the team take small parts home with them in the most awful condition and then beaver away in the garage, eventually bringing the parts back several months later looking like new. This particular Wellington was last used by 20 OTU and was therefore converted to have dual controls. When the bomber was brought up from the Loch only one set of controls came up with the aircraft. The 'second' control column was brought up around a year later, but there was no sign of the co-pilot's floor assembly. One member volunteered to make the entire co-pilot's floor assembly from scratch. This has taken him many hours of spare time work, for the floor is constructed using a corrugated base, and these corrugations for the new floor unit had been hand made using the most basic of tools. Other items like the interior woodwork have been restored off-site using the original material as templates, as have the bomb-bay doors.

During *FlyPast's* visit John demonstrated that some of the Wellington's bomb-bay doors are now functional. Pressure was pumped into the hydraulic system and 'lo and behold' the doors moved to their closed position. Once pressure was released the doors opened again. As one of the other team members explained, the *Wimpey's* bomb-bay doors were spring loaded, so once pressure was released they opened automatically. This explains why, in so many wartime photographs of Wellingtons parked on the ground, the bomb-bay doors are inevitably open!

The Brooklands team have been fortunate in that Lord King of British Airways (BA) took an interest in the restoration project right from the start. He provided a workshop at the rear of Viscount House at Heathrow Airport so that former BA employees could carry out restoration work on various items. BA also restored the Wellington's undercarriage units. As Bob Casbard remarked:

We have been very lucky in receiving help from some of the major companies in British industry. Even in these pressing times companies help if they can. The BA engine shop took one of the

radial engines and the Rolls-Royce Heritage Trust (RRHT) at Filton took the other. Both were returned to us in superb condition. In fact, some of the people at the RRHT were original Bristol engineers who built these engines there in first place, so in terms of expertise the project was well blessed. Without this help from industry it would have been much harder to complete the task.

One vitally important aspect of this major project has been the acquisition of a large quantity of original Vickers drawings. Without these drawings the job would have been impossible! However, the team do not have a full set of drawings, for of the thousands of microfilmed blueprints which were available, only 200 appertain to the Wellington IA, which is the variant the team are working on. But as John Lattimore pointed out:

We were fortunate in having an 'ace' up our sleeve, for one of the team, Gerry Gleason, was a Flight Sergeant on *R for Robert's* unit up at RAF Lossiemouth. Gerry has got an incredible memory and while he was on the team was able to pick up bits and pieces and, nine times out of ten, identify them, AND tell us where they were fitted to the aircraft!

Gerry is no longer an active member of the crew, but still pops in from time to time to keep track of the project.

The Wellington's outer wing assemblies were shipped off to Monarch Aircraft Engineering at Luton, where members of the local branch of the Royal Aeronautical Society put them back into a presentable condition. Transported to Luton by British Aerospace early in 1988, the wings returned to Brooklands, courtesy of National Rescue, late in 1989.

The bomber's gun turrets benefited from work carried out by their original manufacturer Frazer-Nash. The Brooklands Wellington team have since carried out further restorative work on the turrets to bring them up to complete 'operational' condition. Surprisingly, both turrets still have their original perspex in place, which after much cleaning and polishing now looks as good as new.

The aircraft's cockpit area is just one portion of the bomber which has come in for some close scrutiny. Almost everything currently on view in and around the cockpit has had to be built from nothing by the Wellington team. The instrument panel's blind flying panel has had to be built entirely from scratch. Apart from constructing the metalwork in the panel itself,

this also meant many hundreds of miles of travelling for some members of the team, as they searched out the correct sort of instruments from aerojumbles and like events all over the UK. The pilot's seat pan is original, the rest is 'new-build', and the leather padding is original.

Another area which has been constructed from scratch is the mid to rear fuselage. Peering into the mass of geodetics one realizes that just this part of the rebuild programme was itself a massive undertaking. Over the years Bob and John estimate that some 20,000 pop rivets have been used on the Wellington, and the bulk of these have been put in to the airframe manually!

When the team have come to a point where portions of the restoration needed welding or machining, they have been fortunate in being able to call upon the talents and facilities of the nearby Brooklands College. The staff at the College have come to the rescue on a number of occasions.

Alongside Wellington N2980 is a forward fuselage of another *Wimpey*, which in time will be completed as a walk-through exhibit, thus giving visitors to the museum an idea of what life was like 'flying the Wellington'. 'This fuselage will be fitted out internally as complete as we can make it', says John Lattimore. 'We will however have to make certain concessions with regard to visitor safety as there are many things inside a Wellington on which one can easily bang your head or tear your jacket! Nevertheless we hope to give a flavour of the Wellington's interior.'

This second fuselage has proved to be invaluable, for certain parts of its 'sound' geodetic structure have been swapped for parts of a 'lesser quality' from N2980. The benefit of this is twofold, it enables N2980 to keep its structural integrity (which is the aim of the exercise anyway) and it still means that the walk-through exhibit will be as complete as possible.

Wellington N2980 currently has fabric applied to the fuselage top decking and to a portion of the rear fuselage. Bob Casbard explained why. 'We've fabricated these parts of the aircraft for two good reasons. 1st, it stops dust from settling inside the aircraft, and 2nd, the fabric will eventually be given a coat of camouflage paint, complete with squadron codes on the rear fuselage.'

One of the original team responsible for bringing the Wellington to the surface of Loch Ness all those years ago still keeps a close eye over proceedings at Brooklands, indeed he has been 'resident' at Brooklands in one capacity or another for the past sixty-five years! Norman 'Spud' Boorer, now in his eighties, started work with Vickers in September 1931 working in the machine shop. Although 'Spud' really wanted to work in the design department as a draughtsman, he was put initially into

Installation) or as it was known in the workshop, DWI = Down With 'itler!

During his long career at Vickers 'Spud' worked with the famed designer Barnes Wallis on the development of the Dambusting bomb and post-war was involved in the design of the Vickers Viking civil

fruition and his involvement in the recovery of N2980:

We had looked at several options for a museum at Brooklands, but none of them had the potential for a proper museum facility, that was until the tobacco company Gallaher's purchased forty acres

After much work the Wellington begins to take shape. FlyPast Collection

the machine shop, earning the princely sum of 14/2d a week! After attending evening classes he was later offered a job in the Vickers drawing offices. One of his first jobs was to help in the design of the prototype Wellington's rudder assembly. 'Spud' went on to work with George Edwards (who later became one of the 'greats' in the British aircraft industry) on projects like the Wellington with the large anti-magnetic mine ring fitted to it. This was the Wellington DWI (Directional Wireless

airliner. The Viking was a direct descendant of the Wellington using the wings and engines of the bomber mated to a rotund fuselage. Early Vikings even retained the Wellington's geodetic construction in the wings.

'Spud' retired in 1981, after fifty years at Vickers, and almost immediately was approached by Morag Barton, who at that time was formulating plans for a museum in the Brooklands area. 'Spud' remembers how the Brooklands Museum came to

of land which included the museum's present site. Gallaher's only needed ten acres for their office complex, and the remaining thirty acres were made available, at a peppercorn rent, to the local council to start a museum. Shortly after that the Loch Ness Wellington project was initiated. I was 'roped in' to design the lifting gear needed to bring the bomber back to the surface of the Loch. The Vintage Aircraft and Flying Association built the frame, and after some trials here at Brooklands it was moved up to Loch Ness in Scotland and put to work. The rest is history.

Starting to look like the 'real thing'. FlyPast Collection

(Below)
October 1996 and R-Robert looks in fine form; the intention is to leave the majority of the structure uncovered so that visitors can appreciate the geodetic construction. FlyPast Collection

After the bomber was brought back to Brooklands, 'Spud' was co-opted onto the museum's Wellington Restoration Committee and has since helped out on the design and calculations needed during the rebuild process. While he may not be out on the hangar floor 'hammering and banging' 'Spud' Boorer has played a decisive part in the Wellington's future.

The restoration of N2980 *R for Robert* will undoubtedly go down in British aircraft preservation history. The whole project to put this venerable bomber back together has been accomplished by a supremely dedicated band of volunteers, many of whom have 'stayed the course' one way or another.

People from all walks of life have contributed to the rebuild of this unique aircraft, ranging from former Wellington aircrew and groundcrew, former aircraft industry workers, through to keen enthusiasts who just want to be part of this fantastic project. All members of the team, past and present, can feel justly proud to have brought the world's only surviving 'operational' Wellington back from oblivion in the cold waters of Loch Ness.

Type Numbers and Production Data

VICKERS TYPE NO.	MINISTRY SPEC.	SERVICE TYPE NO.
271	B.9/32	
285	29/36	
290	33/37, I/P3(38)NZ	Wellington I
406	II/P1(38), II/P2(40)	Wellington II
408	IA/P1(39)	Wellington IA
415	IC/P1(39)	Wellington IC
417	III/P1(40)	Wellington III
418		Wellington DWI I
419		Wellington DWI II
424	IV/P1(40)	Wellington IV
426	B.23/39	Wellington V
429		Wellington VIII
430	VII/P1(42)	Wellington VII
431/442/449	17/40/V	cabin Wellington
440	X/P1(42)	Wellington X
442	VI/P1(42)	Wellington VI
455	XII/P1 & P2(43)	Wellington XII
458	XI/P1 & P2(43)	Wellington XI
466	GR.XIII/P1 & P2(43)	Wellington GR.XIII
467	GR.XIV/P1 & P2(43)	Wellington GR.XIV
490	XVIII/P1(44)	Wellington T.XVIII

WELLINGTON PRODUCTION BATCHES

SERIALS	NO. OF A/C	SERIALS	NO. OF A/C	SERIALS	NO. OF A/C
K4049	1	Z8328–Z9114	450	MS470–MS496	27
L4212–L4391	175	AD589–AD653	50	NA710–NB766	263
L7779–L7899	100	BB455–BB656	50	NB767–NV408	296
N2735–N2859	100	BJ581–BK564	600	NC414–ND133	500
N2805–N3019	120	DF542–DG197	150	PF820–PG422	400
P2515–P2532	18	DR471–DR600	44	RP312–RR178	226
P9205–P9300	82	DV411–DV953	415	TH450–TH974	(376)
R1000–R1806	550	HD942–HF606	1124		(cancelled)
R2699–R2703	5	HF609–HF816	153	TN250–TN462	(150)
R3150–R3299	100	HF828–HF922	84		(cancelled)
T2458–T3000	300	HX364–HX786	300		
W5352–W5737	300	HZ102–JA645	850		
W5795–W5824	21	LA964–LB251	150		
X3160–X4003	500	LN157–LR210	1382		
X5330–X6517	(750)	ME879–MF742	600		
	(cancelled)	MP502–MP825	250		
X9600–X9993; Z1040–Z1751	710				

Wellington Data

Total production of Wellingtons was 11,461 aircraft, the majority being constructed at Blackpool (5,540), with Chester building 3,406 and Weybridge 2,515. This total far exceeded Lancaster production at a mere 7,377 aircraft!

APPENDIX II

Wellington Units

SQN	MARK	DATES	SQN	MARK	DATES
				IC	May 40–Jan 42
8	XIII	Dec 43–May 45		III	Jan 42–Nov 42
9	I	Jan 39–Dec 39	93	IC	Mar 41–Jul 41
	IA	Sep 39–Sep 40	99	I	Sep 39–Apr 40
	IC	Feb 40–Oct 41,		IA	Sep 39–Apr 40
		May 42–Jun 42		IC	Mar 40–Feb 42,
	II	Mar 41–Aug 41			Oct 42–May 43
	III	Jul 41–Aug 42		II	Jul 41–Oct 41
12	II	Nov 40–Nov 42		III	Apr 43–Aug 44
	III	Aug 42–Nov 42		X	Apr 43–Aug 44
14	XIV	Nov 44–May 45	101	IC	Apr 41–Feb 42
15	IC	Nov 40–May 41		III	Feb 42–Oct 42
24	XV	Feb 43–Jan 44	103	IC	Oct 40–Jul 42
36	I	Dec 42–Jul 43	104	II	Apr 41–Aug 43
	VIII	Feb 43–Sep 43		X	Jul 43–Feb 45
	X	Jun 43–Nov 43	108	IC	Aug 41–Nov 42
	XI	Jul 43–Sep 43	109	I	Jul 41–Sep 41
	XII	Jul 43–Dec 43		IC	Dec 40–Dec 42
	XIII	Jul 43–Dec 43	115	I	Mar 39–Oct 39
	XIV	Sep 43–Jun 45		IA	Sep 39–Aug 40
37	I	May 39–Nov 39		IC	Jun 40–Feb 42
	IA	Oct 39–Aug 40		III	Feb 42–Mar 43
	IC	Jun 40–Apr 43	142	II	Nov 40–Oct 41
	III	Mar 43–Apr 43		III	Sep 42–Aug 43
	X	Mar 43–Oct 44		IV	Oct 41–Sep 42
38	I	Nov 38–Apr 40		X	Jun 43–Oct 44
	IA	Sep 39–Jun 40	148	I	Mar 39–Apr 40
	IC	Apr 40–Aug 42		IC	Apr 40–Oct 41,
	II	Aug 41–Oct 41			Apr 42–Dec 42
	VIII	May 42–Sep 43		II	Oct 41–Apr 42
	XI	Jun 43–May 44	149	I	Jan 39–Dec 39
	XII	Jun 43–Sep 43		IA	Sep 39–Jun 40
	XIII	Sep 43–Jan 45		IC	Mar 40–Dec 41
	XIV	Jan 45–Dec 46	150	IA	Oct 40–Dec 40
40	IC	Nov 40–Feb 42,		IC	Oct 40–Dec 42
		May 42–Jun 43		III	Sep 42–Aug 43
	III	Mar 43–Apr 44		X	Apr 43–Oct 44
	X	May 43–Mar 45	156	IC	Feb 42–Jun 42
57	IA	Nov 40–Nov 40		III	Feb 42–Jan 43
	IC	Nov 40–Jun 42	158	II	Feb 42–Jun 42
	II	Jul 41–Nov 41	162	IC	Jan 42–Feb 44
	III	Jan 42–Sep 42		III	Sep 43–Nov 43
69	XIII	May 44–Aug 45		DW I	Mar 44–Jul 44
70	IC	Sep 40–Jan 43		X	Apr 44–Sep 44
	III	Jan 43–Nov 43	166	III	Jan 43–Apr 43
	X	Apr 43–Jan 45		X	Feb 43–Sep 43
75	I	Jul 39–Apr 40	172	VIII	Apr 42–Mar 43
75(NZ)	I	Apr 40–Aug 40		XII	Dec 42–Oct 43
	IA	Apr 40–Aug 40		XIV	Aug 43–Jun 45

SQN	MARK	DATES
179	VIII	Sep 42–Sep 43
	XIV	Aug 43–Nov 44
192	IC	Jan 43–Mar 43
	III	Jan 43–Mar 43
	X	Jan 43–Jan 45
196	III	Dec 42–Dec 42
	X	Dec 42–Jul 43
199	III	Nov 42–Apr 43
	X	Mar 43–Jun 43
203	XIII	Nov 43–Oct 44
214	I	May 39–ay 40
	IA	Sep 39–Sep 40
	IC	Jul 40–Apr 42
	II	Nov 41–Dec 41
215	I	Jul 39–Apr 40
	IA	Apr 40–May 40
	IC	Feb 42–Sep 43
	X	Sep 43–Aug 44
218	IC	Nov 40–Feb 42
	II	May 41–Dec 41
221	IC	Nov 40–Dec 41
	VIII	Jan 42–Sep 43
	XI	Jun 43–Dec 43
	XII	Sep 43–Oct 43
	XIII	Oct 43–Aug 45
232	XVI	Dec 44–Feb 45
242	XVI	Jan 45–Feb 45
244	XIII	Feb 44–May 45
281	XIII	Aug 45–Sep 45
294	IC	Sep 43–Mar 44
	XI	Mar 44–Jun 45
	XIII	Jun 44–Apr 46
300	IC	Dec 40–Sep 41
	III	Jan 43–Apr 43
	IV	Aug 41–Jan 43
	X	Mar 43–Mar 44
301	IC	Oct 40–Aug 41
	IV	Aug 41–Apr 43
304	IC	Nov 40–Apr 43
	X	Apr 43–Jun 43
	XIII	Jun 43–Sep 43
	XIV	Sep 43–Dec 45
305	IC	Nov 40–Jul 41
	II	Jul 41–Aug 42
	IV	Aug 42–May 43
	X	May 43–Aug 43
311	IC	Aug 40–Jun 43
344	XI	Nov 43–Nov 45
	XIII	Nov 43–Nov 45
405	II	May 41–Apr 42
407	XI	Jan 43–Apr 43
	XII	Mar 43–Feb 44
	XIV	Jun 43–Jun 45
415	XIII	Sep 43–Jul 44
419	IC	Jan 42–Nov 42
	III	Feb 42–Nov 42
420	III	Aug 42–Apr 43
	X	Feb 43–Oct 43
424	III	Oct 42–Apr 43

SQN	MARK	DATES
	X	Feb 43–Oct 43
425	III	Aug 42–Apr 43
	X	Apr 43–Oct 43
426	III	Oct 42–Apr 43
	X	Mar 43–Jun 43
427	III	Nov 42–Mar 43
	X	Feb 43–May 43
428	III	Nov 42–Apr 43
	X	Apr 43–Jun 43
429	III	Nov 42–Aug 43
	X	Jan 43–Aug 43
431	X	Dec 42–Jul 43
432	X	May 43–Nov 43
458	IC	Feb 42–Apr 42, Sep 42–Nov 42
	IV	Aug 41–Jan 42
	VIII	Sep 42–Sep 43
	XIII	Jun 43–May 44
	XIV	Jan 44–Jun 45
460	IV	Nov 41–Sep 42
466	II	Oct 42–Nov 42
	X	Nov 42–Sep 43
524	XIII	Apr 44–Jan 45
	XIV	Dec 44–May 45
527	X	Apr 45–Apr 46
544	IV	Oct 42–Mar 43
547	VIII	Oct 42–May 43
	XI	May 43–Nov 43
	XIII	Oct 43–Nov 43
612	VIII	Nov 42–Mar 43
	XIII	Mar 43–Mar 44
	XIV	Jun 43–Jul 45
621	XIII	Sep 43–Nov 45
	XIV	Jan 45–Dec 45

FLEET AIR ARM

SQN	MARK	DATES
716	XI	Jul 41–Aug 45
728	XIV	1946
758	XI	Sep 43–Dec 43
762	XI	Aug 44–Apr 45
765	X	Jul 45–Apr 46
	XI	Aug 44–Apr 46
783	I	Feb 44–Sep 44
	II	Feb 44–Sep 44

SQN	PREVIOUS TYPE	FIRST WELLINGTON	LAST WELLINGTON	NEW TYPE
8	Blenheim/ Hudson	Dec 43	May 45	Liberator
9	Heyford	Feb 39	Aug 42	Lancaster
12	Battle	Oct 40	Nov 42	Lancaster
14	Marauder	Nov 44	Jun 45	Mosquito
15	Blenheim	Nov 40	May 41	Stirling

SQN	PREVIOUS TYPE	FIRST WELLINGTON	LAST WELLINGTON	NEW TYPE
24	–	Feb 43	Jan 44	–
36	Vildebeest	Dec 42	Jun 45	–
37	Harrow	May 39	Dec 44	Liberator
38	Hendon	Nov 38	Jun 46	Lancaster
40	Blenheim	Nov 40	Mar 45	Liberator
57	Blenheim	Nov 40	Sep 42	Lancaster
69	Baltimore	Aug 42	Aug 45	Mosquito
70	Valentia	Sep 40	Feb 45	Liberator
75	Harrow	Jul 39	Oct 42	Stirling
93	Havoc	Mar 41	May 42	Spitfire
99	Heyford	Oct 38	Sep 44	Lancaster
103	Battle	Oct 40	Jul 42	Halifax
104	(Anson)	Apr 41	Mar 45	Liberator
108	(Anson)	Aug 41	Nov 42	Liberator
109	Anson	Jan 41	Aug 42	Mosquito
115	Harrow	Sep 39	Mar 43	Lancaster
142	Battle	Nov 40	Oct 44	Mosquito
148	Heyford	Mar 39	Dec 42	(Liberator)
149	(Heyford)	Jan 39	Dec 41	Stirling
150	Battle	Oct 40	Oct 44	Lancaster
156	–	Feb 42	Jan 43	Lancaster
158	–	Feb 42	Jun 42	Halifax
162	–	Jan 42	Sep 44	Mosquito
166	(Whitley)	Jan 43	Sep 43	Lancaster
172	–	Apr 42	Jun 45	–
179	–	Sep 42	Nov 44	Warwick
192	–	Jan 43	Mar 45	Mosquito
196	–	Dec 42	Jul 43	Stirling
199	–	Nov 42	Jul 43	Stirling
203	Baltimore	Nov 43	Oct 44	Liberator
214	Harrow	May 39	Apr 42	Stirling
215	Harrow	Jul 39	Aug 44	Liberator
218	Blenheim	Nov 40	Feb 42	Stirling
221	–	Dec 40	Aug 45	–
232	Spitfire	Nov 44	Feb 45	Liberator
242	(Spitfire)	Jan 45	Feb 45	Stirling
244	Blenheim	Feb 44	May 45	–
281	Warwick	Sep 45	Oct 45	–
294	–	Sep 43	Apr 46	–
300	Battle	Oct 40	Apr 44	Lancaster
301	Battle	Oct 40	Apr 43	Halifax
304	Battle	Nov 40	Jan 46	Warwick
305	Battle	Nov 40	Sep 43	Mitchell
311	–	Aug 40	Jul 43	Liberator
344	–	Nov 43	Nov 45	–
405	–	Apr 41	Apr 42	Halifax
407	Hudson	Jan 43	Jun 45	–
415	Hampden	Sep 43	Jul 44	Halifax
419	–	Jan 42	Nov 42	Halifax
420	Hampden	Aug 42	Oct 43	Halifax
424	–	Dec 42	Oct 43	Halifax
425	–	Jul 42	Oct 43	Halifax
426	–	Oct 42	Jul 43	Lancaster
427	–	Nov 42	May 43	Halifax
428	–	Nov 42	Jun 43	Halifax
429	–	Nov 42	Aug 43	Halifax
431	–	Dec 42	Jul 43	Halifax
432	–	Dec 42	Jul 43	Halifax
458	–	Sep 41	Jun 45	–
460	–	Nov 41	Aug 42	Halifax
466	–	Oct 42	Sep 43	Halifax
524	(Mariner)	Apr 44	May 45	–
527	various	Apr 45	Apr 46	–
544	–	Oct 42	Mar 43	Mosquito
547	–	Nov 42	Nov 43	Liberator
612	Whitley	Nov 42	Jul 45	–
621	–	Sep 43	Dec 45	Warwick

WELLINGTON MARKS BY OPERATIONAL SQUADRON USER:

I 9, 37, 38, 75, 99, 109, 115, 148, 149, 214, 215, 783.

IA 9, 37, 38, 57, 75, 115, 149, 150, 214, 215.

IC 9, 15, 36, 37, 38, 40, 57, 70, 75, 93, 99, 101, 103, 108, 109, 115, 148, 149, 150, 156, 162, 192, 214, 215, 218, 221, 294, 300, 301, 304, 305, 311, 419, 457.

II 9, 12, 38, 57, 99, 104, 142, 148, 158, 214, 218, 305, 405, 466, 783.

III 9, 12, 37, 40, 57, 70, 75, 99, 101, 115, 142, 150, 156, 162, 166, 192, 196, 199, 300, 419, 420, 424, 425, 426, 427, 428, 429.

IV 142, 300, 301, 305, 458, 460, 544.

VIII 36, 38, 172, 179, 221, 458, 547, 612.

X 36, 37, 40, 70, 99, 104, 142, 150, 162, 166, 192, 196, 199, 215, 300, 304, 305, 420, 424, 425, 426, 427, 428, 429, 431, 432, 466, 527, 765.

XI 36, 38, 221, 294, 344, 407, 547, 716, 758, 762, 765.

XII 36, 38, 172, 221, 407.

XIII 8, 36, 38, 69, 203, 221, 244, 281, 294, 304, 344, 415, 458, 524, 547, 612, 621.

XIV 14, 36, 38, 172, 304, 407, 458, 524, 612, 621, 728.

XVI 24, 232, 242.

OPERATIONAL TRAINING UNITS

1(C), 3(C), 5(C), 6(C), 7(C), 10, 11, 12, 14, 15, 16, 17, 18, 19, 20, 21, 22, 23, 24, 25, 26, 27, 28, 29, 30, 51, 54, 62, 63, 76, 77, 78, 81, 82, 83, 84, 85, 86, 104, 105, 111.

APPENDIX III

Bomber Command Wellington Availability

DATE	WELLINGTONS + CREWS	TOTAL BOMBER COMMAND FORCE + CREWS
1941		
Jun	204	463
Jul	199	
Aug	191	
Sep	207	
Oct	202	517
Nov209		
Dec	227	
1942		
Jan	174	
Feb	151	374
Mar	191	
Apr	179	
May	183	
Jun	159	402
Jul	170	
Aug	135	
Sep	104	
Oct	132	408
Nov	78	
Dec	107	514
1943		
Jan	n/k	
Feb	137	
Mar	184	
Apr	158	
May	121	764
Jun	117	
Jul	89	
Aug	68	
Sep	38	
Oct	25	828
Nov	15	
Dec	11	
1944		
Jan	7	
Feb	6	984

Wellington U-boat Attacks by Coastal Command

Wellingtons played a significant role within Coastal Command for much of the War, and although never as successful as the Liberators, Catalinas and Sunderlands in respect of positive results (i.e. sunk or damaged targets) in U-boat attacks, they nevertheless achieved a significant measure of success, especially in respect of night attacks. The table below gives details of U-boat attacks that resulted in confirmed damaged or total loss of the enemy vessel.

DATE	SQUADRON/AIRCRAFT	SUBMARINE
4 Jun 42	ES986	*Luigi Torelli*, damaged
6 Jul 42	172 Sqn	U-502
12 Jul 42	172 Sqn	U-159, damaged
27 Jul 42	311 Sqn	U-106, damaged
10 Aug 42	311 Sqn	U-578
2 Sep 42	304 Sqn	*Reginaldo Guiliano*, damaged
22 Oct 42	179 Sqn HX776	U-412
10 Nov 42	172 Sqn	U-66, damaged
19 Feb 43	172 Sqn MP505	U-268
3 Mar 43	172 Sqn MP505	U-525, damaged
21 Mar 43	172 Sqn	U-332, damaged
22 Mar 43	172 Sqn MP539	U-665
10 Apr 43	172 Sqn	U-376
26 Apr 43	172 Sqn	U-566
29 Apr 43	172 Sqn HP630	U-437, damaged
1 May 43	172 Sqn	U-415, damaged
3 Jul 43	172 Sqn	U-126
9 Jul 43	179 Sqn	U-435
24 Jul 43	172 Sqn	U-459
29 Jul 43	172 Sqn	U-614
2 Aug 43	547 Sqn	U-218, damaged
24 Aug 43	179 Sqn	U-134
6 Sep 43	179 Sqn	U-760, damaged (interned)
7 Sep 43	407 Sqn HF115	U-669
11 Sep 43	179 Sqn	U-617
24 Sep 43	179 Sqn	U-667, damaged
21 Oct 43	179 Sqn	U-431
24 Oct 43	179 Sqn HF132	U-566
1 Nov 43	179 Sqn	U-340
10 Nov 43	612 Sqn	U-966 (shared with Liberators)
19 Nov 43	179 Sqn	U-211
28 Nov 43	179 Sqn HF168	U-542
3 Jan 44	612 Sqn MP756	U-373, damaged
4 Jan 44	304 Sqn HF185	U-629, damaged
8 Jan 44	179 Sqn	U0343, damaged
13 Jan 44	172 Sqn HF168	U-231
30 Jan 44	172 Sqn MP813	U-36
10 Feb 44	612 Sqn	U-545
11 Feb 44	407 Sqn MP578	U-283
12 Mar 44	612 Sqn	U-629, damaged
13 Mar 44	172 Sqn HF183	U-575
28 Apr 44	612 Sqn	U-193
4 May 44	407 Sqn HF134	U-846
24 May 44	612 Sqn	U-736, damaged
7 Jun 44	179 Sqn	U-415, damaged
7 Jun 44	407 Sqn HF149	U-989, damaged
13 Jun 44	172 Sqn MP789	U-270, damaged
18 Jun 44	304 Sqn HF331	U-441
20 Jun 44	407 Sqn HF286	U-971, damaged
30 Oct 44	407 Sqn NB839	U-1061, damaged
30 Dec 44	407 Sqn NB855	U-772
2 Apr 45	304 Sqn HF329	U-321

Totals: Sunk 30
Damaged 22

APPENDIX V

Bomber Command Operational Losses

The following tables give details of Bomber Command Wellington losses during operational sorties; the information has been extracted from Bill Chorley's excellent series of volumes *Bomber Command Losses of World War Two*, published by Midland Counties. The volumes covering 1939–40, 1941, 1942 and 1943 are already in print with 1944 planned for release in late 1997 (and 1945 to follow in due course). The entries include only those aircraft lost on operational sorties, although Bill's books include training losses as well and also give full details of the crew and a remarks column with details of the loss. The entries are for those aircraft that were written off and so includes those that made it back to the UK but then crashed. Aircraft that were repaired are not included and so casualties in aircraft that were subsequently repaired are not included; hence, the casualty column is NOT an overall total of aircrew killed.

Where the entry in the target column is left blank it means that the it is the same target as for the previous entry e.g in the first two both losses are on shipping sorties.

Many thanks to Bill for allowing me to use this data; I can certainly recommend the books as references for anyone with an interest in Bomber Command 1939–45.

garden. = gardening (minelaying)
SD = Special Duties

DATE	TARGET	SQN	CAPTAIN	A/C	AIRCREW KILLED
1939					
4.9	Shipping	9	F/S I Borley	L4268	5
		9	F/S A Turner	L4275	5
14.12	Shipping	99	P/O N Lewis	N2870	6
		99	F/S J Healey	N2886	6
		99	F/S W Downey	N2911	6
		99	F/O J Cooper	N2956	6
		99	F/L E Hetherington	N29573	
		99	Sgt R Brace	N2986	6
18.12	Shipping	9	S/L A Guthrie	N2872	6
		9	F/O J Challes	N2939	6
		9	P/O E Lines	N2940	5
		9	F/O D Allison	N2941	6
		9	Sgt R Hewitt	N2983	1
		37	F/O P Wimberley	N2888	4
		37	F/O D Lewis	N2889	4
		37	S/L I Hue-Williams	N2904	6
		37	F/O A Thompson	N2935	5
		37	Sgt H Ruse	N2936	2
		149	F/O M Briden	N2961	6
		149	F/O J Speirs	N2962	5
1939 totals				*20*	*96*
1940					
2.1	Shipping	149	F/O H McBulloch	N2943	6
		149	Sgt J Morrice	N2946	6
20/21.2	Shipping	38	F/O N Hawxby	N2951	6
		38	F/L M Nolan	P2526	0
		99	F/L J Brough	P9219	0
	nickel	99	F/O D Williams	N3004	0
1/2.3	nickel	149	F/O L Field	N2984	6
3.3	nickel	99	P/O A Stewart	N3006	6
22/24.3	nickel	37	F/O P Templeman	P2515	1
	recco	149	F/O F Turner	P9225	0
7.4	Shipping	115	P/O R Gayford	N2949	6
		115	P/O Wickencamp	P2524	6
11/12.4	Stavanger	115	P/O F Barber	P9284	6
12.4	Shipping	9	Sgt C Bowen	P2520	6
		38	S/L M Nolan	P9269	6
		149	Sgt H Wheller	P9246	6
		149	Sgt G Goad	P9266	6
13/14.4	Shipping	38	P/O G Crosby	L4339	6
17/19.4	Stavanger	99	F/O A Smith	P9234	6
21/22.4	Aalborg	149	F/O F Knight	P9218	0
30/1.6	Stavanger	37	S/L R Bradford	P9213	6
		37	F/O G Gordon	P9215	5
		99	F/S J Brent	P9276	6
		115	F/O A Gibbes	R3154	2
15/16.5	Duisburg	115	F/L A Pringle	P9229	5
16/17.5	Gelsenkirchen	9	F/O J Smalley	N3015	0
20/21.5	Cambrai	115	F/S L Moores	P9298	6
21/22.5	Dinant	75	F/O J Collins	R3157	2
		99	F/O J Dyer	L7803	6
		115	F/O D Laslett	P9297	0
		115	P/O D Morris	R3152	6
22/23.5	Namur	9	F/O K Day	L7777	0
23/24.5	comms	149	F/L I Grant-Crawford	P9270	3
25/25.5	comms	37	S/L A Glencross	L7793	3
29/30.5	St Omer	99	P/O J Young	P9241	1
		99	P/O J Brain	P9282	0
		99	P/O C Brain	R3196	0
30/31.5	Diksmuide	38	F/O V Rosewarne	R3162	6
31/1.6	Nieuwport	37	F/O R Simmons	P9288	5
		37	P/O W Gray	L7791	3
5/6.6	Duisburg	9	S/L G Peacock	P9232	2
10/11.6	Soissons	149	F/O J Douglas-Cooper	L7800	6
13/14.6	Pont de l'Arche	9	Sgt R Hewitt	L7787	6
14/15.6	Black Forest	38	Sgt L Morris	N2953	2
18/19.6	Leverkusen	9	P/O F Butler	N2897	6
19/20.6	Ruhr	99	F/L P Pickard	R3200	0

DATE	TARGET	SQN	CAPTAIN	A/C	AIRCREW KILLED
21/22.6	Bremen	9	F/O G Nicholson	L7807	0
5/6.7	Kiel	99	P/O R Willis	R3170	1
6/7.7	Bremen	37	F/O D Lindsay	R3236	5
11/12.7	Bremen	149	P/O J Torgalson	L7805	6
14/15.7	Hamburg	37	Sgt J McCauley	L7792	3
18/19.7	Bremen	115	P/O W Hunkin	P9227	0
19/20.7	Wismar	9	S/L J Monypenny	L7795	6
20/21.7	Gelsenkirchen	37	P/O G Muirhead	R3210	4
	Horst	75	F/O S Watson	R3165	5
25/26.7	Kassel	75	F/O W Coleman	R3235	6
	NW Germany	99	Sgt A Herriot	P9274	0
		99	P/O B Power	P9275	1
2/3.8	Hamburg	115	P/O R Gerry	R3202	6
3/4.8	Horst	75	S/L W Collett	R3176	1
11/12.8	Gelsenkirchen	149	P/O J Miller	P9244	6
16/17.8	Koleda	149	S/L E Thwaites	R3174	3
22/23.8	Mannheim	115	Sgt N Cook	R3276	1
27/28.8	Kiel	149	F.L P Vaillant	P9272	0
30/31.8	Berlin	214	F/O R O'Connor	P2530	0
		214	F/O L Craigie-Halkett	T2559	6
1/2.9	Hannover	37	P/O M Burberry	N2992	5
		75	P/O R Peel	R3159	0
5/6.9	Black Forest	149	F/O H Burton	R3163	0
8/9.9	Boulogne	149	S/L L Andrews	P9245	5
		149	P/O J Leeds	R3175	6
11/12.9	Ostende	38	F/O R Allen	/R	6
18/19.9	NW Germany	99	P/O M Linden	P9242	6
	Le Havre	149	P/O J Pay	R3160	6
20/21.9	ports	75	P/O M Braun	T2463	6
23/24.9	Berlin	311	F/L K Trojacek	L7788	0
25/26.9	Calais	99	F/O F Vivian	L7868	0
27/28.9	Mannheim	214	Sgt J Hall	L7843	3
28/29.9	Hanau	9	F/O A Cox	T2472	0
		149	P/O H Petersen	R3164	1
	Cologne	9	Sgt C Oliver	T2505	5
29/30.9	Bitterfeld	37	F/O A Dingle	R3150	5
	Leipzig	75	P/O F Denton	R3168	1
30/1.10	Leipzig	38	P/O D Maclean	R3219	1
	Osnabruck	115	Sgt C Wessels	R3292	6
		115	P/O A Steel	T2549	4
1/2.10	Berlin	9	F/L C Fox	R3282	6
7/8.10	Berlin	38	S/L R Taylor	P9287	6
		99	P/O Topham	L7896	0
9/10.10	Herringen	149	P/O R Furness	P9273	6
13/14.10	Wilhelmshaven	99	F/O W Keller	P9243	6
14/15.10	Magdeburg	9	S/L J Hinks	T2464	6
16/17.10	Kiel	9	Sgt F Bevan	P9278	0
		75	P/O J Morton	L7857	0
		311	P/O B Landa	L7844	4
		311	S/L J Vesely	N2771	1
		311	F/L J Snajdr	N2773	0
21/22.10	Eindhoven	75	F/O R Elliott	R3158	0
	Hamburg	75	F/L C Gilbert	T2820	0
23/24.10	Berlin	75	P/O R Sanderson	P9292	6
	Emden	149	F/O D Donaldson	T2740	0
24/25.10	Hamburg	38	F/L E Chivers	L7809	6
29/30.10	Berlin	99	F.L K Harvey	T2546	1
5/6.11	Hamburg	214	Sgt G Turner	T2470	6
6/7.11	Ruhr	99	F/L R Jones	R3289	6
7/8.11	Essen	9	P/O P Berry	T2462	0
8/9.11	Dusseldorf	99	Sgt E Fletcher	N2767	0
13/14.11	NW Germany	99	Sgt F Swatton	R3167	0
14/15.11	Berlin	9	S/L S Pritchard	L7852	0
		115	Sgt H Morson	T2509	1
16/17.11	Hamburg	115	Sgt D Larkman	P9286	6
		115	Sgt D English	R3213	6
19/20.11	Berlin	149	P/O K Hide	N2774	6
23/24.11	Berlin	214	Sgt S Chester	T2471	6
25/26.11	Kiel	99	F/S F Swatton	R1176	6
29/30.11	Germany	214	S/L B McGinn	T2893	2?
4/5.12	Dusseldorf	99	F/O F Vivian	T2501	0
7/8.12	Dusseldorf	9	F/O D Stanley	R3220	6
		214	F/L W Harris	R3209	6
		214	F/O D Dadswell	T2476	6
8/9.12	Bordeaux	115	P/O A Tindall	T2520	6
11/12.12	Mannheim	115	Sgt G Hartland	T2466	6
16/17.12	Mannheim	99	Sgt C Muller	T2461	0
		149	Sgt J Marr	P9268	0
		311	Sgt J Krivda	T2577	3
18/19.12	Ludwigshafen	99	F/L G Ogilvie	R1333	4
	Mannheim	99	S/L C Scott-Dickins	T2803	1
21/22.12	Venice	9	Sgt R Harrison	L7799	6
22/23.12	Mannheim	75	Sgt E Chuter	T2474	1
27/28.12	Le Havre	214	P/O J Temperley	L7849	3
	Antwerp	300	P/O A Krynski	R1035	1
29/30.12	Hamm	75	F/L H Newman	R3211	0
		115	P/O P Salmon	T2465	6
1940 Totals				*133*	*446*
1941					
1/2.1	Bremen	301	S/L S Floryanowicz	T2517	6
		301	P/O B Murawski	T2518	5
11/12.1	Torino	9	Sgt S Parkes	R2144	0
12/13.1	Italy	149	Sgt R Hodgson	T2807	0
16/17.1	Wilhelmshaven	40	Sgt A Jones	T2912	6
		311	P/O A Kubiznak	T2519	6
29/30.1	Wilhelmshaven	214	Sgt J Smiles	T2841	0
6/7.2	Boulogne	214	P/O W Spooner	N2776	0
		311	P/O F Cigos	L7842	0
10/11.2	Hannover	103	Sgt W Crich	T2610	0
		115	Sgt H Rogers	R1084	0
11/12.2	Bremen	99	Sgt Robinson	T2888	2
		115	P/O Clarke	R1004	0
		115	Sgt Whittaker	R1238	0
		115	W/C A Evans-Evans	R3238	0
		149	Sgt R Warren	P9247	1
		218	F/O Anstey	R1210	0
		218	Sgt W Adam	T2885	0
15/16.2	Sterkrade	15	P/O C Dove	T2847	4
21/22.2	Wilhemshaven	75	P/O A Falconer	T2503	6
		75	P/O R Hewitt	T2547	0
		149	F/O I Henderson	R1045	6
22/23.2	Brest	115	Sgt E Milton	R1221	6
23/24.2	Boulogne	115	P/O K Arthurs	L7810	6
25/26.2	Dusseldorf	103	P/O J Ralston	T2621	6

DATE	TARGET	SQN	CAPTAIN	A/C	AIRCREW KILLED	DATE	TARGET	SQN	CAPTAIN	A/C	AIRCREW KILLED
		214	P/O H Hordern	L7859	0		Brest	115	Sgt Sayers	R1280	0
		218	Sgt Hook	R1009	0	5/6.5	Mannheim	99	F/O Osborn	T2477	0
1/2.3	Cologne	9	F/O H Lawson	R1228	6	6/7.5	Hamburg	75	Sgt D Nola	R3169	5
2/3.3	Brest	115	Sgt G Pike	R3279	6		Le Havre	304	P/O A Sym	R1443	6
12/13.3	Bremen	9	Sgt B Hall	N2744	4	7/8.5	St Nazaire	150	F/L F Savage	R1374	6
		218	F/O W Crosse	R1326	4	8/9.5	Berlin	99	S/L P Jackson	W5400	6
	Berlin	40	S/L E Lynche-Blosse	R1013	0		Hamburg	149	F/S C Burch	R1506	4
	Boulogne	40	Sgt D Gough	T2515	6			214	S/L F Eddison	R1226	6
13/14.3	Hamburg	57	Sgt J Harvey	T2970	0			214	F/S W Browell	R3208	6
		214	F/O H Matthews	N2746	5		Bremen	301	Sgt T Bojalowski	R1227	6
14/15.3	Gelsenkirchen	149	Sgt L Hawley	L7858	6			304	F/O G Lynes	R1473	5
17/18.3	Bremen	149	Sgt R Warren	R1474	6			305	Sgt J Dorman	R1322	6
18.3	Bremen	311	Sgt Anderle	R1378	0	9/10.5	Mannheim	214	P/O I Woodroffe	R1447	0
18/19.3	Kiel	75	F/O Collins	T2736	1	10/11.5	Hamburg	115	Sgt J Anderson	R1379	1
	Cologne	149	Sgt W Hall	R1159	0			149	Sgt J Keymer	R1512	6
21/22.3	Ostende	57	F/L A Barber	X3162	6			150	F/O V Spiller	R1435	6
	Lorient	150	F/O C Elliot	R3288	5	11/12.5	Hamburg	40	Sgt R Finlayson	R1330	5
23/24.3	Berlin	40	P/O Billyeald	R1166	0			40	Sgt F Luscombe	R1461	6
		300	S/L Cwynar	R1273	0			214	P/O J Toplis	R1462	6
		300	Sgt Hazierczak	T2719	0	15/16.5	Hannover	40	Sgt W Moore	R1167	5
27/28.3	Cologne	9	F/L J Shore	R1335	0			103	P/O R Eccles	R1494	2
		57	Sgt Emmerson	R1441	0	16/17.5	Boulogne	9	Sgt L Mitchell	R1267	1
30/31.3	Brest	103	W/C C Littler	R1043	1	27/28.5	Boulogne	150	Sgt V Huggett	R1044	5
		103	S/L Mellor	W5612	0			304	P/O J Waroczewski	R1392	4
31/1.4	Bremen	15	Sgt B Kelly	T2703	1	2/3.6	Dusseldorf	40	Sgt P Sargent	R1438	5
	Emden	149	Sgt G Morhen	R1229	0		Berlin	214	W/C R Jordan	W5450	0
3/4.4	Brest	115	Sgt C Thompson	R1470	5	9.6	recce.	9	W/C R Arnold	R1758	1
7/8.4	Kiel	40	Sgt T Gamble	R1007	6			9	F/O D Lamb	T2620	5
		214	Sgt R Williams	R1380	6	11/12.6	Dusseldorf	40	S/L M Redgrave	R1323	0
8/9.4	Kiel	149	Sgt J Jago	X3167	6			40	P/O R Payne	R1464	6
		214	Sgt J Cusworth	T2542	6			99	Sgt J Barron	P9281	4
9/10.4	Berlin	9	P/O G Sharp	T2473	6			99	Sgt D Woodward	W5680	6
		57	F/O G Ritchie	T2804	0			149	Sgt W Harrison	W5439	0
		99	S/L D Torrens	R3199	0			300	F/O S Sedzik	W5666	0
	Emden	12	W/C V Blackden	W5375	6	12/13.6	Osnabruck	103	F/O R Chisholm	T2996	6
	Vegesack	57	Sgt D Day	R1437	4			301	F/O Pozyczka	R1348	0
		99	P/O T Fairhurst	R1440	6		Hamm	115	Sgt Robson	R1721	0
10/11.4	Merignac	40	F/L F Bowler	R1493	1	16/17.6	Duisburg	103	S/L D Kelly	N2849	6
	Brest	218	Sgt A Plumb	R1442	6		Cologne	405	Sgt W MacGregor	W5522	6
12/13.4	Merignac	149	Sgt R Morison	T2897	5	18/19.6	Bremen	300	Sgt Paleniczek	W5665	4
15/16.4	Kiel	311	P/O S Zeinert	P9212	0			301	P/O J Krassowski	R1365	6
17/18.4	Cologne	9	Sgt G Heaysman	N2745	2			305	Sgt S Lewek	R1696	2
		149	Sgt J Peel	P9248	6	19/20.6	Cologne	99	S/L B Rogers	R1537	2
	Berlin	9	Sgt R Stark	T2900	6	20/21.6	Kiel	218	Sgt G Jillett	R1339	6
		40	Sgt Jenner	R1331	1			218	Sgt M Fraser	R1713	6
		311	Sgt F Kracmer	R1599	6	22/23.6	Bremen	301	P/O S Pietruszka	R1026	2
20/21.4	Cologne	99	P/O F Cook	T2997	6			311	F/S B Bufka	T2990	5
22/23.4	Brest	115	Sgt Palmer	T2560	1	23/24.6	Kiel	115	P/O Sharpe	T2963	0
		218	Sgt W Swain	L7798	5	24/25.6	Kiel	57	Sgt H Ward	R1608	6
		218	Sgt W Adams	R1368	0		Emden	214	Sgt G Jones	R1609	6
24/25.4	Kiel	15	Sgt A Jones	R1218	0		Boulogne	305	S/L M Kielich	W5723	4
		218	Sgt E Chidgey	T2958	0	25/26.6	Bremen	99	Sgt J Hancock	R1372	6
25/26.4	Kiel	218	F/O G Agar	R1507	6	26/27.6	Cologne	40	P/O D Horrocks	R1406	6
26/27.4	Emden	9	Sgt R Damman	R1281	0			115	Sgt Skillen	R1501	0
29/30.4	Mannheim	99	Sgt F Hewitson	T2721	6		Dusseldorf	150	P/O J Sievers	R1644	6
2/3.5	Emden	305	F/O J Nogal	R1214	2	27/28.6	Bremen	12	S/L G Kitching	W5391	6
3/4.5	Rotterdam	9	Sgt Anderson	T2964	0			57	Sgt M Ross	R1794	6

DATE	TARGET	SQN	CAPTAIN	A/C	AIRCREW KILLED	DATE	TARGET	SQN	CAPTAIN	A/C	AIRCREW KILLED
		142	P/O R Lomax	W5386	6			405	P/O R Trueman	W5537	0
29/30.6	Hamburg	40	F/L A Bird	W5456	5			405	W/C P Gilchrist	W5551	1
		115	P/O A McSweyn	R1509	0			405	Sgt J Craig	W5581	0
	Bremen	115	Sgt F Payne	R1508	0	24/25.7	Kiel	57	Sgt F Green	R1369	4
		115	P/O F Bryant	T2806	6		Brest	103	Sgt M Lund	R1379	4
		300	Sgt P Nowakowski	R1640	0		Emden	304	F/O L Karczewski	X9620	6
		301	F/L L Kozlowski	R1373	1	25/26.7	Hamburg	300	P/O Klecha	R1178	0
1/2.7	Brest	149	P/O S St Vincent-Welch	R1343	6			300	Sgt M Sloma	X9639	5
		149	P/O J Horsfield	R1408	6	30/31.7	Cologne	99	P/O G Bevan	T2957	6
	Cherbourg	311	Sgt O Helma	R1516	6			142	F/S H Vidler	W5364	6
2/3.7	Bremen	12	F/L W Baxter	W5419	6			150	Sgt P Parrott	W5719	5
3/4.7	Essen	57	Sgt W Hoskins	R1589	5	2/3.8	Hamburg	101	P/O Buncley	R1088	0
		75	Sgt I Reid	W5621	6			101	Sgt W Davey	R1800	6
		99	P/O J Dunn	T2984	3			103	Sgt Kelsey	X3204	0
	Bremen	300	F/O K Kula	R1642	4			405	P/O R Cox	W5527	6
		301	F/O Butkiewicz	R1492	1		Berlin	104	P/O R McGlashan	W5580	6
6/7.7	Brest	12	S/L A Baird	W5360	6			405	F/L T Kipp	W5483	0
	Munster	40	P/O J Marksteeds	N2843	5	3/4.8	Hannover	218	P/O J Maxwell	X9747	2
		115	Sgt O Matthews	R1063	6			218	W/C J Fletcher	Z8781	4
	Dortmund	405	F/O R Fraas	W5490	2	5/6.8	Aachen	12	F/L R Langlois	W5421	0
7/8.9	Cologne	9	P/O D Jamieson	R1040	6		Frankfurt	103	Sgt Greey	W5656	6
		99	F/L E Masters	T2880	0			305	S/L S Scibier	W5593	3
		214	F/O R Jenkyns	T2992	5		Karlsruhe	104	P/O B Jones	W5485	6
8/9.7	Munster	9	Sgt B Pitt	T2973	6		Saarbrucken	104	Sgt W Stephenson	W5517	0
9/10.7	Osnabruck	40	F/O G Conran	R1770	2		Mannheim	115	F/L F Litchfield	R1471	0
		305	Sgt J Mikszo	R1762	1			149	Sgt F Fowler	R1524	6
10/11.7	Cologne	9	Sgt S Retter	W5729	3	6/7.8	Mannheim	57	Sgt B Cleaver	Z8704	0
		300	P/O J Kuflik	R1184	0			75	Sgt L Millett	R1648	2
13/14.7	Bremen	75	Sgt F Minikin	X9634	4			149	Sgt J Farmer	X9633	6
		115	Sgt W Reid	R1502	1			214	P/O C McD Didsbury	X9750	6
14/15.7	Hannover	104	P/O W Rowse	W5513	6		Frankfurt	150	P/O C Landreth	W5721	6
		405	Sgt D Thrower	W5534	0			300	F/L H Cichowski	X9676	6
	Bremen	149	P/O P Dixon	T2737	0	8/9.8	Hamburg	301	F/O M Liniewski	T2625	4
		214	P/O J Crampton	R1613	1	12/13.8	Hannover	9	Sgt E Lewin	R1341	6
		214	P/O V Brown	R1614	6			149	P/O F Beemer	R1024	6
		304	P/O J Ostrowski	R1002	0			149	P/O Fox	T2716	1
		305	F/O J Janota-Bzowski	W5726	6		Kiel	9	F/L K Ball	R1513	6
15/16.7	Duisburg	57	Sgt Rishworth	N2784	6		Boulogne	99	P/O G Eccles	R1503	0
		57	Sgt G Osborne	R1624	6		Berlin	104	Sgt R Holyman	W5443	6
		75	Sgt R Fotheringham	R3171	6			104	S/L H Budden	W5461	0
		115	F/S N Cook	R1222	6			142	F/L A Gosman	W5433	0
		218	F/L J Stokes	R1536	6		Essen	115	P/O Wood	T2563	1
16/17.7	Hamburg	40	S/L R Weighill	X3220	6			115	Sgt J Wallace	Z8835	6
		40	Sgt A Bird	X9630	5	14/15.8	Rotterdam	12	Sgt Cameron	W5536	1
		150	P/O E Betheridge-Topp	R1495	5		Hannover	104	P/O J Drewsen	W5486	6
		311	Sgt G Nyc	R1718	1			115	Sgt C Alway	R1500	6
17/18.7	Cologne	149	Sgt D Stewart	N2853	1			150	Sgt J Elder	R1016	1
	Rotterdam	301	F/O B Kuzian	N2840	6			150	Sgt A Perry-Keane	R1394	6
19/20.7	Hannover	311	Sgt V Netik	R1371	6			218	P/O A Mitchell	R1008	6
21/22.7	Mannheim	115	Sgt N Johnston	Z8788	6			218	P/O W Wilson	X9753	5
24.7	Brest	12	Sgt H Heald	W5380	6			405	P/O G Fleming	W5496	6
		40	Sgt M Evans	T2986	6	16/17.8	Cologne	12	F/L C McVeigh	W5444	3
		75	Sgt D Streeter	N2854	6			104	Sgt W Stephenson	W5532	6
		101	F/L F Craig	R1702	4			305	Sgt S Przeclawski	W5463	6
		103	Sgt J Bucknole	N2770	6		Duisburg	99	P/O G Wells	X9700	5
		104	P/O M Nicholls	W5438	0	18/19.8	Duisburg	149	P/O J Lynn	X9704	2
		218	P/O M Jully	R1726	4			149	P/O Gregory	X9746	0
								218	Sgt K Shearing	N2844	6

DATE	TARGET	SQN	CAPTAIN	A/C	AIRCREW KILLED
		218	Sgt H Huckle	W5457	1
		300	Sgt K Ceglinski	R1641	2
19/20.8	Kiel	9	Sgt C Everitt	R1455	6
		101	Sgt W Fisher	W5715	6
		104	F/L W Burton	W5416	6
25/26.8	Karlsruhe	40	Sgt D Youlden	T2514	6
		40	S/L A Martin	X9749	6
26/27.8	Cologne	9	S/L H Bufton	W5703	0
27/28.8	Mannheim	115	P/O Foster	R1468	0
		115	S/L Sidnall	W5710	0
		115	P/O Pooley	X9672	0
		150	Sgt E Nicholson	W5722	0
28/29.8	Duisburg	40	P/O J King	Z8839	3
		104	Sgt G Spickett	W5595	6
		405	P/O E Watts	W5488	4
29/30.8	Mannheim	103	P/O W Oldfield	R1213	4
		115	Sgt J Murdoch	X9826	5
		214	Sgt E Foxlee	R1604	6
30/31.8	Hamburg	101	P/O Reynolds	Z8860	1
31/1.9	Boulogne	12	P/O C Khosla	W5577	6
	(includes two Indian Air Force personnel)				
	Cologne	99	P/O G Eccles	R1411	5
		101	P/O J Ashton	R1703	3
2/3.9	Ostende	40	P/O A Fitch	R1030	2
		218	S/L Gibbes	X9810	0
	Frankfurt	40	P/O Baker	X9669	0
		57	Sgt L Hutchison	W5434	6
		104	P/O R Doherty	W5435	0
		150	Sgt Dickenson	Z8815	0
		214	F/L R May	R1717	6
		305	Sgt Molata	W5563	0
3/4.9	Brest	115	P/O Scholes	W5684	0
6/7.9	Huls	75	P/O J Johnson	X9767	6
		57	Sgt N lake	Z8794	6
7/8.9	Berlin	9	Sgt T Wilmot	R1499	0
		9	Sgt J Saich	Z8845	6
		12	S/L P Edinger	W5598	5
		12	S/L S Fielden	Z8328	0
		104	Sgt F Richardson	W5362	6
		115	Sgt I McH Gordon	R1798	6
		214	W/C G Cruckshanks	R1784	6
		218	S/L H Price	W5449	0
		405	Sgt J Saunders	W5521	0
	Kiel	115	Sgt R Hill	R1772	1
10/11.9	Torino	101	P/O Allen	R1699	0
		103	P/O D Petrie	R1396	6
		104	S/L D Strong	W5576	0
11/12.9	Kiel	75	Sgt K Roe	R1038	6
		149	Sgt D Bennett	X9879	6
12/13.9	Frankfurt	40	S/L J Atkins	R1328	2
		218	Sgt C Dare	X9670	0
13/14.9	Brest	57	Sgt S Gray	R1792	0
		99	Sgt J Watt	X9703	0
		214	Sgt Nicholls	N2802	0
15/16.9	Hamburg	57	Sgt A Witherington	X9923	2
		75	Sgt J Ward	X3205	4
		75	Sgt A Hawkins	X9759	4
		311	Sgt V Soukup	R1015	6
	Le Havre	305	W/C J Drysdale	W5526	6
17/18.9	Karlsruhe	75	Sgt W Smyth	X9834	3
19/20.9	Stettin	142	P/O I Burke	W5384	5
		405	Sgt T Dougall	Z8344	0
20/21.9	Berlin	57	Sgt J McGeach	R1271	1
		75	Sgt J Matetich	R1518	0
		75	P/O A Raphael	T2805	0
		103	F/O T Wardhaugh	9609	2
		103	P/O I Murchie	X9665	6
		214	P/O Barnard	R1712	0
		214	Sgt L Kissack	W5452	5
	Frankfurt	57	Sgt E Backhouse	R1706	0
		103	P/O K Wallis	L7886	0
		103	Sgt A Rex	R1539	5
		150	Sgt Dickenson	X9811	0
	Ostende	101	Sgt W Dil	X9922	4
26/27.9	Emden	9	Sgt J Gingles	X3222	2
		115	Sgt M Farnan	R1332	6
	Cologne	305	Sgt E Buszko	W5557	1
28/29.9	Genova	9	F/S W Kitson	R1279	6
		57	S/L Warfield	Z8789	0
		57	Sgt J Paul	Z8868	6
	Frankfurt	75	Sgt S Isherwood	R1177	0
		99	Sgt J Parry	T2879	6
		99	P/O K Rumbo	W5436	3
		99	Sgt E Coleman	X9761	0
		99	Sgt J Watt	Z8869	6
29/30.9	Hamburg	115	Sgt L Ellis	X9673	6
		115	Sgt A Hulls	X9910	5
	Stettin	142	P/O G Bull	W5378	6
		214	Sgt L Hancock	X9884	0
30/1.10	Hamburg	9	Sgt A Humble-Smith	X3347	0
		57	Sgt G Johnson	W5445	0
10/11.10	Cologne	12	P/O D Faint	W5379	4
		12	Sgt F Tothill	Z8379	6
		57	Sgt E Backhouse	X9756	6
		57	Sgt M Young	Z8897	6
		75	Sgt R Curlewis	Z8909	6
		75	Sgt Taylor	Z8945	6
		101	P/O G Imeson	R1219	1
	Bordeaux	218	Sgt V Haley	R1511	1
		218	Sgt McLean	X9677	3
12/13.10	Nurnberg	12	Sgt C Elsdon	W5552	0
		40	P/O I Field	X9619	6
		57	Sgt A Jeffries	R1757	5
		75	S/L P Chamberlain	X9981	6
		214	Sgt J Key	X9762	0
		218	Sgt J McGlashan	Z9810	0
	Bremen	40	Sgt G Bateman	X9822	6
13/14.10	Dusseldorf	101	Sgt R Betts	T2846	0
	Munich	115	Sgt F Deardon	Z8844	6
14/15.10	Nurnberg	40	Sgt J Hiscock	X9882	6
		40	P/O G Buse	X9926	6
		40	Sgt K Edis	Z8782	6
		218	Sgt K Fisher	Z8865	0
15/16.10	Cologne	57	P/O K Miller	X9978	6
		75	Sgt R Barker	W5663	4
		75	Sgt J Matetich	X9916	6

DATE	TARGET	SQN	CAPTAIN	A/C	AIRCREW KILLED	DATE	TARGET	SQN	CAPTAIN	A/C	AIRCREW KILLED
16/17.10	Duisburg	40	S/L T Kirby-Green	Z8862	5			458	P/O R Furey	R1775	6
		103	P/O Jones	R1217	0		Kiel	99	Sgt Russell	X9740	0
		218	F/L Dunham	Z8957	0			115	P/O Stock	Z8848	0
	Dunkirk	305	Sgt S Hildebrandt	W5579	6			218	Sgt A Cook	R1135	6
20/21.10	Bremen	99	Sgt L Faunt	R3222	6			218	Sgt Forsyth	Z8853	1
		99	Sgt Morgan	Z8891	0			311	Sgt S Linka	Z8966	4
		149	P/O A Hodge	Z8795	6	26/27.11	Emden	75	Sgt Giddens	Z1144	0
		311	Sgt V Prochazka	R1046	0			103	P/O Ward	T2999	0
	Emden	304	Sgt N Zykow	N2852	6			214	F/S N Hettrick	Z8373	6
	Antwerp	458	Sgt P Hamilton	Z1218	5			218	Sgt Helfer	Z1103	0
21/22.10	Bremen	12	Sgt J Miller	W5393	5	27/28.11	Dusseldorf	9	Sgt W Ramey	X3287	2
		142	Sgt T Parker	Z1210	6	30/1.12	Emden	75	Sgt F Harrison-Smith	Z1099	6
		301	Sgt L Cieslak	Z1217	0		Hamburg	101	Sgt D Willisson	R1778	4
22/23.10	Mannheim	57	P/O R Tong	Z8792	0			101	Sgt P Winfield	R3295	0
		75	Sgt C Taylor	X9914	6			142	F/S K Barnfield	Z1202	6
		99	Sgt T Mahon	W5454	6			142	Sgt A Gilmour	Z1292	6
		150	Sgt A Bradshaw	T2967	6			214	Sgt M Fitzgerald	Z8953	6
	Le Havre	405	Sgt C Hall	Z8419	6			304	P/O J Zajac	X3164	0
		458	F/L J Sargeaunt	R1765	1			405	S/L R Bisset	W8426	6
24/25.10	Frankfurt	101	P/O G Bundey	X9828	6	7/8.12	Dunkirk	104	Sgt R Anson	Z8426	6
		103	P/O R Keefer	T2506	0		Aachen	99	Sgt Firth	Z8958	1
		150	Sgt Wilkenshaw	T2960	0	11/12.12	Le Havre	57	Sgt D Watson	T2959	6
		405	P/O Frizzle	W5489	0		Brest	218	Sgt Brewerton	W5727	0
26/27.10	Hamburg	57	P/O J Watson	R1722	1	16/17.12	Brest	218	Sgt Vezina	X9785	0
		57	P/O Walters	Z8946	3		Ostende	304	S/L J Blazejewski	R1064	6
		75	Sgt S Isherwood	Z1168	1			305	Sgt Cusowski	Z8427	0
		304	P/O E Ladro	W5720	1	22/23.12	Wilhelmshaven	405	Sgt Mather	W5560	0
31/1.11	Bremen	115	W/O J Snowden	X9873	0	23/24.12	Brest	75	F/S L Bentley	Z8834	1
5/6.11	SD	109	P/O Bull	T2565	0		Cologne	305	Sgt H Rozpara	W5374	6
7/8.11	rover	57	Sgt S Gray	Z8903	6	27/28.12	Dusseldorf	57	W/O T Purdy	Z1097	5
		57	Sgt A Cook	Z8985	3			101	P/O G Pelmore	Z1115	6
	Berlin	75	P/O W Methven	X9951	1		Brest	75	Sgt Machin	Z8971	0
		75	Sgt J Black	X9976	6	28/29.12	Wilhelmshaven	311	Sgt A Siska	T2553	3
		99	P/O C Gilmore	T2516	6		Emden	405	Sgt E Williams	W5561	6
		99	F/L J Dickinson	T2554	1						
		99	P/O W Moore	X9739	2	*1941 Totals*				*467*	*1,810`*
		101	P/O W Hardie	R1701	6						
		149	Sgt S Dane	X9878	5	*1942*					
		214	P/O L Ercolani	X3206	0	3/4.1	Brest	99	P/O R Thomas	R1519	6
		218	Sgt J McGlashan	Z1069	0	6.1	Brest	9	P/O M Hodges	X3388	1
	Mannheim	103	F/L E Lawson	X9794	1			57	F/S D Richardson	Z1096	5
		142	Sgt S Hart	Z1211	1	6.1	Brest	458	P/O H Moran	Z1182	2
		150	Sgt L Atkins	R1606	6	6/7.1	Brest	12	P/O J Garlick	L5514	1
		300	Sgt K Sobczak	R1705	0			12	Sgt P Voller	W5523	6
		300	Sgt P Nowakowski	Z1271	0	9.1	Cherbourg	12	Sgt D Butterworth	W5356	3
		301	Sgt H Bolcewicz	Z1277	0			458	F/O B Hickey	R1785	6
		304	P/O T Bilcharz	R1215	0			458	Sgt D Garland	Z1312	4
8/9.11	Essen	75	Sgt K Smith	X9628	1	9/10.1	Brest	311	Sgt J Fina	W5682	0
		75	Sgt G Nunn	X9977	6	10/11.1	Wilhelmshaven	12	F/S C O'Connell	W5611	4
		75	Sgt J Wilson	Z8942	5			40	P/O P Sanders	X9824	2
9/10.11	Hamburg	9	P/O H Wilgar-Robinson	X3280	6			304	Sgt P Obiorek	Z1982	6
		9	Sgt W Pendleton	X3352	0			304	P/O T Zajac	DV432	6
15/16.11	Emden	99	F/S T Patterson	L7873	6	14/15.1	Hamburg	40	P/O E Broad	X9742	6
		99	Sgt G Farmery	Z8975	6		Emden	99	Sgt Carter	Z8947	0
		115	Sgt A Homes	X9888	6	15/16.1	Hamburg	104	Sgt B Adams	W5417	6
		149	Sgt R Bramhall	R1627	6			150	Sgt L Hunt	Z1078	1
		150	P/O Leddra	T2618	0			214	F/S E Hale	R1759	6
		214	Sgt Campbell	Z8900	0			300	F/L J Bak	Z1265	6

DATE	TARGET	SQN	CAPTAIN	A/C	AIRCREW KILLED	DATE	TARGET	SQN	CAPTAIN	A/C	AIRCREW KILLED
		301	P/O Liszka	Z1397	0		Essen	75	P/O A Slater	X3652	1
		419	P/O T Cottier	Z1145	4			103	Sgt G John	R1393	0
	Emden	104	Sgt J Wilmot	W5493	4			142	Sgt D White	Z1321	6
17/18.1	Bremen	142	P/O A Pickett	Z1320	6	26/27.3	Essen	12	W/C A Golding	W5372	6
		311	Sgt J Svoboda	T2971	3			12	F/S F Lowe	W5371	6
		405	S/L W Keddy	Z8329	4			57	F/S R Snook	X3665	6
20/21.1	Emden	12	F/L W Thallon	Z8370	2			115	Sgt H Taylor	X3589	6
		101	S/L P Chapman	Z1110	6			115	P/O G Soames	X3604	6
		142	P/O J Scott	Z1207	6			142	P/O J Tillard	Z1283	6
21/22.1	Bremen	311	F/S M Plecity	DV515	6			214	P/O E Creed	Z1143	6
22/23.1	Munster	301	Sgt J Socoko	Z1285	6			300	F/O B Zelazinski	Z1269	6
26/27.1	Hannover	12	Sgt J McKnight	W5585	4			301	F/S Porada	R1590	5
		305	Sgt L Molota	Z8372	0			301	P/O W Jaroszyk	Z1262	6
28/29.1	Munster	214	P/O G Webster	X9890	6	28/29.3	Lubeck	75	P/O M Bell	X3462	6
6/7.2	Brest	12	F/O C Barnes	Z8491	0			103	P/O J Ward	R1061	6
		142	F/L W St C McNeilly	Z1247	6			109	P/O J Maygothling	X9913	8
		300	F/O H Kracinski	Z1282	3			115	Sgt W Ballard	X3341	6
11/12.2	Le Havre	12	P/O N Nowell	W5355	6			142	P/O J Hall	Z1203	0
	Mannheim	40	P/O Ackland	Z8904	0			142	Sgt G Leather	Z1274	6
	Brest	150	Sgt R Dick	Z1076	6			305	Sgt F Wasinski	W5567	0
12.2	Op Fuller	103	S/L I Cross	Z8714	2			419	P/O K Hobson	X3477	2
		214	W/C R MacFadden	Z1081	6	1/2.4	Le Havre	12	Sgt J Woodhead	W5395	0
		419	F/S J Vezina	Z1091	6		Hanau	57	S/L G De L Harvie	X3410	6
		419	P/O R Laing	Z1146	6			57	Sgt T Roper	X3425	6
21/22.2	Intruder	150	P/O Birkes	R1463	4			57	F/S J Nevill	X3607	6
		150	P/O J Green	X9830	6			57	F/S R Knobloch	X3748	2
25/26.2	Kiel	12	P/O E Bairstow	W5440	6			57	Sgt W Paterson	Z1565	5
		12	S/L R Abraham	Z8410	0			214	Sgt R Burtwell	R1789	6
		214	P/O E Baker	X9939	0			214	P/O J Baker	X9979	6
		214	S/L C Miles	Z8858	0			214	W/O W Page	Z1052	5
		301	F/O J Jablonski	Z1377	6			214	Sgt A Ferguson	Z1156	6
26/27.2	Kiel	158	F/S R Robb	Z8536	6			214	Sgt E Dixon	Z8805	6
		305	F/O J Orczechowski	W5423	6			214	F/L E Baker	Z8842	6
		405	F/L J Robson	W5516	6			214	P/O R Hayes	Z8979	6
3/4.3	Billancourt	311	Sgt B Hradil	Z1070	6		Poissy	405	F/S M Howson	Z8527	5
	Emden	311	Sgt K Danihelka	Z1167	6	2/3.4	Poissy	150	P/O R Powell	X9814	5
8/9.3	Essen	9	Sgt R Lovell	X3411	5		garden.	101	Sgt J Weaver	X3709	6
		9	Sgt J Doughty	X3641	6	5/6.4	Cologne	9	P/O P Brooke	X3415	6
		12	Sgt M Duder	Z8409	5			75	W/C R Sawrey-Cookson	X3489	6
		101	P/O C Luin	X3656	6			75	F/S G Thomas	X3661	0
		115	P/O R Runagall	X3419	6			304	P/O A Osadzinski	X9764	6
9/10.3	Essen	9	Sgt J Cartwright	X3643	6	6/7.4	Essen	142	F/S G Mays	Z1205	6
		12	P/O R Buchanan	W5442	3	8/9.4	Hamburg	57	P/O N Morse	X3757	6
		101	Sgt Ward	X3642	0			158	Sgt J Wisher	Z8511	6
		150	S/L J Nicholls	DV447	6			405	P/O R Lake	Z8358	6
		158	F/L G Duff	W5431	5			419	F/O A Crighton	X3467	1
10/11.3	Essen	405	P/O K Durbridge	Z8428	6	10/11.4	Essen	9	F/O A Mactaggart	X3702	6
		419	Sgt J Foy	Z1077	0			12	P/O H Cook	W5570	6
12/13.3	Kiel	9	Sgt Webb	X3603	0			214	P/O J Murray	HF586	6
		75	Sgt J Parnham	X3282	6			301	P/O J Wasilewski	Z1333	0
		75	F/O J Sandys	X3585	6			304	Sgt J Janik	R1320	1
		75	S/L P Kitchin	X3588	6			305	F/O Czolowski	W5519	0
		301	F/O S Zakrzewski	Z1257	6			311	F/S J Kalensky	Z8838	6
		311	Sgt J Fina	R1802	6		nickel	158	Sgt W Amos	W5482	6
13/14.3	Dunkirk	12	F/S L McK Scott	Z8578	6	12/13.4	Essen	9	Sgt F Davidson	X3722	5
		406	F/S P Cooney	Z1251	6			103	F/S R Gillespie	W5664	6
	Cologne	305	F/O C Rymkiewicz	Z8438	4			115	Sgt A Holder	X3596	6
25/26.3	St Nazaire	12	Sgt E Due	W5578	4			158	P/O P McMillan	W5358	0

DATE	TARGET	SQN	CAPTAIN	A/C	AIRCREW KILLED	DATE	TARGET	SQN	CAPTAIN	A/C	AIRCREW KILLED
		158	S/L W Protheroe	W5525	6	3/4.5	Hamburg	300	F/L W Wolski	Z1183	5
		300	Sgt J Zalejko	Z1213	5			305	F/O S Karpetowski	W5590	0
		301	F/O J Goldhaar	Z1252	0			305	F/O A Jankowski	Z8406	6
		304	P/O W Misniakiewicz	9687	1	4/5.5	Nantes	103	F/S J St G Arrowsmith	Z8833	4
		304	Sgt Lozowicki	DV437	0	5/6.5	Stuttgart	12	F/O N Richardson	Z8495	5
		405	F/S D Lyold	W5531	2			150	Sgt R Bell	X3407	6
14/15.4	Dortmund	150	P/O C Mardon	DV593	1			150	F/S R Davenport	X3451	0
		158	Sgt P Winkle	Z8490	5			150	Sgt R Baxter	X3673	0
		214	F/S R Lawrence	Z1148	6			305	P/O Ginter	W5573	0
		301	P/O M Rzemyk	Z1379	4			305	F/O S Krawczyk	Z8599	0
		301	Sgt S Krzystyniak	Z1468	0	6/7.5	Stuttgart	115	F/L N Paterson	X3466	2
		305	F/O S Sznidel	Z8586	2			115	F/L J Sword	X3591	2
		311	Sgt V Para	Z1098	3			419	F/S L Roberts	X3717	5
		405	P/O P Toft	W5390	0			460	S/L C Gilbert	Z1254	5
		405	Sgt D MacFarlane	W5427	5			460	F/O W Kennedy	Z1413	1
		405	F/S H Chinn	Z8530	0	7/8.5	garden.	57	P/O J Sligo	Z1564	5
		419	F/S J Norris	X3484	6	8/9.5	Warnemunde	9	F/L J Eliott	X3369	5
15/16.4	Dortmund	101	Sgt J Nesbitt	X3694	6			12	F/S F Roddy	W5574	6
		156	P/O A Griffith	X3697	6			158	Sgt E Seaward	W5387	4
		214	P/O L Leech	Z8951	6			158	F/S I Davies	W5562	5
16/17.4	garden.	156	P/O J Sheffield	X3417	6			158	F/S A Reid	Z8439	6
17/18.4	Hamburg	12	F/L W Castello	Z8398	5			158	Sgt J Davison	Z8600	4
		57	S/L G Phipps	X3478	0			419	F/S H Giddens	X3480	1
		57	F/S W st G Wilson	X3542	3			419	F/S C Shannon	X3703	6
		101	Sgt R Cowley	X3356	6	15/16.5	garden.	9	Sgt S Richards	Z1615	1
		101	P/O E House	X3655	4			75	F/S M Fraser	X3482	5
		158	F/S E Olliver	W5575	5	17/18.5	Boulogne	9	Sgt H Wanostrocht	X3276	5
		300	F/O J Kusmierz	Z1267	6			57	S/L J Laird	DV806	0
		305	F/O Wielochowski	W5566	0			115	Sgt F Butterworth	X3644	5
19/20.4	garden.	156	P/O R Fox	X3485	6			419	F/S F Pikula	Z1562	5
		156	F/O L Pinion	X3708	0	19/20.5	Mannheim	12	P/O W Fulton	W5458	6
22/23.4	Cologne	9	P/O A Hale	X3358	1			101	Sgt J Beecroft	X3472	1
		9	Sgt O Barnes	X3638	2			103	F/L P Rees	Z1141	6
		9	Sgt W Ramey	X3759	5			156	S/L T McGillivray	X3671	6
		75	P/O E Jarman	X3487	1	29/30.5	Gennevilliers	156	W/C P Heath	X3706	6
		75	F/S T Mahood	X3667	6			419	P/O E Cavaghan	X3715	5
23/24.4	Rostock	101	W/O J Chaundy	X3701	5			460	F/O T Bourke	Z1388	4
		304	F/O J Kwak	X9829	6			460	F/O R Jones	Z1391	3
24/25.4	Rostock	150	Sgt H Thorogood	X3305	6	30/31.5	Cologne	9	Sgt S Langton	X3469	0
25/26.4	Rostock	9	S/L D Holmes	X3226	6			9	F/L M Hodges	BJ674	5
		103	F/S C Bray	DV579	6			12	F/L A Payne	W5361	6
		115	Sgt A Fone	X3633	6			12	P/O A Waddell	Z8376	5
26/27.4	Rostock	301	F/O C Nowacki	Z1317	0			12	Sgt G Everatt	Z8598	5
27/28.4	Cologne	115	Sgt L Harris	X3639	4			12	P/O W Shearer	Z8643	1
		150	Sgt A Hutchinson	X3288	6			57	P/O Ravenhill	X3387	0
		150	P/O V Bailey	X3700	6			101	P/O A De F Gardner	X3670	5
		300	P/O J Fusinki	Z1276	0			101	P/O C Read	Z1612	0
		304	P/O J Morawski	W5627	0			103	F/S W Onions	DV452	6
		304	F/O R Szczurowski	Z1088	5			109	Sgt T Eddy	Z1113	3
28/29.4	Kiel	9	Sgt G Sampson	X3716	6			115	Sgt E Edwards	Z1614	5
		12	Sgt N Spray	Z8342	6			142	Sgt N Lowden	Z1208	5
		158	F/S L McKay	Z8521	0			142	P/O G Chaffey	Z1209	5
		214	Sgt S Avent	DV768	6			150	Sgt S Shaw	X3448	6
		460	F/S L Shephard	Z1290	6			156	Sgt P Malin	DV715	5
29/30.4	Gennevilliers	57	F/O K Heald	X3640	5			156	P/O J Bain	X3598	6
		115	Sgt W Reynolds	X3593	6			158	Sgt R O'Brien	5392	5
		156	F/O L Pinion	Z1571	5			158	S/L D Harkness	Z8577	5
	Ostende	158	Sgt J Saunders	Z8525	5						

DATE	TARGET	SQN	CAPTAIN	A/C	AIRCREW KILLED

(in addition to these squadron losses on this first 1,000 bomber raid, the following OTU losses were recorded: 11 OTU - 1, 12 OTU - 1, 14 OTU - 3, 15 OTU - 2, 22 OTU - 4, 23 OTU - 1, 25 OTU - 1, 26 OTU - 4.)

DATE	TARGET	SQN	CAPTAIN	A/C	AIRCREW KILLED
1/2.6	Essen	57	F/S J Kormylo	DV816	0
		115	F/O L Williams	X3721	5
		142	P/O D McDonald	Z1410	5
		305	W/C R Hirszbandt	Z8583	6
		460	Sgt J Walsh	Z1311	6
		460	F/O A Holland	Z1344	2
2/3.6	Essen	12	F/S H Dimmock	Z8533	3
		57	F/S V Cummock	X9787	5
		75	P/O C Carter	X3408	0
		156	Sgt P Powell	DV786	5
		301	P/O W Glowacki	R1615	6
		460	Sgt S Levitus	Z1249	5
		460	F/O J Keene	Z1394	4
3/4.6	Bremen	101	F/L N Edwards	X3473	3
		115	Sgt T Wood	X3635	5
		115	F/S J Hutchison	X3724	5
		115	P/O H Acourt	X3749	0
		300	P/O D Mendela	Z1291	0
5/6.6	Essen	57	Sgt W Barnes	HF915	5
		103	F/L W McD Morison	DV699	4
		150	F/S T Kay	X3674	6
		156	Sgt W Thompson	DV812	5
		156	P/O E Smith	X3339	6
		301	F/O D Plawski	Z1331	6
		301	F/O F Witakowski	Z1467	6
		305	Sgt Przybyla	Z8601	0
		419	F/S J Dutton	X3486	5
6/7.6	Emden	9	P/O J Cowan	Z1575	0
		150	F/O M Blunt	X3279	6
		156	F/S T Terris	HF918	5
		301	Sgt M Bober	R1390	5
8/9.6	Essen	12	Sgt W Clayton	Z8652	6
		75	P/O R Smith	X3587	5
		75	P/O G Murdoch	Z1573	5
		103	P/O J Firman	DV773	5
		150	F/O W Love	X3725	5
		300	F/L M Michalowski	R1725	6
		460	Sgt D Hurditch	Z1412	1
11/12.6	garden.	9	P/O V Saul	X3695	5
16/17.6	Essen	150	P/O J Myall	Z1608	1
		419	Sgt C Leblanc	X3359	1
		419	F/S A Harris	X3723	5
19/20.6	Emden	57	Sgt D Ashworth	Z1611	5
		101	Sgt F Keen	X3669	5
		300	Sgt C Dziekonski	Z1215	6
		300	Sgt J Kropacz	Z1256	6
		305	Sgt A Gusowski	Z8339	4
		460	Sgt D Kitchen	Z1486	5
20/21.6	Emden	9	W/C L James	X3713	5
		75	F/O A Fraser	X3760	5
		305	F/O Konowski	Z8537	0
21/22.6	garden.	460	F/S R Buckingham	Z1383	5
22/23.6	Emden	57	Sgt J Larkins	X3758	5
		103	W/C O Godfrey	DV818	5

DATE	TARGET	SQN	CAPTAIN	A/C	AIRCREW KILLED
		115	P/O M Freegard	X3555	0
		301	F/O Z Dubas	Z1345	5
23/24.6	St Nazaire garden.	9	Sgt K Kingdon	X3423	4
		103	Sgt T Emmott	T2921	5
		103	Sgt S Vickery	DV831	5
25/26.6	Bremen	115	115 P/O W Croxton	X3554	5
		156	Sgt W Thompson	BJ594	0
		301	W/C S Krzyztyniak	Z1479	0
		305	F/L E Rudowski	Z8528	1
		1481	S/L M Atkinson	X9812	5

(the major Wellington losses on this 1,000 bomber raid to Bremen fell on the OTUs – 11 OTU – 3, 12 OTU – 4, 15 OTU – 2, 16 OTU – 1, 18 OTU – 3, 20 OTU – 1, 21 OTU – 1, 22 OTU – 2, 23 OTU – 2, 26 OTU – 1, 27 OTU – 1.)

DATE	TARGET	SQN	CAPTAIN	A/C	AIRCREW KILLED
27/28.6	Bremen	150	F/O D Osborne	X3309	5
		150	Sgt A Nightingale	Z1616	6
		150	S/L B Hooper	BJ666	0
		156	Sgt H Owen	Z1619	5
29/30.6	Bremen	57	S/L J Franks	Z1578	6
		57	Sgt Moore	Z1618	3
		75	P/O W Monk	X3539	5
		75	P/O R Bertram	Z1616	5
		115	F/O K Stanford	BJ796	1
2/3.7	Bremen	12	Sgt J Keats	Z8531	0
		12	Sgt I Dunn	Z8579	3
		103	Sgt D Spooner	R1617	3
		103	P/O A Little	DV611	4
		109	P/O P Sullivan	AD605	5
		300	F/S T Kubiak	Z1204	6
		300	P/O M Kubacki	Z1326	0
		301	S/L M Brzozowski	Z1314	0
		460	Sgt A Johnston	Z1381	3
		460	Sgt A Whittick	Z1470	4
6/7.7	garden.	156	Sgt A Galley	X3345	5
		156	Sgt A Attwater	Z1576	5
		419	F/S P Murphey	Z1597	6
8/9.7	Wilhelmshaven	75	P/O T Smith	X3557	6
		101	P/O J Tregea	X3634	5
		300	Sgt L Szychowiak	Z1489	1
9/10.7	garden.	142	F/O S Critchison	Z1324	5
10.7	Dusseldorf	75	Sgt J Wilmhurst	X3720	5
11/12.7	garden.	101	S/L F Freeman	Z1751	5
		101	P/O A Angel	BJ583	5
12/13.7	garden.	460	Sgt A Moyle	Z1328	6
13/14.7	Duisburg	12	P/O D Welch	W5397	5
		115	F/S H Mooney	X3560	0
		142	F/S J Richardson	Z1341	4
		150	Sgt J Sykes	X3797	3
		419	W/O W Sargant	X3416	5
19.7	Essen	150	P/O M Wilding	X3755	4
19/20.7	garden.	12	P/O J Muirhead	W5414	5
21/22.7	Duisburg	12	F/L J Langley	Z8420	5
		57	Sgt T Wakefield	X3584	5
		101	F/S E Fortin	X3312	6
		115	P/O M Freegard	X3561	6
		115	P/O K Stanford	X3726	1
		115	Sgt J Fletcher	X3750	5
		142	Sgt J Vandersteen	Z1408	5

DATE	TARGET	SQN	CAPTAIN	A/C	AIRCREW KILLED	DATE	TARGET	SQN	CAPTAIN	A/C	AIRCREW KILLED
		150	P/O J Skrender	X3590	2			101	W/O A Vautour	BJ841	5
		301	P/O H Bock	Z1405	5			156	P/O R Woof	Z1622	5
		301	F/O C Lewicki	Z1406	5	4/5.8	garden.	142	Sgt C Love	Z1487	5
22.7	ASR	301	P/O A Majcherczk	Z1472	3			460	P/O A Grand	Z1422	5
23/24.7	Duisburg	9	F/O H Brown	Z1577	1	5/6.8	garden.	301	Sgt W Gohres	Z1386	4
		57	Sgt A Davies	BJ673	5		Essen	419	P/O R Krefting	X3360	6
		115	F/S E Boutiller	BJ595	0	6/7.8	Duisburg	12	Sgt G Leats	Z8585	6
25/26.7	Duisburg	12	Sgt W Foster	W5437	0			150	F/S R Baxter	X3698	4
		12	S/L P Lemon	Z8502	1	9/10.8	Osnabruck	150	Sgt J Hughes	Z1593	5
		12	W/C R Collard	Z8591	1			150	Sgt S Glover	BJ608	4
		115	P/O D Felt	Z1606	5			460	F/S J Finlay	Z1463	5
		142	P/O N Sprake	Z1287	5	11/12.8	Mainz	57	Sgt R Riddell	BJ830	5
		150	Sgt D Horsleman	X3795	1			57	F/S T Barclay	BJ625	4
		460	F/L C Burgess	Z1399	5			75	P/O G Bradey	X3646	5
		460	S/L J Leighton	Z1462	3			75	F/L L St G Dobbin	BJ767	2
26/27.7	Hamburg	12	F/S A Holgate	W5367	4			150	P/O R Munson	X3744	1
		12	P/O D Rowe	Z8526	0			156	F/S F Harker	X3798	2
		57	Sgt K Hudson	Z1654	5			156	S/L J Beavis	Z1595	6
		75	F/S C McPherson	X3714	6			156	P/O C Taylor	BJ603	5
		75	P/O I Shepherd	Z1596	4	12/13.8	Mainz	150	Sgt D Beaton	BJ588	3
		101	Sgt D Raymond	BJ590	5			460	F/O W Clegg	Z1404	5
		115	Sgt J Howells	X3412	0	15/16.8	Dusseldorf	156	F/S C Newlove	DF666	5
		115	W/C F Dixon-Wright	BJ615	6	17/18.8	Osnabruck	101	P/O E Brown	X3654	6
		115	Sgt B Feredey	BJ670	2			101	Sgt C Foderingham	BJ844	1
		115	Sgt J Smith	BJ723	0			300	Sgt I Konderak	Z1409	0
		142	S/L C Olsson	Z1319	2	18/19.8	Flensburg	12	P/O D Rowe	Z8538	5
		142	F/S N Carrel	Z1376	5			57	P/O R McLaren	X3371	5
		142	P/O C West	Z1461	5	20/21.8	garden.	75	W/O E Andersen	BJ774	5
		300	Sgt P Bakalarski	Z1270	1			115	F/S J Newman	X3989	5
		460	F/L V Keyser	Z1335	5			305	F/O K Borowski	Z1471	0
		460	F/O F Breen	Z1483	5	24/25.8	Frankfurt	101	F/S C Elkington	Z1594	2
27.7	Bremen	57	W/C M Peters-Smith	X3653	5			150	Sgt J Scorer	X3414	3
		156	F/S R Munday	Z1659	1			150	Sgt E Bound	BJ651	5
28/29.7	Hamburg	9	Sgt H Hannaford	X3456	5			101	F/S H Thompson	BJ831	3
		9	P/O J Mullins	X3475	6			300	Sgt B Koscien	Z1488	0
		9	S/L H Ledger	X3606	4	27/28.8	Kassel	12	P/O A Norman	Z8403	5
		57	F/L J Dean	Z1650	6			12	P/O D Jones	Z8656	5
		75	Sgt C Croall	X3452	1			12	Sgt D McNeil	X3802	4
		75	F/S A Sutherland	X3558	5			12	P/O D Macnaughton	X3988	5
		75	F/L P Wilson	X3664	6			57	Sgt V Saunders	X3331	3
		75	F/S A Johns	Z1570	5			75	F/L A Osborn	BJ708	5
		75	F/S G Hutt	BJ599	5			101	F/S G Brown	X3649	2
		75	F/S J Gilbertson	BJ661	3			101	Sgt J Spinney	X3657	0
		101	Sgt P Teall	X3668	5			101	P/O E Beale	BJ698	6
		115	Sgt A Williamson	Z1605	5			115	F/O W Skelton	Z1266	1
		115	P/O L Mason	Z1624	2			142	F/O A Paget	Z1338	4
		156	F/S E Borsberry	X3710	5			142	F/S A Harker	Z1396	5
		156	F/L J Wilson	BJ592	6			142	P/O C Keddy	Z1411	5
		156	W/C H Price	BJ840	6			142	P/O M Johnson	Z1424	5
		419	W/C J Fulton	X3488	6			150	Sgt G Coombes	X3418	5
29/30.7	Saarbrucken	12	Sgt W Foster	W5424	5			156	F/S M Savage	X3367	6
		142	Sgt G Cooper	Z1316	6			156	P/O J Longhurst	Z1613	6
		150	S/L L Cohen	BJ881	5			156	Sgt R James	DF667	5
		419	W/O N McH Moore	X3712	4			305	Sgt J Pytlak	Z1245	3
31/1.8	Dusseldorf	9	Sgt W Hall	BJ876	4			460	Sgt C Viney	Z1212	4
		9	P/O R Pink	BJ878	5			460	F/O J Summers	Z1259	5
		12	Sgt W Good	Z8499	5	28/29.8	Nurnberg	57	Sgt L Brooks	BJ619	0
		57	F/S T Murphy	BJ607	5			57	F/S J Rowney	BJ701	5

DATE	TARGET	SQN	CAPTAIN	A/C	AIRCREW KILLED
		75	F/S E Perks	X3389	5
		75	F/S S Davis	DF673	5
		101	F/L P Harper	X3391	0
		101	F/L J Follett	X3754	4
		115	P/O J Duffy	X3464	0
		115	Sgt W Allen	X3647	4
		115	W/O J Smith	X3675	3
		115	P/O J Berry	Z1607	0
		115	P/O C Pafford	BJ688	5
		150	P/O J Birke	BJ649	0
		156	F/L W Gilmour	X3728	5
		301	P/O J Tyszko	Z1491	0
		305	P/O S Turski	Z1281	5
	Saarbrucken	419	Sgt P Zaparynuk	DF665	4
		460	F/O R Elrington	Z1485	5
1/2.9	Saarbrucken	115	P/O R Shires	BJ893	6
		142	Sgt R Dolan	Z1478	0
		156	Sgt J Douglas	BJ716	3
2/3.9	Karlsruhe	12	F/S C Alt	Z8529	2
		142	Sgt H Heath	Z1466	5
		150	F/S L Clarke	X3313	5
		419	W/C A Walsh	X3711	5
3/4.9	Emden	75	Sgt J Law	X3396	5
		75	F/S E Hunting	X3794	5
4/5.9	Bremen	12	Sgt T Smith	Z8595	4
		101	P/O N Gill	BJ891	5
		115	P/O F Davies	BJ663	5
		115	Sgt G Keith	BJ771	0
		142	Sgt I Lamont	Z1214	5
		150	Sgt J Tortman	Z1671	0
		300	Sgt L Szychowiak	Z1320	5
		419	Sgt A Kertson	BJ602	5
6/7.9	Duisburg	12	Sgt J Dunlop	Z8517	5
		12	F/S G Littlejohn	BJ691	5
		75	F/S W Parkes	X3867	5
		75	Sgt G Sharman	BJ765	5
		101	F/S R Williams	BJ769	5
		115	F/S C Lanceley	BJ724	3
7/8.9	garden.	12	F/S J Barker	BJ777	5
8/9.9	Frankfurt	12	P/O C Moseley	Z8644	5
		75	Sgt E Johnson	BJ596	0
		142	F/S J Heddon	Z1342	1
		150	Sgt G Sherratt	X3304	0
		150	Sgt J Glaves	X3745	0
		150	Sgt D Bowker	BJ591	1
10/11.9	Dusseldorf	75	Sgt E Lees	BJ828	5
		75	F/S F Burrill	BJ698	5
		75	Sgt T Metcalfe	BJ974	5
		142	P/O S McHugh	Z1477	5
		300	F/L S Waszkiewicz	Z1258	5
		460	Sgt J Pearson	R1695	3
		460	F/S J Bryden	Z1216	5
13/14.9	Bremen	12	Sgt H Feast	Z8523	5
		12	F/S A Harrison	Z1728	5
		150	Sgt H Grace	Z1651	5
		156	P/O V Brough	BJ600	6
		156	S/L R Collier	BJ789	5
		419	F/S E Brasher	Z1385	5
14/15.9	Wilhelmshaven	12	Sgt H Pryce	Z8505	5
		115	P/O F Boaden	BJ693	6
16/17.9	Essen	101	P/O C Grant	BJ897	5
		142	S/L D Barnard	DF550	0
		142	F/S J Marriot	Z1380	5
		142	P/O A Sandon	Z1480	5
		150	Sgt W Randle	BJ877	0
		156	Sgt G Proudfoot	X3822	0

(the raids of 10/11, 13/14 and 16/17 included significant participation – and losses – by the Bomber OTUs)

DATE	TARGET	SQN	CAPTAIN	A/C	AIRCREW KILLED
18/19.9	garden.	115	P/O R Owen	X3718	5
19/20.9	Munich	101	P/O E De Bartok	BJ689	6
	Saarbrucken	150	Sgt D Northey	X3762	5
		156	Sgt V Bastable	BJ883	0
21/22.9	garden.	101	F/S J Rimmer	X3457	5
		101	S/L V Paterson	X3815	3
		115	Sgt D Evans	BJ962	5
23/24.9	garden.	142	F/S L Seamark	Z1219	5
		305	Sgt T Sekowski	Z1476	5
26/27.9	garden.	12	F/O J Ward	BJ776	5
28.9	Lingen-Ems	115	S/L R Parsons	Z1663	3
30/1.10	garden.	12	Sgt G Mitchell	BJ964	5
2/3.10	Krefeld	115	Sgt F Adsett	BK271	5
		419	F/S S Stowe	BK269	5
5/6.10	Aachen	142	P/O G Edgett	BK281	4
		150	F/S A Makay	BJ829	0
		156	F/S T Case	X3811	0
		156	Sgt W Chiddick	BK203	1
		419	Sgt K Crewe	Z1623	5
		419	F/S T Powell	BJ729	5
		425	Sgt M O'Driscoll	X3943	5
6/7.10	Osnabruck	75	Sgt G Rhodes	DF639	5
		115	F/O L Smith	BK313	5
8/9.10	garden.	12	P/O J Simpson	BJ780	0
		301	Sgt S Bielec	Z1255	4
11/12.10	garden.	75	Sgt G Shalfoon	BK341	5
		301	Sgt M Blachowski	R1585	0
12/13.10	garden.	12	Sgt K Simmonds	Z8532	2
13/14.10	Kiel	12	W/O J Heddon	BJ653	0
		75	Sgt V Watters	X3954	5
		75	Sgt C Davey	BJ837	0
		156	F/S J Taylor	BJ775	3
		300	F/L J Wojcik	X1250	6
		419	Sgt W Wakeman	DF664	5
		420	P/O B Adilman	X3963	0
		420	F/S W Croft	DF636	5
		425	Sgt R Clinton	BJ783	0
15/16.10	Cologne	12	Sgt R Bayley	BJ606	6
		142	F/S R Cole	X3960	5
		142	Sgt B Shaddick	DF642	0
		150	Sgt E Smith	X3552	5
		156	S/L J Hobbs	BK339	5
		300	Sgt C Szymen	Z1475	5
		419	Sgt J Jolley	BK270	5
		420	F/S L White	X3808	5
16/17.10	garden.	115	Sgt D Gordo	X3946	5
		115	S/L C Wright	BK312	5

DATE	TARGET	SQN	CAPTAIN	A/C	AIRCREW KILLED
23/24.10	Genoa	115	Sgt K Pudsey	Z1574	0
		150	F/O H Rees	BK309	2
24/25.10	Milan	12	Sgt J Wilcox	W5394	5
		75	Sgt H Hugill	Z1652	2
		75	Sgt J McConnell	BJ725	5
		115	Sgt D Oldridge	BK306	5
		142	Sgt B Shaddick	X3455	5
		142	Sgt J Young	BK385	5
28/19.10	garden.	150	F/O W Crane	X3957	5
		150	Sgt W Woodcock	BK310	1
29.10	Essen	115	F/S R Urwin	X3540	5
		115	F/O Rawlings	Z1738	5
		115	Sgt F Barker	BJ660	5
31.10	Emden	150	F/S A Makay	BK360	5
		150	Sgt H Brook	Z1625	5
31/1.11	garden.	305	F/O A Rogowski	Z1279	5
3/4.11	garden.	300	P/O I Sawicki	Z1421	5
7/8.11	garden.	142	Sgt R Hill	BK198	5
	Genoa	156	P/O D Chell	X3422	5
8/9.11	garden.	142	Sgt R Evison	BJ728	5
		300	Sgt S Chmielewski	Z1343	3
9/10.11	Hamburg	142	P/O W Bent	BJ711	6
		150	Sgt D Prosser	X3310	6
		420	Sgt W Beale	Z1679	5
		425	Sgt R Foltz	BJ764	4
		425	Sgt N Raitblat	BK557	5
11/12.11	garden.	425	Sgt J Larche	BJ846	3
15/16.11	garden.	150	F/S J Perry	BK301	5
16/17.11	garden.	115	Sgt T Gill	X3597	5
		142	P/O H Stower	BK278	0
19/20.11	garden.	305	Sgt L Werschner	Z1496	5
20/21.11	Turin	142	W/O G Gregory	BK536	0
		150	P/O J Sweet	BK538	4
22/23.11	Stuttgart	115	Sgt E Coates	BJ842	2
		115	Sgt A Robertson	BK206	4
		156	F/L E Fletcher	X3672	3
25.11	Essen	300	Sgt W Kazimierczak	Z1495	1
28/29.11	garden.	150	Sgt G Ceeney	BK194	5
2/3.12	Frankfurt	115	W/O A McCrae	BK338	5
6/7.12	Mannheim	115	F/O H Larkins	BJ898	5
		115	F/O M Dixon	BK513	5
		300	Sgt J Furmaniak	Z1401	5
		301	F/P K Suszczynski	Z1337	3
		305	Sgt Z Cipirski	Z1278	1
		425	P/O G Cronk	BJ657	5
9/10.12	Turin	115	Sgt R Smith	X3393	0
11/12.12	Turin	199	W/C C Hattersley	BK514	1
17/18.12	Fallersleben	115	F/O A Campbell	BK274	5
		115	Sgt R Crisp	BK336	5
		1474 Flt	P/O D Couper	DV892	7
20/21.12	Duisburg	156	W/O F Watkins	Z1660	2
		156	F/S G Proudfoot	BJ589	3
		425	F/S L Causley	Z1729	4
21/22.12	Munich	156	F/S S Cybulski	BK386	5
31/1.1	garden.	115	P/O L Hickman	X3351	0
1942 Totals				645	2,537
1943					
9/10.1	garden.	301	F/O T Tyrala	R1535	4
12/13.1	garden.	305	F/O F Krawczyk	Z1272	5
14/15.1	Lorient	300	Sgt S Gosiewski	Z1387	5
		426	P/O G Milne	BK165	6
	garden.	466	Sgt R Babington	HE152	6
15/16.1	Lorient	427	S/L M Williams	BK364	5
21/22.1	garden.	420	Sgt S Gergley	BJ966	6
		427	F/L D Shead	X3873	5
		429	F/O I Johnson	BK432	5
		466	F/S G Emerson	HE410	1
26/27.1	Lorient	301	Sgt M Krol	Z1318	0
		424	Sgt V McHarg	BJ714	3
		427	P/O C Taylor	X3348	0
		429	Sgt L Rodgers	BK163	5
		466	Sgt D McKenzie	HE368	3
27/28.1	garden.	115	Sgt F Plum	X3936	0
29/30.1	Lorient	166	F/S R Currie	BK159	0
		166	W/O R Gray	BK515	5
		420	P/O E Stanton	DF615	5
		420	Sgt D Sanderson	DF626	5
		424	Sgt R Buie	BK436	0
	garden.	305	F/O A Pankiewicz	Z1415	5
30.1	Hamburg	426	F/L R Lowe	Z1680	6
	Oldenburg	427	P/O C Bennett	BK389	5
	Emden	466	F/L C Simmonds	HE397	5
		466	Sgt L Axby	HE471	5
3/4.2	Hamburg	115	P/O C Tuma	BK127	5
		300	Sgt P Marciniszyn	BK511	6
		305	Sgt M Seredyn	Z1392	4
	garden.	300	Sgt W Sowa	BK303	5
4/5.2	Lorient	427	P/O C Parsons	BJ668	4
6/7.2	garden.	199	Sgt G Moses	BK367	5
		424	Sgt E Cox	BJ658	6
		425	Sgt J Poirier	Z1742	6
		466	Sgt J Murdoch	HE393	0
7/8.2	Lorient	166	Sgt M Clements	X3544	5
		199	F/L K Powell	BK507	6
12/13.2	garden.	427	Sgt O Adlam	BJ778	5
13/14.2	Lorient	115	Sgt T Rait	BK166	4
		166	F/S G Ashplant	BK460	1
		199	F/O J Bell	X3870	6
		420	P/O L Gibson	BK330	5
14/15.2	Cologne	196	F/L R Milne	HE169	5
		426	W/C S Blanchard	X3420	6
		466	F/S W Martin	HE153	1
		466	F/L W Kirk	HE164	3
16/17.2	Lorient	427	Sgt J Holloway	Z1676	0
19/20.2	Wilhelmshaven	166	Sgt H Bastick	BJ973	5
		305	Sgt K Ignatowski	Z1288	0
		426	Sgt J Gauthier	BJ919	6
		466	Sgt R Rosser	HE531	1
20/21.2	garden.	424	Sgt I Baulf	BK435	6
24/25.2	Wilhelmshaven	424	F/S J Banks	HE369	3
26/27.2	Cologne	166	Sgt E Twigg	BJ961	5
		199	P/O J Waterfield	Z1600	0
		420	Sgt H Hansen	BK468	5

DATE	TARGET	SQN	CAPTAIN	A/C	AIRCREW KILLED	DATE	TARGET	SQN	CAPTAIN	A/C	AIRCREW KILLED
		426	Sgt H Rands	Z1599	5	10/11.4	Frankfurt	166	F/S A Urquhart	X3334	5
		427	Sgt W Harwood	BJ886	6			166	F/O J Everill	BK549	5
		427	Sgt G Taylor	BK268	5			166	Sgt P Hall	BK464	5
27/28.2	garden.	426	Sgt L Sutherland	X3364	0			420	P/O C Jackson	HE422	1
28/1.3	St Nazaire	425	Sgt J Broussaeu	BJ918	0			424	Sgt R Buie	HE159	4
		427	Sgt L Southwood	X3563	0			426	P/O J Sammet	HE652	5
		427	Sgt W Hartney	BK343	5			429	W/O D Jeffries	HE636	5
1/2.3	garden.	466	Sgt W Barrow	HE376	5			431	Sgt W Bidmead	HE213	2
2/3.3	garden.	115	Sgt S Hunt	BK495	5			466	P/O F Booy	HE506	5
		427	Sgt L Lymburner	X3390	6	11/12.4	garden.	425	Sgt E Carvajal	HE491	5
		429	Sgt J Black	HZ260	4	14/15.4	Stuttgart	420	S/L F Taylor	HE550	2
3/4.3	Hamburg	115	Sgt D Laidlaw	Z1620	5			420	Sgt P Cozens	HE863	5
		425	Sgt J Gauthier	BK334	6			424	Sgt A Harrison	HZ273	0
5/6.3	Essen	300	F/O K Romaniszyn	BK150	1			425	P/O A Doucette	X3763	6
		420	P/O R Graham	HE280	6			425	Sgt R Dingman	HE733	0
		426	P/O C Trask	BK401	6			428	Sgt W Harris	HE176	1
		429	F/S S Conroy	BJ755	1			431	Sgt J Avery	HE374	0
		466	Sgt A Yielder		6			431	Sgt L Denby	HZ357	4
7/8.3	garden.	431	Sgt D Pitts	HE202	0	16/17.4	Mannheim	166	F/O S Lupton	HE862	2
9/10.3	garden.	166	F/S J Kavanagh	BK368	4			196	P/O I Morgan	HE387	5
		426	P/O G Baker	X3284	6			196	W/C A Duguid	HE469	0
		429	Sgt K Hollbech	BK429	5			420	Sgt L Horahan	HE682	4
12/13.3	Essen	115	Sgt L Fallon	BJ756	5			425	Sgt P Bujold	HE475	2
		199	Sgt D Clifford	HE519	4			426	Sgt L Thompson	HE591	5
		199	F/L W King	HZ263	5			427	Sgt S Tomyn	HE547	1
		420	Sgt G Cooke	HE690	1			427	Sgt B Chambers	HE745	0
		424	P/O R Caldwell	BK348	0			429	S/L F Holmes	BK162	5
		425	Sgt J Lanontagne	BK340	0			431	Sgt H Sutterby	HE379	1
13/14.3	garden.	300	Sgt T Kuzminski	BK516	5			466	F/S C Tozer	HE501	5
		420	Sgt C Tidy	BK296	5	20/21.4	garden.	429	Sgt R Ellison	HE414	0
23/24.3	garden.	196	Sgt H Duckmanton	HE167	4	22/23.4	garden.	300	F/L E Przysiecki	HE291	5
26/27.3	Duisburg	426	Sgt E Hall	X3696	5	26/27.4	Duisburg	196	Sgt G Fletcher	HE168	5
		429	F/O G Fox	MS487	3			196	P/O W Mallison	MS491	0
		431	F/L G Eades	HE503	5			420	Sgt E Newburg	HE693	5
29/30.3	Bochum	166	Sgt O Collins	X3965	5			426	W/C L Crooks	HE867	0
		166	Sgt J Hodgson	HE545	5			427	Sgt G Hall	HE771	1
		196	F/O E Culff	HE548	5			428	Sgt L Coutts	HE365	4
		420	Sgt R Brandow	X3814	5			429	Sgt S Hanah	HE382	6
		420	P/O B Grant	MS484	4			429	Sgt J Cairns	HE737	3
		426	Sgt R Todd	BJ762	3			431	Sgt J Reynoldson	HE476	0
		427	Sgt McFadden	HE744	5	28/29.4	garden.	166	P/O L Clark	HZ278	4
		428	Sgt J Cartier	BK564	3			196	Sgt F Swain	HE170	5
		428	Sgt J Martyn	HE175	5			196	Sgt J Atkins	HE220	5
		429	Sgt K Burini	BJ920	5			196	F/L I Bonard	HE395	5
		429	Sgt H Carty	BK540	5			428	Sgt R Parkinson	HE543	5
		431	Sgt E Aspden	HE182	4			428	Sgt K Radcliff	HE728	5
3/4.4	garden.	166	Sgt A Radbourne	HE631	5	4/5.5	Dortmund	166	Sgt A Starck	HE244	5
4/5.4	Kiel	426	F/O D Kennedy	X3699	3			166	Sgt A Uditsky	HE923	5
		428	F/O R Tighe	HE432	5			196	Sgt J Staniforth	HE162	5
6/7.4	garden.	166	F/L N Brown	BK299	0			428	W/O R Moulton	HE727	3
8/9.4	Duisburg	166	Sgt C Barclay	BK361	0			428	Sgt D Johnson	HE864	2
		166	P/O D Morgan	HE658	3			466	Sgt L James	HE530	1
		300	P/O S Tomicki	HE148	6	12/13.5	Duisburg	196	Sgt J Greenfield	HE398	5
		420	P/O W Walkinshaw	MS479	5			199	Sgt L Waldorf	HE702	5
		425	F/S J Smith	HE592	5			300	Sgt S Werner	HE295	5
		428	P/O R Buckham	DF635	0			426	Sgt K Fighter	HE157	5
		466	Sgt S Wood	HE155	5			426	Sgt I Runciman	HE905	1
	garden.	199	Sgt K Pinchin	HE495	5			428	Sgt A Hatch	HE321	5

DATE	TARGET	SQN	CAPTAIN	A/C	AIRCREW KILLED	DATE	TARGET	SQN	CAPTAIN	A/C	AIRCREW KILLED
		428	Sgt W Mann	HE656	5	13/14.6	garden.	199	P/O W Sawdy	HF597	5
		429	P/O B Geale	HE423	5	21/22.6	Krefeld	166	Sgt A Burgess	HE924	5
		429	Sgt A Halstead	HE913	5			300	Sgt M Bronicki	HE327	6
		431	Sgt G Wood	HE440	5			300	F/S M Bialobrowka	HE985	5
		466	F/S C Trinder	HZ530	5			305	Sgt S Szpalinski	HE347	2
13/14.5	Bochum	166	P/O W Wahl	HZ280	2			429	F/O J Lown	HE981	5
		426	Sgt J Pettigrew	HE243	5			429	P/O G De Bussac	HZ517	5
		426	Sgt J Thomson	HE697	5			429	Sgt E Star	HZ519	5
		429	Sgt F Windibank	LN349	4			429	F/S E Eames	HZ520	2
		431	S/L T Marshall	HE183	5			431	W/C J Coverdale	HF518	5
		466	Sgt E Hicks	HZ271	0	22/23.6	Mulheim	429	W/O W Sneath	HF457	3
		466	P/O T Sampson	MS473	1			429	W/C J Savard	HZ312	5
16/17.5	garden.	466	Sgt J Lawson	HE386	5			431	F/O D Hine	HE394	5
21/22.5	garden.	428	Sgt A Simpson	HE177	4			466	P/O A Ford	HE326	4
		428	Sgt C Magnusson	HE899	5	23/24.6	SD	192	P/O E Eastham	HZ41	6
		431	Sgt R Buck	HE200	5	24/25.6	Wuppertal	166	P/O R Currie	HF594	5
		466	Sgt E Horner	HZ257	5			300	Sgt J Jawoszek	HF606	5
23/24.5	Dortmund	166	Sgt E Morris	HE290	5			300	F/O W Turecki	HZ376	3
		166	Sgt C Westwood	HE655	5			429	F/S L O'Leary	HZ521	5
		166	F/O A Steward	HF486	5			432	Sgt N Goldie	HF572	5
		199	Sgt H Austin	HZ585	3			432	Sgt J Mercier	HZ518	4
		300	F/O H Piatkowski	HZ374	5	25/26.6	Gelsenkirchen	166	F/S C Mattress	HE346	5
		426	Sgt L Sutherland	HE281	5			166	F/S M Arthur	HF589	3
25/26.5	Dusseldorf	166	Sgt R Batterbee	HE235	5			196	P/O N Smyth	HE412	4
		166	Sgt R Lowe	HE699	5			466	F/S A Airy	HF544	5
		199	F/O D Makin	HF488	4	26/27.6	garden.	432	F/S W Horn	HF568	5
		426	F/S S Pennington	HE590	6	28/29.6	Cologne	166	P/O W McGinn	HE922	1
		428	Sgt W Pepper	HZ476	6			300	F/S M Kleinschmidt	HZ438	5
		431	Sgt R Barclay	HE990	3			431	F/S J Parker	HE443	5
	SD	192	F/S G Bell	HE228	1		garden.	466	Sgt G Coles	HF481	5
27/28.5	Essen	166	F/L D Tonkinson	HE752	5	3/4.7	Cologne	166	S/L A Cookson	HF595	5
		199	Sgt J Waller	HE634	5			196	Sgt P Gee	HE980	5
		428	F/S D Thompson	HZ485	5			196	F/O E Eastwood	HZ478	6
		428	Sgt W Lachman	MS481	1			429	F/L R Brinton	LN296	5
		432	P/O R Taylor	HE294	5			431	Sgt N Apperley	LN284	4
29/30.5	Wuppertal	428	Sgt F Shelnutt	HF471	5			432	Sgt J Baker	HE630	3
		428	Sgt J Ferguson	LN424	0			432	Sgt R Burgess	HF493	1
		429	F/O B Richmond	HZ471	5			432	Sgt P Chambers	HZ481	5
		431	Sgt A Smith	HE203	5			432	P/O W Taylor	LN285	5
		432	Sgt F Dingwall	HE553	2			466	P/O J Edmonds	HF569	5
		432	Sgt W Griggs	LN435	2	5/6.7	garden.	466	W/C J Owen	HF601	5
		466	Sgt H Lloyd	HE212	5	8/9.7	garden.	166	Sgt D Scott	HF453	5
		466	P/O J Launder	HZ269	0	13/14.7	Aachen	432	Sgt C Dyson	HE353	5
		466	Sgt L Upjohn	MS494	1			466	F/S W Gunning	LN288	5
1/2.6	garden.	196	F/O J Deans	HE163	0	24/25.7	Hamburg	166	W/O G Ashplant	HZ314	5
11/12.6	Dusseldorf	196	F/O J Jackson	MS486	2			305	F/O S Grzeskowiak?	HF472	0
		199	Sgt C Andrews	HE277	5	25/26.7	Essen	300	Sgt E Garczynski	HZ486	2
		426	W/O N Hayes	HZ261	5			429	P/O K Johnston	HE803	1
		428	Sgt W Lachman	HE322	4			432	S/L C Sinton	HE514	0
		429	F/S R Conroy	HE593	4			466	Sgt R Thorpe	HZ580	5
		429	P/O R Davies	HF542	5	27/28.7	Hamburg	429	W/C J Piddington	JA114	3
		429	F/S R Ellison	HZ355	1	29/30.7	Hamburg	166	P/O R Birbeck	HE810	5
		431	Sgt W Eaglesham	HE184	5			432	W/C H Kerby	LN294	4
		431	S/L W Mulford	HE392	5	2/3.8	Hamburg	166	Sgt H Nash	HE464	5
		431	Sgt H Apperley	HF543	0			166	W/O R Burton	HE578	5
		432	F/L L Bourgeois	HE729	5			300	F/L J Spychala	HE807	0
		466	F/O F MacKelden	HE150	6			300	F/O W Smyk	HF605	2
		466	Sgt F Green	HE154	5			305	F/S S Grzeskowiak?	HZ467	5

DATE	TARGET	SQN	CAPTAIN	A/C	AIRCREW KILLED
		432	P/O D McDonald	HE906	5
5/6.8	SD	192	Sgt M Rice	LN349	2
11/12.8	garden.	466	W/O E Fogden	LN442	5
12/13.8	garden.	166	F/O W McGinn	HF483	5
		432	P/O S Noble	HE348	5
15/16.8	SD	192	F/S D Aubrey	HE230	4
	garden.	166	F/S A Bates	HF596	5
		300	F/S M Rech	HE768	3
27/28.8	garden.	166	W/O J Newman	HE901	5
30/31.8	Monchengladbach	166	Sgt H Heron	HE988	5
		166	F/O E Cook	LN397	5
		300	F/L L Osmialowski	JA116	5
		432	F/S J Pendleton	JA118	5
		466	F/S M Smart	HZ531	5
		466	Sgt J Harwood	LN292	5
22/23.9	Hannover	432	Sgt L Tierney	LN547	0
		432	Sgt R Barlow	LN554	2
27/28.9	Hannover	432	P/O S Atkinson	HE817	4
7/8.10	garden.	300	S/L S Morawski	HF490	5
		300	F/S J Zoltznski	HF590	0
8/9.10	Hannover	432	F/S D Baker	LN451	5
(this was the last Main Force loss)					
7/8.11	garden.	300	F/S J Drobny	LN508	0
11/12.11	garden.	300	F/L J Winiarek	LN393	2
1943 Totals				*312*	*1,066*

BOMBER COMMAND AIRCRAFT LOSSES BY SQUADRON

SQN	1939	1940	1941	1942	1943
9	7	17	28	28	80
12			15	63	78
15			4		4
37	5	11			16
38		10			10
40		32		3	35
57			32	34	66
75		13	33	47	
99	6	27	32	2	
101			15	35	
103			21	16	
104			15	2	
109			1	4	
115		19	39	65	6
142			9	45	
149	2	21	30		
150			17	54	
156				44	
158				17	
166					44
192					4
196					18
199				1	13
214		9	28	17	
218			34		

SQN	1939	1940	1941	1942	1943
300		1	14	25	23
301			12	26	2
304			10	9	
305			14	23	6
311		5	30	8	
405			18	9	
419				29	
420				4	16
424					8
425				7	9
426					21
427					16
428					20
429					30
431					20
432					21
458				3	
460				29	
466					35

OTU OPERATIONAL LOSSES

These are not included in the main tables above.

UNIT	1939	1940	1941	1942	1943
11 OTU	–	1	1	12	
12 OTU				8	1
14 OTU					
15 OTU			2	6	
16 OTU				12	2
18 OTU				4	1
20 OTU				3	
21 OTU				5	1
22 OTU				14	1
23 OTU				9	
25 OTU				9	
26 OTU				11	1
27 OTU				8	2
28 OTU					2
29 OTU				1	2
30 OTU					2

LOSSES BY AIRCRAFT MARK 1939–43

Losses here are for operational and training sorties, squadrons and OTUs.

I	3
IA	45
IC	563
II	171
III	430
IV	141
X	229
Total	*1879*

Glossary

A&AEE – Aircraft & Armament Experimental Establishment

AACU – Anti-Aircraft Co-operation Unit

AFDE – Air Fighting Development Establishment

AFV – Armoured Fighting Vehicle

AHB – Air Historical Branch

ALG – Advanced Landing Ground

ASV – Air to Surface Vessel radar

ASW – Anti-submarine warfare

ATA – Air Transport Auxiliary

auw – all-up weight

BCIS – Bomber Command Instructors School

BDU – Bombing Development Unit

CAS – Chief of the Air Staff

CSU – Constant Speed Unit

DAF – Desert Air Force

DR – Deduced Reckoning

DWI – Directional Wireless Installation (cover name for mine warfare equipment)

E-boat – German fast attack craft

E/A – enemy aircraft

EFTS – Elementary Flying Training School

ELINT – Electronic Intelligence

Flak – anti-aircraft fire

Freya – German radar system

FTR – Failed to return

'Gardening' – minelaying

HC – High Capacity (bomb)

HCU – Heavy Conversion Unit

Knickebein – German radio navigation system

Meaconing – sending out a false radio signal to decoy the user

MEC – Middle East Command

METS – Middle East Torpedo School

MT – Motor transport

MT – Motor Transport

MU – Maintenance Unit

MV – Motor Vessel

Navy O – Japanese Mitsubishi A6M 'Zero' fighter

Nickel – leaflet-dropping raid

Oboe – navigational aid

ORB – Operational Record Book

ORBAT – Order of Battle

ORS – Operational Research Section

OTF – Operational Training Flight

OTU – Operational Training Unit

PFF – Pathfinder Force

PR – Photo Reconaissance

PRFU – Pilots Refresher Flying Unit

RAE – Royal Aircraft Establishment

RCM – Radio Counter Measures

RSU – Repair and Salvage Unit

RTB – Returned to base

SBO – Strategic Bombing Offensive

SFTS – Service Flying Training School

'Shaker' – marking technique

SSR – Special Signals Reconnaissance

u/s – unserviceable

UE – Unit Establishment

Bibliography

Andrews, C. F., *Vickers Aircraft Since 1908* (Putnam, 1988)

Bergal, Hugh, *Flying Wartime Aircraft* (David & Charles, 1972)

Bury, George, *Wellingtons of 115 Squadron Over Europe*

Chorley, Bill, *Bomber Command Losses of World War Two*, four vols (Midland Counties)

Delve, Ken & Jacobs, Peter, *Six Year Offensive* (Arms & Armour Press, 1992)

Delve, Ken, *The Source Book of the RAF* (Airlife Publishing, 1994)

Gee, John, *Wingspan – recollections of a bomber pilot* (self published, 1988)

Harris, Sir Arthur, *Bomber Offensive* (Greenhill Books, 1990)

Harris, Sir Arthur, *Despatch on War Operations* (Frank Goss, 1995)

Jary, Christopher, *Portrait of a Bomber Pilot* (Sydney Jary Ltd, 1990)

Lihou, Maurice, *It's Dicey Flying Wimpeys in Italian Skies* (Air Research, 1992)

Orange, Dr Vincent *et al*, *Winged Promises* (RAF Benevolent Fund Enterprises, 1996)

Searby, John, *Everlasting Arms* (William Kimber, 1988)

Walker, Nigel, *Strike to Defend* (Neville Spearman, 1963)

Index